BRIDGING CHANGE

A Wyoming Valley Sketchbook

SALLY TELLER LOTTICK

To Rick —
With my very best wishes
Sally Teller Lottick
12/5/92

Wyoming Historical and Geological Society
Wilkes-Barre, Pennsylvania 1992

Published by the Wyoming Historical and Geological Society
49 South Franklin Street, Wilkes-Barre, PA 18701

Designed and composed by The Bookmakers, Incorporated, Wilkes-Barre, Pennsylvania
Halftones prepared by Graphic Arts Services, Inc., Wilkes-Barre, Pennsylvania
Cover color separation by Llewellyn & McKane, Wilkes-Barre, Pennsylvania
Manufactured by Capital City Press, Montpelier, Vermont

Manufactured in the United States of America

ISBN 0-937537-03-9

BRIDGING CHANGE

FRONT COVER: "From the Market Street Bridge," by Charles Burrott Zimmerman, captures the gateway to the city as it was in the mid-1950s. D. LEONARD CORGAN LIBRARY, KING'S COLLEGE, EDWARD WELLES, JR., COLLECTION

FRONTISPIECE: Surmounted by one of the bridge's four guardian eagles, this pillar of the Market Street Bridge is called "Prosperity" and states: "To the industry builded by human hand and brain on our mineral resources we owe growth, influence and welfare." This eagle has seen depression and recovery, as well as prosperity, since assuming its station atop the bridge in 1929. The bridge itself, survivor of both the 1936 and 1972 floods, is a symbol of strength and hope to many of Wyoming Valley's inhabitants. PHOTO BY MARK COHEN

INDUSTRY
PROSPERITY

To my father

STEPHEN ANDREWS TELLER

whose encouragement and support brought this publication to fruition

To the memory of my grandmother

SARAH FELL HUGHES TELLER

whose wonderful stories embedded in me a deep love of local history

And to the memory of my son

NOAH ANTRIM LOTTICK

whose enjoyment of the original articles has made him a part of this book, too

The fourth and current Luzerne County Courthouse was erected on the site of the abandoned canal basin at the height of the valley's prosperous days. Construction of the cruciform neo-classical building took four years and two million dollars—an astronomical amount in 1910 and symbolic of the wealth of the county in the era of "black gold". The building's rotunda rises from one mosaic and marble gallery to another up to the dome. Listed on the National Register of Historic Places, it has received recognition for its successful historic preservation.
PHOTO BY RALPH C. VIVIAN

Contents

Preface

NO BOOK ON HISTORY is written through the efforts of one person alone. If no one took the trouble to save and store the boxes of letters, journals, and records, if no one valued old pictures sufficiently to treat them with respect, if no one found the time and energy to care for these extremely fragile pieces of other people's passage, there would be no material with which to work.

Most important among the contributors to this work are Mary Ruth Kelly, Executive Director of the Wyoming Historical and Geological Society; and F. Charles Petrillo, Chair and Editor of its Publications Committee. Ruth Bevan's help has been invaluable, as has been that of the society's librarians and archivists over the years: Margaret Craft, Theresa Plummer, and Wendy Franklin. In fact, without the support of the entire staff of the Historical Society, this book could not have been written. I would also like to thank both John Beck and Rita Wolberg for their very valuable editing.

Many of the articles in this book were written for *Valley Panorama,* a monthly magazine published in Wyoming Valley from 1986 to 1988, when it merged with *Panorama,* a Hazleton publication. Special help for individual articles has come from a number of people: Sr. Agnese Post, Sisters of Christian Charity; Mary Callahan, Mary Mulderig, and Maria Pendleton, alumnae of St. Ann's Academy; Alice Patterson Patience, widow of Edgar Patience; Betty Frith, now retired, and Ronald Petrilla of the Association for the Blind; Sharon Ward, researcher for the Greater Wilkes-Barre Partnership; Sr. Mary Roche, Sisters, Servants of the Immaculate Heart of Mary, and Sr. Joan Quinn, IHM, former principal of Seton Catholic High School; John Orlandini, Frances Dorrance Chapter 11 of the Society for Pennsylvania Archeology, Inc.; Elena English Horrigan Parkhurst; and many others who have helped me learn about and find valuable sources of information. Richard Ross and Michael Thomas have provided invaluable help with photographs, rescuing images from very faded and fragile sources.

I have leaned heavily on *A History of Wilkes-Barre and Wyoming Valley*, the work of Oscar Jewell Harvey, completed by Ernest G. Smith. Harvey's encyclopedic detail on any topic in the valley's early history is always impressive. I have tried to mention each source of information where it is used. The bibliography that concludes this book may prove helpful to those wishing to locate more material.

It is a great pleasure to thank my immediate family: Edward Antrim Lottick, my husband, who has taken significant time from his more pressing interests to do critical reading and editing; Adam Teller Lottick, our son, who has cheered me on; and Karen Anna Lottick, our daughter, whose message has been, "Keep it readable, Mom. Remember it's for nonhistorians!" I hope it is both.

Sally Teller Lottick

OCTOBER 1992

BRIDGING CHANGE

This sketch views the city of Wilkes-Barre from Redoubt Hill—probably from a spot on the hilltop above Our Lady of Fatima's Shrine on North Street. The view is centered on Franklin Street. The covered bridge at Market Street is the major landmark to the right, and the steeple of Old Ship Zion dominates Public Square to the left. The second Court House, also on the Square, is visible. The steeple on Franklin Street belongs to the structure dedicated in 1833 as the First Presbyterian Church. It was replaced in 1848 by a Gothic revival building which has served as the home of the Osterhout Free Library since 1890.

Since the Wyoming Division of the North Branch Canal was constructed between 1831 and 1834, one might expect the cart in the foreground to be crossing the bridge over the canal. However, since the rock toward the left of the picture is clearly on dry ground, the path crossing just behind the cart could be Union Street.

This sketch is so similar to a painting that hangs in the Eugene S. Farley Library of Wilkes University that one cannot avoid concluding that they are closely related. The painting is dated to the 1840s, but no part of the canal is visible in it, nor is there any indication of active coal mining. Artistic license can be very frustrating for historians. WYOMING HISTORICAL AND GEOLOGICAL SOCIETY, HEREAFTER CITED AS WHGS

A Treasure House of History

WE HAVE A WONDERFUL and unique local history in Wyoming Valley, with tales of heroism, suffering, romance, and achievement. And from our historical roots a wonderful and unique community has emerged that nurtures us all today. But despite our focus on this limited geographic area, events here reflect the worldwide developments that have determined the fate of our world, our nation, and our state. In fact, at times, events here have been the first step in a new direction and have, in turn, led to much larger developments.

The late Edward F. Hanlon, history professor at King's College, saw the history of Wyoming Valley as the history of a people who were leading the way. In *The Wyoming Valley: An American Portrait,* Hanlon showed that what was happening here was defining the future of America. It often happened here first.

Our local history records our participation in the broad forces of history. It gives us examples on this much smaller scale of how the great movements of history have had specific meaning right here for each of us.

The Wyoming Valley

THE NORTH BRANCH of the Susquehanna River dramatically changes course where it is joined by the Lackawanna. At that point, the river swings sharply to the southwest. The next seventeen miles of wide plains, river flats, rising foothills, and surrounding mountains are known as Wyoming Valley.

The valley begins just below the massive rocky outcropping, called both Campbell's Ledge and Dial Rock, north of Pittston. It ends where the mountains narrow to a gorge at Tilbury's Knob—once called Rampart Rocks—above West Nanticoke.

From its mountains to the northwest flow Abraham's, Toby's, and Harvey's creeks. The mountains on the southeastern side give rise to Mill Creek, Laurel Run, Solomon's Creek, Warrior Run, and Nanticoke Creek. The valley is bounded on its northwestern flank by Back Mountain, Larksville Mountain, and Plymouth Mountain. On the other side are Wilkes-Barre Mountain, with Wyoming Mountain behind it, and Penobscot Mountain to the southwest. This is the setting for the ebb and flow of events that have created the Wyoming Valley we live in today.

The Westward Movement

THAT TREMENDOUS westward migration of the descendants of the seaboard settlers began with the settlement of Wyoming Valley. During the eighteenth century, Great Britain maintained a policy of keeping the colonies confined to the seaboard, east of the Appalachians. This way England could hold down the costs of frontier defense, and make it easier to control the existing settlements.

The formation of the Susquehannah Company by a group of Connecticut citizens demonstrated the force of the westward thrust. The Susquehannah Company settled in Wyoming Valley, far inland from the coastal plain and west of King George's Proclamation Line of 1763. They settled here despite Wyoming Valley's inaccessibility to wagons; despite its prior occupation by a group of Delaware Indians under Teedyuscung; despite the forceful claims of the Pennamite settlers (and the somewhat shadowy nature of their own claim); despite the opposition of Great Britain; and despite the opposition of the Colony of Pennsylvania and, after the American Revolution, the opposition of the Commonwealth of Pennsylvania. That westward thrust was powerful indeed and truly became the wave of the future.

What was the nature of this area that the Susquehannah Company moved into? Archeology has given us many insights into thousands of years of Native American occupation of the valley. It was originally a hunting and fishing site. It was also farmed by the Indians for several hundred years. Stockaded towns were occupied by these farming populations, whom the archeologists and anthropologists are still tracing.

But the stories I learned about the Native Americans as a child were not about our prehistory. They were not about the settled Indian communities' fishing, farming, and hunting. They were not about the spring migrations to net the shad, nor even about the summer migrations during the early historical period when the area was an unoccupied buffer zone between the Indian territories and the white settlers.

Instead, the stories were about savages who surrounded and killed a brave and stalwart band fighting for America, who then massacred their prisoners and fired all the buildings. Just months later, these same savages carried off a little girl whose family searched for her for a generation. Sullivan's March was mentioned as a mere footnote to these events, and then chiefly because of his road-building operation. That battle, however, the world-famous Battle of Wyoming for which one state, sixteen counties, and sixty-four lesser municipalities have been named, has been celebrated annually since 1832 in a secular ritual on the 3rd or 4th of July at the Wyoming Monument in Wyoming, Pennsylvania.

The actual facts of that thirty-minute battle are less exciting than the history of the propaganda derived from it. Our understanding of its significance requires that we also try to understand why the myth of a massacre that may never have taken place is so persistent.

Dr. Clement Valletta of King's College believes that the significance of the Battle of Wyoming lies in its role as an Edenic myth: Wyoming Valley as Eden or paradise, promised by the English King Charles II both to the Connecticut settlers and to the Pennsylvania settlers, and claimed and possessed and occupied by them. This paradise was violated, not by people defending their lands against loss, but by savages. Dr. Jeremy Packard of Wyoming Seminary points out that the settlers found it absolutely necessary to demonize the Indians in order to rationalize the seizure of their lands and the destruction of their culture.

The land was finally restored to the settlers, who were both literally and figuratively the ancestors of the valley's current inhabitants. And because of the Battle of Wyoming, the valley was not just restored but was now earned and truly belonged to the settlers, thanks to the blood of their martyrs. The Battle of Wyoming made this land their land.

Why are none of the battles of the Yankee-Pennamite Wars remembered and celebrated with similar fanfare? There are no ceremonies at Tilbury Terrace or at the site of Fort Wyoming on the River Common in Wilkes-Barre. Not much is left to remind us of the redoubts once constructed where the Luzerne County Court House officials now park their cars.

There certainly was little of mythic stature or quality about the Yankee-Pennamite Wars. Two groups of settlers claimed the valley, each cast aspersions on the other's claims and motivations, neither side won a complete victory, and the conflict finally ended in court with the precedent-setting Decree of Trenton. The decision went in favor of Pennsylvania mostly because the land was contiguous to Pennsylvania and not to Connecticut. The Trenton Court, however, organized under the Articles of Confederation, totally failed to address the issue of conflicting land claims.

When Pennsylvania then denied citizenship to the Connecticut settlers who had cleared and worked the land, the second Yankee-Pennamite War erupted. Timothy Pickering, once George Washington's quartermaster general and later his postmaster general, proposed a practical compromise and began the process of working out the details. The land disputes were finally settled with the Compromise Act of 1799.

The migrants who had moved inland from the Atlantic coastal and riverine towns did indeed acquire the land they had sought. Family by family, the titles were cleared and ownership was established. But what kind of community emerged? Dr. William Price, local educator and historian, in his thesis on this subject, concludes that an American community grew from that clash of New England and Pennsylvania cultures in Wyoming Valley.

The New Englanders and the Pennsylvanians, living side by side, were forced to seek solutions to a number of specific differences in their government and in their religious institutions. "The Connecticut culture was more democratic, more progressive, and more capitalistic, while Pennsylvania projected the opposite profile," Price contends. Pennsylvania was still the feudal domain of the Penn family—a proprietary colony. Connecticut's township governments were democratic and accountable to their citizens. On the other hand, Connecticut had an established church, supported by taxes, whereas Pennsylvania allowed no establishment of religion. William Penn had purposely reached out to settlers of many faiths. The peaceful coexistence of these two different cultures required constant effort. It demanded that both cultures adapt.

A specific example, cited by Price, of the pressure of the Yankee-Pennamite conflict creating social change through adaptation can be seen in the allocation of land. Like the other Connecticut settlement groups of the time, the Susquehannah Company had developed a plan for a closed community. The valley was to be surveyed; the townships mapped out; and the town lots, farm lands, and woodlands allocated by lot to members of the Susquehannah Company only. This gave each member far more land than one family would have been able to use and would have left large areas effectively unoccupied.

After the first round of conflict with the Pennamites, the Yankees abandoned this closed system and adopted instead a pattern of settlement that would win over the Pennsylvania settlers to the Connecticut cause by making it possible for them also to become land owners with freehold titles.

This open land system, making land readily available through a lottery to anyone who wanted to settle in Wyoming Valley, was designed to attract a rapidly growing population that would quickly stabilize the area. The economic incentive was privately owned land of family-farm size—that is, a size that a family could cultivate effectively and therefore occupy fully, which would give that family a vested interest in the community. In fact, the Settlers' Committee took back the settling rights of absentee proprietors and reallocated them to those who would actually occupy the land. Lazarus Stewart, whose story is told later in this book, was a beneficiary of this policy.

The Connecticut system of land ownership contrasted sharply with that of Pennsylvania. Pennsylvania allocated lands through a system of tenancy and quitrents payable to the Penn family. Land was leased rather than granted outright. Many settlers, regardless of origin, naturally preferred the Connecticut system of outright ownership. The valley's rapid population growth under the Yankee auspices reflected this preference.

Abijah Smith began mining at this opening in Plymouth in 1807, joined by his brother John a year later. Between 1807 and 1820, they sent six thousand tons of anthracite on 90- by 16- by 4-foot arks to Havre de Grace, Maryland, where the Susquehanna River empties into the Chesapeake Bay. One out of every three arks foundered on the trip downriver. The coal was then shipped by coastal vessels to New York City. Markets developed very slowly, and the profit margin was small for these industrial pioneers. FROM OSCAR J. HARVEY'S *History of Wilkes-Barre*

One result of the open plan of settlement was to minimize extremes of ownership. Most residents (92.5 percent) owned between ten and fifty acres. Between 1770 and 1800, only five families acquired land in excess of fifty acres.

A further result of the open plan of settlement was the intermarriage of the Connecticut and Pennsylvania families from the time the children of the first settlers were old enough to marry. One has only to read the lists of applications for marriage licenses today to recognize that intermarriage of the valley's families, regardless of religious, national, and ethnic backgrounds, is the rule rather than the exception.

The story of the settlement of this valley is one of Yankees versus Delaware Indians and Iroquois, Yankees versus Pennamites, Yankees and Pennamites versus the British, Tories, and Senecas; then, following the Revolution, another round of Yankees versus Pennamites before the final resolution of conflict through the courts. These were certainly very determined settlers. As we all know, the westward movement continued across the entire continent until settlers had filled the land to the Pacific Ocean.

An Industrial Economy

THE INDUSTRIAL REVOLUTION—that massive change in our culture's mode of economic production—started here with the recognition of the potential usefulness of stone coal. The settlers in Wyoming Valley were subsistence farmers, with some specialized crafts and trades to supplement their income.

The Gores, for example, were blacksmiths as well as farmers, and from the time of their arrival here, used the stone coal with a forced draft in their forge. But because it was deemed useful only with a forced draft, the stone coal was not regarded as an item for successful trade or production.

In 1808, however, it became clear locally that this hard coal could be burned in an ordinary fireplace on an open grate, providing a marvelous source of home heat. Jesse Fell, a blacksmith as well as an innkeeper and magistrate, conducted an experiment to show this in Wilkes-Barre. Immediately upon its success, he made a number of grates for his friends and neighbors. Some local entrepreneurs began to work harder on getting this useful stuff to a bigger market.

The valley's underground wealth of anthracite gave it the potential to be part of industrial America. Despite its mountain-bound isolation, it became an important goal to include Wyoming Valley in the great transportation network that was evolving. The canals, specifically the North Branch Canal, made Wyoming Valley reasonably accessible to Harrisburg, Baltimore, and Philadelphia. Later, when the North Branch Extension was completed, the valley could have access to the markets of upstate New York and the midwest by way of the Erie Canal. These canals made it possible for Wyoming Valley to be a participant in the great nationwide burst of industrial growth.

The canals, however—although far better-suited for transporting coal than freight wagons could ever be on the steep, winding, rough roads over the mountains—had a limited season. Both ice and flooding were great hazards. The railroads, the canals' successors, had a long-term advantage despite their greater cost. The railroad links established in the valley maintained their viability as part of the American industrial complex of the nineteenth century. Today, the great twentieth-century highways keep us in the national transportation network.

Even more important to Wyoming Valley were the people who traveled here and subsequently became part of the community because of the canals and railroads. Irish and Germans who came to build the canal settled here. And as the mining industry developed, the earlier settlers—whose ancestry was largely English and Scots Irish, along with smaller percentages of other groups, including African-Americans—were joined by Welsh and English miners brought to the valley to share their expertise and skill. German and Eastern European Jews arrived, establishing businesses to supply the expanding population. Then as coal production increased and the demand for workers grew, Poles came from the three regions governed by Russia, Austro-Hungary, and Germany. They were followed by Magyars, Slovaks, Lithuanians, Tyroleans, Russians, Ukrainians, Ruthenians, Italians, Greeks, Syrians, and Lebanese. Since World War II, Hispanics, Asian Indians, Chinese, Koreans, and Vietnamese have also made their homes here.

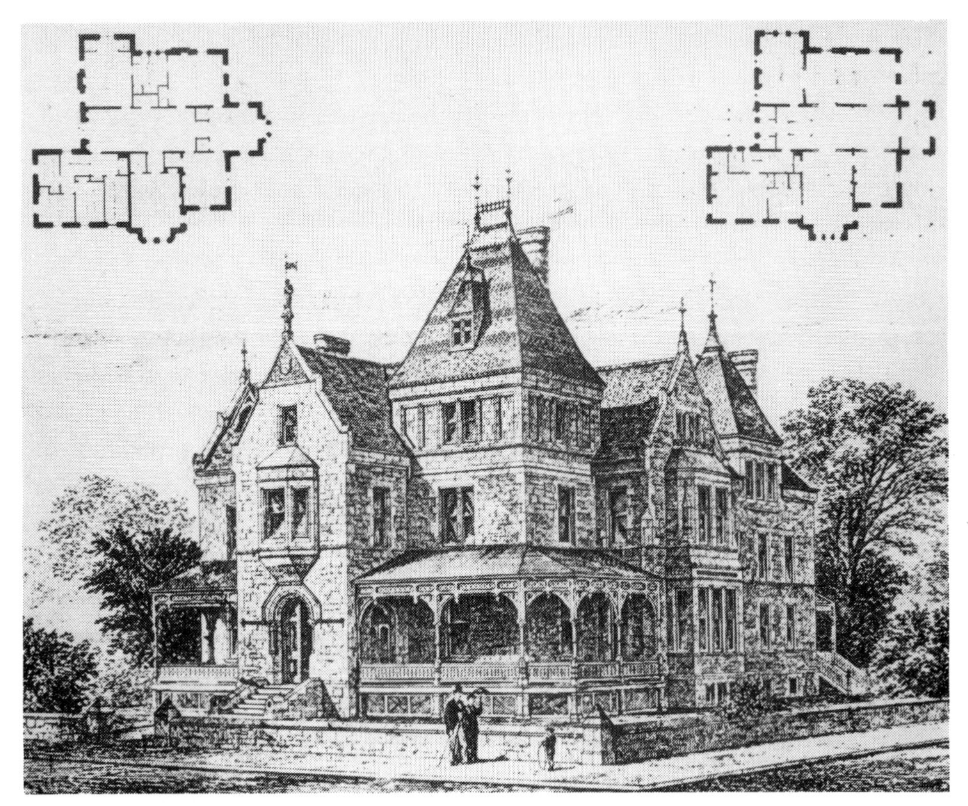

This famous house was featured in an 1879 issue of *The American Architect and Building News.* Located at 202 South River Street in Wilkes-Barre, it was designed by Frederick Clark Withers, widely known for his church designs and best remembered for the Jefferson Market Court House in Greenwich Village. It became the home of Fred Kirby, 5-and-10-cent-store magnate, and was donated to Bucknell Junior College (now Wilkes University) by his son. Wilkes has successfully incorporated a number of Wilkes-Barre's prominent historic houses into its campus. Almost all of Wilkes University's main campus and a significant part of King's College are within Wilkes-Barre's National Register Historic District. WHGS

Without the development of the anthracite industry and the transportation network it required, Wyoming Valley could very easily have remained a farming community, not very different from the many small towns nestled in valleys to the north and west.

A Mixed Economy

THE SOURCE OF the Wyoming Valley's current livelihood did not just happen. The fading of the anthracite industry led the valley into depression almost ten years before the Great Depression hit the rest of the nation. By the 1950s, the population was steadily declining and Luzerne County was on the Depressed Areas list. In 1902, 140,000 workers were employed in the mines. By 1959, there were only 5,000 left. Thus the Knox Mine Disaster in 1959 signaled the end of deep mining in Wyoming Valley.

The 1950s also saw the beginnings of the comeback, however. The needle trades had helped keep the valley going during the worst period and by 1960 employed 10,000 workers. The presence of the federal government was a key to survival. Construction of the Veterans Hospital in Wilkes-Barre, as well as the Veterans Administration Building, the location here of the Social Security Administration, and the establishment of a major U.S. Post Office data processing center have provided many good jobs. Urban Redevelopment and the Model Cities Program were among the resources that a strong congressional presence, in the person of Dan Flood, helped fund. Also, federally funded housing supplemented the aging housing stock in the 1960s and 1970s.

The Agnes Flood of 1972 was devastating, but the federal response enabled us to rebuild, in some cases from below the street level. This dramatic reconstruction of the infrastructure has given the valley a significant advantage. At the same time, we still retain a few historic structures. These survivors are, we hope, sufficient still in number and variety to demonstrate our uniqueness and maintain our dignity and pride.

Expansion of the local educational institutions has greatly enhanced the service industry. Penn State Extension, which moved from central Wilkes-Barre to its new campus in Lehman in 1964, has since become the Pennsylvania State University Wilkes-Barre Campus. The Luzerne County Community College was established in 1967 in the old Sterling Hotel annex in Wilkes-Barre then moved to its new Nanticoke campus in 1974. College Misericordia, King's College, and Wilkes University have all expanded significantly. The transformation of Bucknell Junior College into Wilkes College and then into Wilkes University is only one indicator of this continuing growth and development. Similar expansion of the health care industry has provided another economic advantage.

Perhaps most important has been citizen initiative. In the 1950s, William O. Sword organized the Committee of 100 and worked under the aegis of the Greater Wilkes-Barre Chamber of Commerce to draw in new industry. Citizen initiative continues to be a major factor in Wyoming Valley's economic development, demonstrated by the Committee on Economic Growth and the Greater Wilkes-Barre Partnership, as well as by the work of such individual entrepreneurs as the late Marvin Roth and Al Boscov.

We entered the 1990s with a renewed urban base. Having once moved from an agrarian to an industrial economy, we have succeeded in shifting from that to a service economy and have survived the distress and displacement that accompanied those changes. Our history of overcoming obstacles and solving problems gives us not only great potential for the future, but also an under-

This unusual photograph shows the Baltimore Coal Breaker with its whole range of workers—bosses to breaker boys—in 1854. The breaker was constructed to handle coal from the important coal seam in Wilkes-Barre's East End that was first utilized for profit in 1814 by Lord Butler. The mine was sold for $35 per acre to a Mr. Thomas Simington and others from Baltimore in 1829 and reorganized as the Baltimore Coal Company. In 1836 it became the site of the first gravity railroad in the valley, designed by Alexander Gray to take coal from the mine to the new canal. Loaded cars rolled downhill to the canal aided by the weight of the coal, and horses drew the empties back uphill along the wooden rails.

After 1842, the demand for coal to power locomotives required that large lumps be broken up and sorted by size. This led to the development of breakers—mechanical devices for breaking down the huge rocks and sorting them by size through a series of screens. The first successful breaker elevating coal to a height and breaking it as it slid down chutes was developed in 1853 by the Delaware, Lackawanna and Western Railroad and installed in Scranton. WHGS

standing of our uniqueness within the national and international networks that provide our livelihood.

No understanding of Wyoming Valley is complete if it does not recognize the significance of its patchwork of neighborhoods, boroughs, and towns. It must be cognizant of the ties to church and synagogue and extended family.

And it must appreciate the continuity of cultural tradition that impels a Jewish family to observe Christmas Eve with a Russian Orthodox dinner on January sixth; or why a Mr. and Mrs. O'Brien have become pillars of the Lithuanian church; or how a young professional of Italian descent and her husband, a young professional of Polish descent, can have great difficulty deciding whether to send their offspring to St. Hedwig's, Wyoming Seminary, or Wyoming Valley West. Would Holy Name be a possible compromise or just make the decision more difficult?

No wonder newcomers to Wyoming Valley can suffer a mild degree of culture shock. Where does the individual leave off and the community begin? And which, if any, of our many communities takes precedence in each person's life? Will we continue to grow both as individuals and as members of these communities into a larger and more integrated whole? I believe we are indeed becoming more cohesive, but I hope we will always find room for both the rich fabric of a multicultural community and the new cultures that are now being established in our midst. The stories that follow focus on some of the details of our rich cultural evolution.

Settlements in the Wilderness

From the days of its nearly unknown first inhabitants—people whose existence and way of life is known only from evidence unearthed by archeologists—through the time of its occupation by various Native American tribes to its first settlements by British colonists and its role in the American Revolution, the Wyoming Valley remained nearly unspoiled amid the vast wilderness of the North American Continent.

This rock shelter at the base of Campbell's Ledge provided a rich archeological yield during Max Schrabisch's 1923 explorations: cord-marked pottery fragments, charred deer bones, fragments of fresh water mussels, chips of flint and chert, and evidences of repeated fires—charcoal and heat-cracked pebbles—to a depth of two feet. Schrabisch concluded that the shelter was used by deer hunters as a campsite where arrowpoints were manufactured and venison cooked. WHGS

Our Unknown Predecessors

The Archeological Record

WYOMING VALLEY'S EARLIEST INHABITANTS lived here long before any written records were kept, and their story can be learned only from the artifacts they left behind. However, if these artifacts, when discovered, are carefully and professionally excavated, analyzed, and interpreted, they can give us a great deal of information. Even a small piece of broken pottery, when it is properly examined in the context in which it is found, can help us learn more about our predecessors.

From this archeological evidence, we know that humans found their way to Wyoming Valley 12,000 years ago, shortly after the glaciers of the last Ice Age receded from the area. This assertion is based on the Clovis points—carefully chipped spear points used in big game hunting—found on a site in Duryea. But we know very little about the people who hunted here at this extremely early date.

Archeologists have divided prehistoric cultures into broad patterns. The earliest, the creators of the Clovis points, were nomadic hunters. After about 8000 B.C., the Archaic cultures developed, in which small populations migrated according to seasonal cycles. As agriculture was introduced and populations increased in size, the transition from Archaic to Woodland cultures took place. From 1000 B.C. until the European settlement period, living patterns are divided into the Early Woodland Period (1000 B.C. to 300 B.C.), Middle Woodland Period (300 B.C. to A.D. 1000) and Late Woodland Period (A.D. 1000 to the historic period). In the Early and Middle periods, corn was increasingly cultivated, but it was a small part of the diet compared to food obtained by hunting and gathering. In the Late Woodland period, however, dependence on corn, beans, and squash superseded the hunting and gathering pattern, and much larger settlements developed.

Pottery, which enters the archeological record during the Woodland periods, is one of the most important clues for developing our knowledge and understanding of prehistory. When people began to stay longer in one place, they started to make pottery. Pots made of fired clay survive the ravages of time, unlike leather, bone, and most other materials used to create tools and artifacts. Pots, like the worked stone of the Clovis points, take on the character of their creators, and each culture developed its own characteristic shapes and patterns. It is through such clues as the variations in the decorations of pot rims that we can identify different cultures prior to European settlement. The distribution of distinctive artifacts helps us learn not only where people lived but where they traveled.

Airport II Site

THERE ARE SEVEN recorded prehistoric sites in Wyoming Valley with some components from the Late Woodland period. One of these is Airport II, first noted in 1914 by Christopher Wren and discovered anew in 1985. Located at the Wyoming Valley Airport in Forty Fort, it was about to be bulldozed for a playing field when the Frances Dorrance Chapter 11 of the Society for Pennsylvania Archaeology got permission from the Forty Fort Borough Council to test it for artifacts. The site was professionally excavated by John Orlandini and Francis D. Garrahan in 1986. Garrahan's article about it, "A Clemson Island/Owasco Settlement on the North Branch of the Susquehanna," was published in *Pennsylvania Archeologist* in February 1990.

Radiocarbon dating of charcoal found at the Airport II Site places it at about A.D. 980. Findings indicate that hunting and fishing were still a part of the inhabitants' lives, but there are several indications that the people living there may have been using hunting and fishing merely to supplement the corn that they grew. In other words, they were well on their way to living in a permanent settlement.

We know that the inhabitants ate nuts and freshwater mussels and smoked tobacco in pipes. A stockade protected part of their village site. It may have been built for protection from harsh weather only and therefore never completed. Perhaps the evidence for the rest of the stockade, if it was built as a total enclosure for protection from enemies, has been eroded by floods. There are indications of both circular and oblong houses and of an elongated structure that could have been a longhouse or a pen. Not all of these structures are inside the partial stockade. There is also evidence of rebuilding, indicating successive occupations. This could mean that the site was occupied seasonally. But rebuilding could also indicate long-term occupation with changes required because of a growing population.

Parker Site

In the spring of 1967, Robert and Alice Parker were working ahead of bulldozers removing soil from Jacob's Flats, northwest of Plains Township and across the Susquehanna River from Forty Fort, when they discovered a large deposit of freshwater mollusk shells. Probing the deposit, they uncovered fragments of fish and animal bone, potsherds (fragments of pottery), and projectile points (for example, arrowpoints). Ira F. Smith III, in 1973 the field archeologist and associate curator of archeology at the William Penn Museum in Harrisburg, published a description and analysis of the findings at the Parker Site in *Pennsylvania Archeologist* (September 1985). He described how the Parkers enlisted the aid of the Frances Dorrance Chapter of the Society for Pennsylvania Archaeology to help explore the site. It turned out to be part of a large ancient garbage dump that had collected beside a dirt causeway. The causeway had been built across a wide ditch. And the ditch, in turn, completely surrounded a prehistoric stockaded village. A 15,000-square-foot area of the village area was excavated in the summer of 1968.

The ditch surrounding the village was about four feet deep and eleven to fourteen feet wide. It seems to have been dug by the inhabitants to provide fill to throw around their stockade. Six feet inside the ditch was the stockade. It was eight feet wide and made up of five lines of posts protecting the living area, with a long, narrow gateway passing through them. Eight depressions, eight to ten feet in diameter, were inside the main palisade. Within these depressions were layers of charred marsh grasses, burned logs, fire-cracked rocks, charred corn kernels, and a variety of broken potsherds—critical evidence for purposes of dating and identification.

Closer to the center of the village were a variety of pits. There was not enough evidence to determine the function of most of these, but one deep, bell-shaped pit contained a badly deteriorated human skeleton and shale objects (probably digging tools), along with a variety of potsherds, shale fragments, chips, and miscellaneous animal bones.

In 1845, Charles Miner reported an Indian burial site uncovered during the early 1830s while the canal was being dug. Located less than 168 yards from the Parker Site, it is possible that these skeletons, found in the same flexed position as the one in the Parker Site, were in the cemetery for the village. The burial in the abandoned storage pit may have been a temporary mid-winter expedient, the cemetery ground being frozen too hard for stone hoe and digging stick.

Numerous tools found on the site were used for securing food (points, flints, netsinkers, and hoes); for processing food (teshoa—blades used for cut-

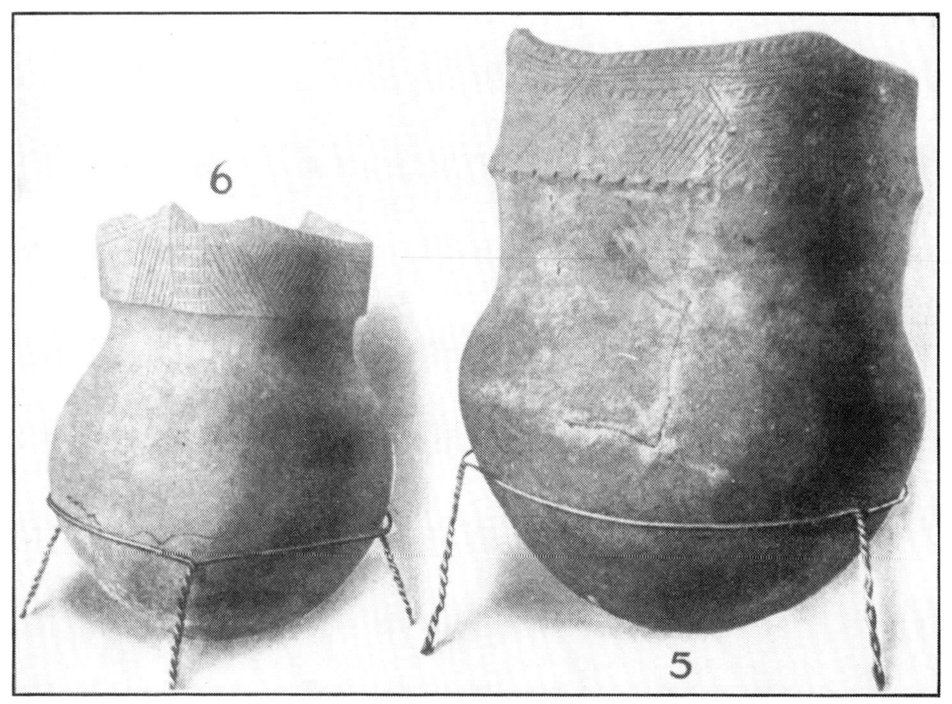

These pots from the collection of the Wyoming Historical and Geological Society were used to illustrate Arthur C. Parker's article in its 1910 "Proceedings and Collections." Parker described them as Iroquoian (Figures 5 and 6), Algonquin (Figure 8) and Mixed (Figure 7). In 1984, Barry C. Kent's analysis in *Susquehanna's Indians* of the same and similar pots was much more complex. Shapes, styles of decoration, and clay content—especially the addition of crushed

ting, scraping, and chopping; milling stones and pestles); for securing wood (celts); and for processing raw materials (honing stones, hammerstones, and anvils). A number of bone and antler artifacts survived—hairpins, ornaments, beads, fishhooks, awls, and fragments from cups or ladles. There were also some botanical remains—butternut shells, plum stones, hickory nuts, persimmon seeds, and some fragments of bean. The great bulk of this food sample was Northern Flint corn, which according to Ira F. Smith III was "the major reason why permanent villages like this one could be built and occupied for long periods of time." While the people living at the Airport II Site were on their way to becoming permanently settled, the people at the Parker Site were firmly entrenched, both literally and figuratively, in their stockaded town.

A key clue to the dating of this site is that no European trade goods were found. Paul Wallace points out in *Indians in Pennsylvania* that when the first permanent trading post in the northern hemisphere, Tadoussac, was established on the St. Lawrence River by the French in 1603, European goods had already reached many Indians from trading vessels along the Atlantic coast. At the same time that Champlain was founding Quebec in 1608, John Smith noted

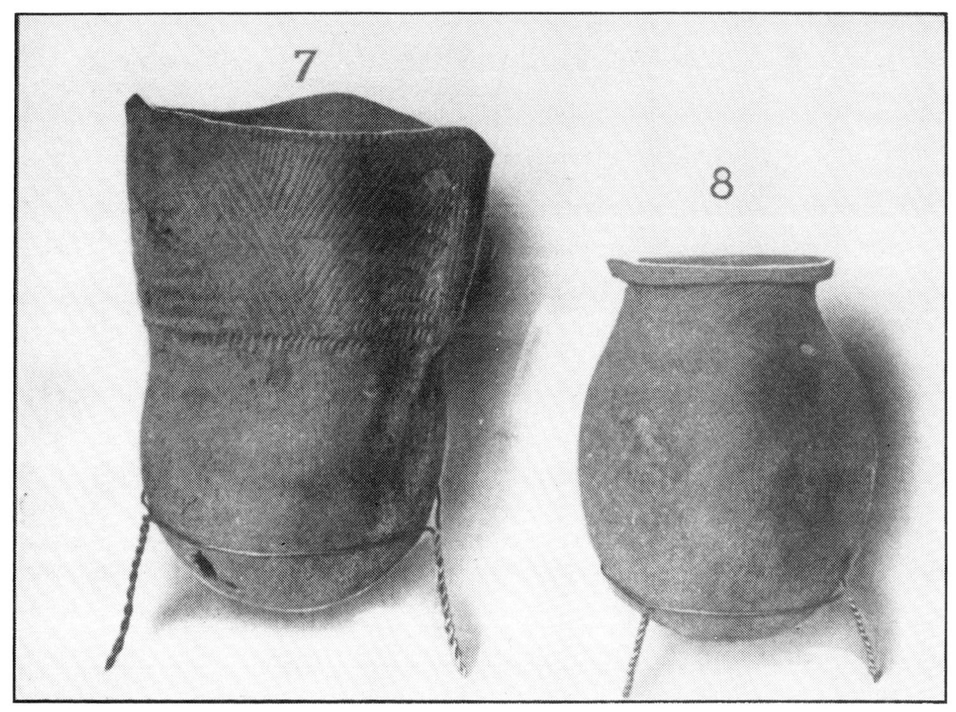

mussel shell—provide many clues to this area's early cultures. "One thing is certain [says Kent]. Throughout Iroquoia and in adjacent areas of parallel or related pottery development such as the upper Delaware, the Wyoming Valley, and the upper Susquehanna, there was a basic, common theme of pottery decoration, involving increasingly higher collars, added to which was a great deal of exchange of local decorative ideas by all participants in the theme." WHGS

that the Susquehannocks to the north of the Chesapeake Bay were already in possession of trade goods.

Analysis of the layering of the pottery shards, the variety of types and designs, and the ratios of these to each other, suggests that the Parker Site dates to the early part of the sixteenth century, about 1525. Radiocarbon dating of logs brackets this period between about 1470 and 1600, plus or minus ninety years.

Wyoming Valley appears to have contained three sites enclosed by complex stockades and external ditches. Two are mentioned in early historical writing. One, described by Isaac A. Chapman in 1817 *(A Sketch of the History of Wyoming)*, stood on the flats in Kingston Township north of Toby's Creek, about one-half mile from the Susquehanna River. The second, described by Charles Miner in 1845 *(History of Wyoming in a Series of Letters from Charles Miner to his son William Penn Miner, Esq.)*, appears to be identical with the Parker Site. The third is the Schacht Site, one mile upriver from Nanticoke on the west side of Warrior Creek, excavated between 1960 and 1962. Near the Schacht Site is the Dundee excavation done between 1967 and 1971, apparently related to the Schacht Site. The pottery complex found at these three sites is designated as the Wyoming Valley Culture.

Rock Shelter Sites

THE WYOMING VALLEY CULTURE is also evident in the rock shelters in the mountains surrounding the valley. These were explored by Max Schrabisch and described in an article published in 1926, "Aboriginal Rock Shelters of Wyoming Valley and Vicinity" in the *Proceedings and Collections of the Wyoming Historical and Geological Society* 29 (1926). Rock shelters were created by overhanging rock ledges. Those that faced south could capture the sun's warmth; and when they were located near a convenient water supply, provided enough height for comfort, and had relatively smooth dirt floors, these rock overhangs were used by Indians both as overnight lodgings while traveling and as hunting and fishing campsites. Schrabisch carefully documented the shelters' locations and the artifacts he found during his excavations. These artifacts included many potsherds of the same content and design periods as those found in the stockaded sites. Ira F. Smith III believed these finds suggested a "complex settlement system composed of semipermanent riverine towns and seasonal satellite camps within a prescribed hunting territory . . . most certainly of the same culture, but perhaps at different points in time."

It is interesting to note that pottery of the Wyoming Valley Culture has also been found in the same kind of dense concentration in the Mohawk area of east central New York State and in the Upper Delaware Valley of Pennsylvania and New Jersey. In locations between these three areas, the pottery is either not found or occurs only infrequently. Less dense findings indicate forays from these three major settlement areas to the West Branch of the Susquehanna, the Upper Susquehanna, and the Middle Delaware, and indicate that certain paths acted as the connecting links between them.

From the evidence at the Parker Site and at the Rock Shelter Sites, Smith concludes that these early citizens of Wyoming Valley lived

> *year round in large towns surrounded by elaborate earthen and timber stockades and entrenchments traversed by dirt causeways. Straight passages of parallel lines of posts controlled access to the interior of the village where residents occupied bark-covered, smaller versions of the Iroquoian longhouse, occasionally rested in rounded, domed sweat lodges [Wallace points out that the Indians of the 1600s were much cleaner than their European counterparts], and erected special purpose circular or oval-shaped semi-subterranean structures against the inner perimeter of the stockade wall. . . . The material remains indicate a culture characterized by a bone, stone, and clay technology, supplemented certainly by wood, bark, skin, and fabric, . . . heavily dependent upon pebble or cobble tools.*

Who were they? We know they were not the Susquehannocks, the tribe that inhabited much of the rest of the Susquehanna River valley, particularly the area to the north of Wyoming Valley, near the New York state border in the Bradford County area. The artifact patterns of the Susquehannocks are distinctly different from those of the Wyoming Valley Culture. According to Barry C. Kent, author of *Susquehanna's Indians,*

> *Sometime prior to 1575, the people responsible for the early Schultz Incised pottery [the Susquehannocks] began to abandon their small villages on the upper Susquehanna. Most of them eventually settled in Lancaster County on the lower Susquehanna. . . . Where they [stayed along the way] and how long it took them to move from one place to the other are something of a mystery. . . . It seems logical to propose that their movement south and the coalition of their scattered villages may have been in response to eventual political and economic strife with the Iroquois. There is little or no archeological evidence for such conflict, but nevertheless, the possibility for such still exists. There is some evidence for hostilities between [the] Susquehannocks and certain of their neighbors to the south, viz., the people of the Wyoming Valley . . . None of these people survived as [a] distinct culture after 1575. Their demise is suspected to be the result of internecine warfare among themselves, followed by Susquehannock aggression during the period of [the Susquehannock's] southward migration.*

Were these early inhabitants defeated in war? As Kent says above, there is no strong indication for this in the archeologic record.

Were they wiped out by smallpox, measles, or influenza? Whole villages were known to have been annihilated by these diseases, which swept through the Indian population after contact with Europeans. Sometimes these diseases moved far in advance of the Europeans, carried from one village to the next among people who had never before been exposed to them and who, unlike the Europeans, had developed no immunity. David K. Richter noted recently in *Pennsylvania History* that once these diseases hit any given area, native populations declined by as much as 90 to 95 percent.

One economic theory for the inhabitants' departure is that they had simply used up the land. The intensive farming practices of other cultures in the northeast, Paul Wallace notes, forced villages to move every ten or twenty years. Prodded by the need to find new, fertile fields for their corn, Wyoming Valley's inhabitants may have voluntarily left the area. We can only speculate whether they emerged elsewhere as a distinct group that has shown no known association with the Wyoming Valley region. Or they may have been assimilated into other developing Indian cultures.

Another economic theory for the events leading to the abandonment of the stockaded towns in Wyoming Valley is presented by Barry Kent. He suggests that instead of war it may have been a taste for European trade goods that caused the Susquehannocks to make this sixteenth century migration, moving from the Bradford County area, north of Wyoming Valley, to what is now Lancaster County, south of the valley. In the pursuit of their migration, they may have come into conflict with the people of the Wyoming Valley Culture and caused their demise. It may be, Kent says,

> *that [trade goods envy] was enough to stimulate [the Susquehannocks'] need to have and control their own direct access to the [European] trade. This could only come about through their residential proximity to a coastal area, or through their hegemony over other peoples on the coast or seaports. Their forays down the Delaware, as marked by scattered occurrences of [their] pottery there, may have been precisely to seek such access or control in that area. In any event, it does appear that they did band together and move rather quickly into the lower Susquehanna Valley. We also know that other indigenous cultures along their route ceased to exist at about this time. The people of the Wyoming Valley . . . did not survive into the contact period of the second half of the sixteenth century. . . . We can only guess at the role of the migrating Susquehannocks in this disappearance.*

We know that these sixteenth-century inhabitants of Wyoming Valley raised corn, lived in towns, made good pottery, dressed in decorated leather garments, and expressed their artistic instinct by carving ornaments. We can only speculate as to why they left.

Careful professional excavation and study of such archeological sites continues to be the goal of the Society for Pennsylvania Archeology, Inc., Frances Dorrance Chapter 11. In addition to its work on Airport II at the Wyoming Valley Airport, the organization has recently worked on the Cremard Site and the Golumb Farm Site and has now begun work at a new location not far from the Susquehanna River. Each site is different, and each has a story to tell.

A Postscript

According to Max Schrabisch's research in the 1920s, Captain John Smith, at the time of his explorations of the Chesapeake Bay (1607), believed that Wyoming Valley was occupied by the Wassawomeke, a tribe with an earlier Algonquin rather than a Susquehannock/Iroquoian culture. In fact, Schrabisch speculates that their name, "Wassawomeke," is the origin of the Lenni Lenape/Delaware name for this valley, "M'cheuwaming," (spelled "Maughwauwama" by Ira Smith) which means great plains or flats, and is the origin of our word "Wyoming." According to Schrabisch's interpretation of John Smith, the Wassawomeke were the mortal enemies of the Susquehannocks. Schrabisch, who made a careful review of all the materials available to him before he began his study of the rock shelters, states that the Wassawomeke were destroyed not by the Susquehannocks but by the Iroquois in 1652. However, C. A. Weslager suggests that "Wassawomeke" was actually the Algonquin name for the Susquehannocks, whose own language was in the Iroquoian language group, and who were at war with the Iroquois confederacy in the mid-1600s. Present day archeologists Ira F. Smith III and Barry C. Kent and Indian historian Paul A. W. Wallace make no mention of the Wassawomeke. And the absence of any European influence on the Wyoming Valley Culture artifacts indicates very strongly that the stockaded town sites were abandoned in the 1500s, long before 1652.

The late Charles C. Clark, Chief Little Owl of the Nanticoke Tribal Council, is pictured above. His son, Kenneth S. Clark, is the present elected leader of the Nanticoke Indian Association. The association's museum is located in Milsboro, Delaware. PHOTO BY L. T. ALEXANDER. COURTESY C. A. WESLAGER. FROM *The Nanticoke Indians—Past and Present*

Known Indian Inhabitants

THE ARCHEOLOGICAL RECORD tells us that, as early as the 1550s, migrations were taking place that drastically affected Wyoming Valley's inhabitants. After 1600, written records increasingly supplement the archeologic record; and the journals of European soldiers, traders, and missionaries provide a wealth of interesting detail.

As the period of indirect contacts with European culture (about 1550 to 1625) gave way to the Indians' responses to the European invasion (about 1625 to 1675), many Indian communities were disrupted and their people forced to move from the eastern seaboard areas. These displaced persons became Wyoming Valley's new inhabitants. These newcomers had no real claim to the valley, however, since they were here at the invitation of the Iroquois Confederacy.

The Iroquois Confederacy

ALSO KNOWN AS the Six Nations of the Iroquois, the confederacy was an alliance of the Mohawk, Onondaga, Cayuga, Seneca, Oneida, and after 1722, Tuscarora tribes. The terrible Beaver Wars (1638–1674), fought among the Indian tribes over control of the fur trade, led to the Iroquois' expansion of their territory. By 1675, they were overlords of an area that now comprises large parts of New York, Delaware, Maryland, New Jersey, and Pennsylvania, as well as vast territories to the west and to the north. This territory, from at least 1675, and perhaps much earlier, included the North Branch of the Susquehanna River.

The Iroquois believed that Wyoming Valley was critical to the preservation of their territory—the region they called their Longhouse. The valley lay on the southern flank of their territory and controlled the trails important in both war and diplomacy from the junction of the North and West Branches of the Susquehanna River at Shamokin (now Sunbury) to Onondaga (now Syracuse). For at least the hundred years prior to the white settlement of the valley in 1769, the Iroquois viewed Wyoming Valley as the southern door of their Longhouse.

The Susquehannocks, who called themselves the Andaste, had been the dominant tribe along the North Branch prior to its inclusion in the Iroquois territory. As described in the preceding chapter, the disappearance of the prehistoric inhabitants of the valley and of those at Shenk's Ferry on the lower Susquehanna River seems to coincide with the Susquehannocks' sixteenth-century migration from their northern villages to a single heavily fortified village at Conestoga in the Lancaster County area. As a result of this migration, a vacant area was created along the North Branch.

Wyoming Valley seems to have been without permanent residents for some time, although it continued to be used as a hunting and fishing territory. The Iroquois, who now claimed the area, were far too small in number to colonize it. Instead, they were forced to rely upon the displaced Indians from the seaboard to fill the vacuum.

As Paul A. W. Wallace points out, welcoming the tribes of Indians who had been uprooted by white settlements to shelter under the branches of the Iroquois' Tree of Peace was not blind altruism. It was instead an act of enlightened self-interest intended to keep out those white settlers already beginning to hammer on the southern door of the Longhouse.

In 1758, Christian Frederick Post, Moravian missionary to the Indians, wrote,

> *they settle these New Allies on the Frontiers of the White People and give them this as their Instruction: "Be Watchful that no body of the White People may come to settle near you. You must appear to them as Frightful Men, and if notwithstanding they come too near give them a Push we will secure and defend you against them. . . ." The Chain of Union between the several Indian Nations is that of nature, that if we have War with one of them, we have also war with them all.*

The Shawnee were the first displaced persons to settle in the valley. Some bands of Shawnees may have found their way to Wyoming Valley as early as 1701. As a people, they had been uprooted about 1680 from the southeastern coastal area of what is now the United States and had begun a series of migrations that eventually took separate groups to both the Delaware and Susquehanna River valleys.

When the Iroquois had some difficulty with the Shawnee living in the Upper Delaware valley in 1728, they ordered them to go west. Those already settled in Wyoming Valley moved on to Ohio, and Chief Kakowatchiky brought his people to the valley from the Delaware River. They settled at the present site of Plymouth until 1744, when most of them moved on to Logstown on the Ohio River with Kakowatchiky. A few, however, remained at Shawnee Flats until 1756 when Paxinosa, their leader, decided to move closer to the Six Nations. They resettled further north on the Susquehanna River at Tioga before also moving west to Ohio.

The Mahicans were invited to join the Shawnee in Wyoming Valley by Paxinosa. The Mahican chief and Christian convert Abraham, his wife Sarah, their family, and some other Mahicans accepted the invitation and moved to Wyoming Valley in 1753. They came from the Moravian mission village of Gnadenhutten (Huts of Grace), where they had moved earlier when they became Christian converts. Gnadenhutten was located on the Lehigh River at the mouth of Mahoning Creek where Lehighton is located today.

The Mahicans stayed on in Wyoming Valley when Paxinosa and the Shawnee moved north in 1756. In fact, the village at Shawnee Flats is shown on the survey map of the Manor of Sunbury in 1768. This specific Indian village at Shawnee Flats was often called "Wyoming" in the 1700s, although the name was already in common use for the valley as a whole and sometimes was used for the area comprising all of northeastern Pennsylvania.

The Mahicans apparently remained in the valley until 1768–69 when the last Indians left to join the Delawares of the Ohio Territory to the west or the Moravian Indian villages on the Lehigh. Abraham's Creek is said to be named for the Mahican chief Abraham.

Mohegans were also living in Wyoming Valley at the Upper Kingston Flats in 1736, according to Conrad Weiser's notes in his journal for that year. Very little is known about this early Mohegan settlement, but we do know that the Mohegans eventually settled at Tioga.

Barry C. Kent points out that the Mahicans and Mohegans were frequently confused with each other, but research has shown that they were separate peoples, despite the similarity of their names and languages. Coming from the Hudson Valley, the Mahicans had strong cultural and linguistic ties with the Munsee, the Lenni Lenapes of the Upper Delaware River. The Mohegans came from eastern Connecticut. Both were experiencing the same cultural breakdown as other East Coast Indians during the seventeenth and eighteenth centuries. And many people from both groups were migrating toward the Iroquois territory to escape white pressure.

Lenni Lenape of Munsee origin from the Minisink area of the Delaware River moved their main settlement from the Upper Delaware River valley to the mouth of the Lackawanna River in the vicinity of present day Pittston at about the same time that the Shawnee were settling in the area that is now Plymouth. According to Oscar J. Harvey, their village "stood between the bold precipice famed as Campbell's Ledge and the mouth of the Lackawanna River." The Munsee settlement is first mentioned in official Pennsylvania documents in 1727. Their village was called Candowsa, probably after the name of their chief, Kindassowa. The village was also known as Asserughney or Assarockney, most likely derived from the Iroquois name for the Lackawanna River, Hazirok. After the Munsees' involvement in the destruction of the Moravian mission at Gnadenhutten in 1755, they moved further north to establish a new town near present day Corning, New York.

Lenni Lenape of Unami origin, who were living at the Forks of the Delaware, were ordered by the Iroquois early in 1742 to leave that region. The Iroquois were responding to the request of the lieutenant governor of Pennsylvania, a request made because of numerous disturbances in the region. The Forks of the Delaware is the area where the Lehigh River joins the Delaware and is now occupied by Easton, Bethlehem, and Allentown. Some of the Lenni Lenape went to the Ohio River in western Pennsylvania, others to the Shamokin area on the Susquehanna, and still others to Nescopeck Creek, about twenty-five miles south of Wilkes-Barre.

By far the largest number came to Wyoming Valley. They built their village on the flats on the right bank of Solomon's Creek in what is now the Firwood area of Wilkes-Barre. The village stood near an apple orchard then surviving from a prehistoric settlement. The group was decimated by an epidemic and moved upriver to Jacob's Plains (now Plains) late in 1743. The new village became known as Matchasaung or Mejauchsin, meaning 'union' or 'united,' indicating to Harvey that its inhabitants came from both the Unamis and Munsees. This small village seems to have continued to exist, becoming part of Teedyuscung's domain in 1753.

The Lenni Lenape were also known as the Delawares, because of their occupancy of the Delaware River Valley when the Europeans arrived. *Delaware* is not an Indian word but comes from the name of the British Lord De la Warr. As noted above, the two Lenape groups in Wyoming Valley were the Munsees and the Unamis or Wanamies. The Munsees were the "people of the stony country," whose council fire had been at Minisink. The Unamis had had their traditional council fire in the general area of what is now Trenton, New Jersey.

The increasing use of the name "Delawares" indicated the merging of the interests of the Munsees and the Unamis. Those who settled in the eastern areas of Pennsylvania became known as the Eastern Delawares and tended to ally with the British. Those who moved to western Pennsylvania and Ohio (generally referred to as the Ohio Territory) were called the Western Delawares, and in the French and Indian War (Seven Years War) they threw in their lot with the French.

C. A. Weslager has traced the westward movement of the Delawares (Lenape) from New Jersey and Pennsylvania to Ohio, the Indiana Territory, Missouri, Kansas, and finally Oklahoma. Nora Thompson Dean (Touching Leaves) of Dewey, Oklahoma, is pictured here. She wears traditional deerskin clothing which she made from early patterns. A fluent speaker of the Delaware Indian language and a member of the Wolf group of the Lenape, she assisted Weslager in gathering data for his work on the Delawares. COURTESY C. A. WESLAGER. FROM *The Delaware Indians, A History*

Tuscarora were observed in Wyoming Valley by the Moravian missionary De Watteville in October 1748. They were occupying the area just south of the mouth of the Lackawanna River. A village called Adjouquay at this location is noted in the official records in 1755. Listed as an Iroquois village, it may refer to this Tuscarora settlement.

The Tuscarora had begun migrating north from North Carolina about 1710 in order to join the Iroquois. They officially became the sixth nation of the Iroquois in 1722, but the migration continued over many years with prolonged stops along the way.

Nanticokes living in Maryland in the 1740s found their position untenable and asked the permission of the Iroquois chief Shickellamy at Shamokin (now Sunbury) to move into Pennsylvania. They also asked the colonial authorities of Pennsylvania for a safe conduct for their journey north. In 1748 these Nanticokes moved to Wyoming Valley, settling on the flats at the site of present-day Nanticoke. Described by another Moravian missionary, David Zeisberger, as "clever, modest people," they had a reputation as poisoners and as the inventors of witchcraft. Paul Wallace suggests that they encouraged this reputation as a protective device. Their settled homeland had been the Eastern Shore of the Chesapeake Bay in Maryland. They had become tributary to the Iroquois about 1680. This did not mean that they were humiliated or denationalized but that they accepted the Iroquois protection and became loyal "props of the Longhouse."

For five years the Nanticokes occupied the Nanticoke Flats of Wyoming Valley, making seasonal excursions to the Eastern Shore, along the Nanticoke Path, to enjoy the seafood that had been their customary diet. In 1753 they moved on to Chenango in New York where they were subsequently adopted into the Iroquois Confederacy.

Teedyuscung's Settlement was the result of the search of the Nanticokes, with the backing of the Iroquois, for a leader who could stabilize and maintain Indian possession of Wyoming Valley. The Shawnee had just persuaded the Mahicans, Abraham and Sarah and their family and followers, to relocate from Gnadenhutten to Wyoming Valley, as mentioned earlier.

Shortly before the Nanticokes left Wyoming Valley, they visited the Christian Indians at Gnadenhutten and invited them to move into Wyoming Valley, particularly urging Teedyuscung to assume the role of chief. Teedyuscung responded positively to the Nanticokes' invitation.

Teedyuscung organized a band of sixty-five to seventy Indians and moved to the valley in April 1754. They occupied the Firwood area of Wilkes-Barre near the ancient apple orchard, the site of the first village of the Unami group of Lenni Lenape that had been decimated by disease ten years earlier.

The Iroquois promised to protect Teedyuscung's band and promised the colony of Pennsylvania that they would never part with the land at Wyoming: "Our bones are scattered there, and on this Land there has always been a great Council Fire." Chief Hendricks of the Mohawks, one of the Six Nations, made this statement in 1754—the year the Susquehannah Company accomplished the Susquehannah Purchase from the Mohawks by means the Iroquois Confederacy regarded as clearly illegal.

The Six Nations proclaimed that the purchase of Wyoming Valley by the Susquehannah Company was a fraud. Paul Wallace quotes John Shickellamy (son of Shickellamy, who had given the Nanticokes permission to settle here) who was then the Iroquois chief at Shamokin:

> *Whosoever of the white should venture to Settle any land on Wyomock [Wyoming] or thereabouts, belonging hitherto to the Indians, will have his Creatures killed first, and If they did not desist they them self would be Killed, without distinction, let the Consequence be what it would.*

These Nanticoke children are participating in the Ribbon Dance at a powwow. C. A. Weslager quotes Chief Kenneth S. Clark, "[The] powwow is intended to preserve and enhance the cultural identity of the Nanticoke people and to renew the bonds of friendship and cultural exchange with Indian and non-Indian friends." In 1987 the Nanticoke Downtown Revitalization Committee invited the Nanticoke Tribal Association to hold their annual powwow in Nanticoke, Pennsylvania. The area near the Nanticoke–West Nanticoke Bridge is thought to be the site where the Nanticokes, for whom the city is named, most likely lived during their occupation of the area in the middle of the eighteenth century. PHOTO BY PEGGY TOWNSEND. COURTESY C. A. WESLAGER. FROM *The Nanticoke Indians—Past and Present*

Teedyuscung warned off the advance surveyors of the Susquehannah Company in 1762, but died when his cabin burned in April 1763. Within weeks, the Connecticut settlers had moved in, built homes and planted crops. That October, a Western Delaware war party under Captain Bull, Teedyuscung's son, fulfilled the promise of the Iroquois and captured or killed all but a few of the settlers who had already fled back to Connecticut.

By the end of the decade, however, more settlers arrived from both Connecticut and Pennsylvania, and the Iroquois officially gave up their title to the land in the Fort Stanwix Treaty of 1768. But the treaty did not end the Iroquois' resentment over their loss.

The Iroquois had hoped to stay neutral during the American Revolution, but eventually they split and took sides. The Oneida and Tuscarora sided with the Americans, while the Mohawk, Onondaga, Cayuga, and Seneca stayed with their long-time ally, the British, as did the Shawnee and Delaware.

The Seneca Raids against the American settlements throughout central Pennsylvania in May 1778 led to the Great Runaway when settlers all along the West Branch of the Susquehanna River abandoned their homes. The Senecas and their allies, the British and Tories, then invaded Wyoming Valley under Major John Butler's command in July 1778.

When they engaged the Wyoming Valley settlers in the Battle of Wyoming, the Senecas were following a strategy based on their widely recognized claim to this land. The Iroquois Confederacy, to which the Senecas belonged, believed that they had been deviously cheated by the valley's white settlers. According to Dr. Arthur Parker, they had developed their plan for winning back the land a year earlier at a meeting of the whole Iroquois Confederacy at Onondaga. Although one purpose of the expedition against the settlers was to help the British cause by eliminating this outlying white settlement, the Senecas, like the Iroquois as a whole, had as their primary goal the recovery of their lost valley.

On July 3, 1778, the Battle of Wyoming succeeded, as the Senecas intended, in again emptying Wyoming Valley of its white settlers. It did not stay empty for long, however, and the American reprisals were severe. According to his official report, General John Sullivan's 1779 expedition wiped out forty Indian towns. "A vast quantity of vegetables of every kind was demolished, (and) the quantity of corn destroyed, at a moderate computation, must amount to 160,000 bushels." He does not mention the plum, peach, and apple orchards they cut down or girdled. Despite Iroquois raids against Wyoming Valley in 1780 and 1782, Sullivan's march marked the effective end of any Indian claim to Wyoming Valley.

Teedyuscung
Opportunist or Diplomat?

TEEDYUSCUNG, self-styled "King of the Delawares" in the mid-eighteenth century, was a critical figure in Wyoming Valley's early history. He was described by the Moravian missionary and historian John Heckewelder as a "portly, well-looking man endowed with good natural sense, quick of comprehension, and very ready in answering the questions put to him. While passing and repassing to and from the enemy with messages, he was called the War Trumpet."

Teedyuscung was born about 1706 near Trenton, New Jersey, where his ancestors of the Lenni Lenape had lived from time immemorial. He was the son of Old Captain Harris, "a noted man among the Indians," according to Anthony F. C. Wallace. The family were Unami and members of the Turtle Clan, the greatest and most dignified of the three clans of the Lenni Lenape, for they believed that a great tortoise, first of all created beings, bore the earth upon its back. Traditionally, Harvey states, the chief of the Unamis was the chief of the entire Lenni Lenape tribe. However, according to the historic resource study done by the Hugh Moore Historical Park and Museums for the Delaware and Lehigh Canal National Heritage Corridor,

> *at the time of the first European contact the Lenape were living in village bands that contained no more than a few hundred members. . . . In each village group one particular lineage appears to have supplied the village chief. The chiefs acted as mediators to help settle local disputes and performed key roles in ceremonial functions. In reality, their social status was primarily that of being "first" among equals since tribal custom did not grant to them coercive powers. Chiefs did play a major role in directing hunting, but all important decisions had to be made by a general village council. This lack of a strong political organization would later place the Lenape at a grave disadvantage when they were confronted by the unified power of the Iroquois.*

About the time William Penn landed in Pennsylvania (October 1682), the once proud and powerful Lenni Lenape or Delawares had been subjugated by the Iroquois Confederacy. No longer allowed to make war, they were subject to the sovereignty of their conquerors. Even the land they possessed could not be sold without the Iroquois' consent. For example, Penn's Great Treaty of 1683 for much of southeastern Pennsylvania (most of Philadelphia, Delaware, Montgomery, and Chester counties and the part of Bucks not included in the 1682 treaty) purchased the right of possession from the Lenni Lenape but was supported by the purchase of the right of sovereignty from the Iroquois.

By 1737 the Lenni Lenape had no effective recourse from the scam of the infamous Walking Purchase. On September 19 of that year, three strong young men began the timed walk that the Penn family agents had supposedly negotiated in 1686. This questionable treaty was a grant to William Penn for a tract of land north of Neshaminy Creek in Bucks County to extend "as far as a man can walk in a day and a half and thence eastward to the Delaware River." According to Anthony F. C. Wallace, the Lenapes understood this to mean a walk along the bank of the Delaware River and Tohiccon Creek at the usual pace for woods travel. Instead, one of the men, Edward Marshall, succeeded in covering sixty miles in the allotted day and a half, along a direct northerly route that had been secretly cleared in advance. Then James Logan, agent for proprietor Thomas Penn, demanded that the northern boundary of the land to be ceded should be drawn at right angles to the Delaware River from the point where Marshall stopped. The difference between a line drawn "eastward" to the river and a line drawn at a right angle to the river is the territory encompassing most of Northampton, Monroe, and Pike counties. This very large tract included some of the Lenape's most important hunting areas.

Settlers poured into the newly opened area, which encompassed the Forks of the Delaware. Numerous disturbances developed between them and the Lenape, and in 1742 the Iroquois at the behest of the Pennsylvania government ordered the Lenape to leave the area. Compliance with this order brought the first settlement of the Unamis of the Lenape to Wyoming Valley as described in the preceding chapter.

During the first half of the eighteenth century, the Shawnees, the Nanticokes, and the Munsees, a group of the Lenni Lenape, had all located villages in Wyoming Valley at the Iroquois' invitation. With the addition of the Unamis from the Forks of the Delaware, Wyoming Valley was becoming an active trading center although still only sparsely occupied.

Meanwhile on Christmas Eve 1741, another element affecting Wyoming Valley entered the scene. The new Moravian settlement on the Delaware River received the name "Bethlehem" from Nicolaus Ludwig, Count von Zinzendorf, who had just arrived there; and the work of the Moravian missionaries among the Indians in northeastern Pennsylvania got under way in earnest. The Moravians visited the Indian villages in Wyoming Valley several times during the next few years. Their carefully kept notes are one of the best sources of information about the occupants of Wyoming Valley during this period.

Wyoming Valley had been written off earlier by the Moravians when the Shawnees refused to listen to them, but the missionaries were more successful with the later arrivals, especially the Lenni Lenape. They also found a number of willing converts among the Lenape's relocated villages along the northern stretches of the Delaware and Susquehanna Rivers and the mountains between them.

Among the Moravians' converts was Teedyuscung. About 1730, Teedyuscung had emigrated from his home near Trenton, abandoning his livelihood as a broommaker. He resettled in the Kittatinny Mountains in what is now Monroe County, Pennsylvania. There a group of Delawares had established a village along the Pocopoco Creek northeast of what is now Brodheadsville.

Teedyuscung first heard the Moravians preach in 1742. In 1749 he was admitted into the Moravian mission village called Gnadenhutten. Teedyuscung said at his baptism in 1750, "I cannot describe it—but I wept and trembled." Because he was "so desirous to be delivered from sin," he was renamed "Gideon." He did not spend all his time at Gnadenhutten, however, and seems to have kept in close contact with the Lenape in Wyoming Valley. Then, in 1753, Abraham, a Mahican, left Gnadenhutten with his family to settle in Wyoming Valley.

In 1754 Wyoming Valley's Indian inhabitants, particularly the Nanticokes, urged Teedyuscung to move there and assume leadership responsibility for the valley. Teedyuscung responded positively to their invitation, and "dazzled by the prospect of a crown, trafficked his peace of mind for the unrest of ambition." The Moravian historian, William C. Reichel, believed that the visitors who were pushing him to assume leadership had touched that "resentment that burned within his soul when he remembered how his countrymen were being injured by the whites, and how they had been traduced and were being oppressed by the imperious Iroquois, and he agreed to become chief of the Eastern Delawares."

Teedyuscung and sixty-five Delawares and Mahicans left Gnadenhutten on April 24, 1754, for Wyoming Valley. They settled in the Firwood area of Wilkes-Barre, where they were joined by a number of unconverted Delawares from the Minisink region in the Poconos.

The Wyoming Valley had now become the object of mutually exclusive and conflicting claims. On June 24, 1754, the Moravian missionary, John Martin Mack, observed in his journal:

Wyoming is in a critical condition. The New Englanders in right of a Royal Charter, lay claim to Wyoming. The Pennsylvanians hold it is within the Pro-

Teedyuscung, leader of the Indian inhabitants of Wyoming Valley, ably represented the interest of the Lenapes in the pursuit of their tribal integrity until his death by fire in 1763. WHGS

prietary grant, and wish the Indians to sell it to them. Thus the Indians are in a dilemma, for if they yield to the solicitations of the Pennsylvanians and oppose the New Englanders who desire to settle here, and threaten to shoot their horses and cows, they know there will be a war, as the New Englanders are a people who refuse to regard the Indians as lords of the soil, and will subjugate them if they refuse to evacuate the Valley.

In the summer of 1754, a New York trader, John Henry Lydius, secured the purchase of Wyoming Valley from a small number of Iroquois chiefs. This sale was accomplished with the liberal application of liquor and bribery, and the contract was immediately declared illegal by the Iroquois. But the purchaser, the Susquehannah Company of Connecticut, used it to justify its claim to the valley and began to organize to settle there.

In the fall of 1754, several representatives of the Susquehannah Company came to look over the lands they had "purchased." In one account described by Oscar Harvey, when the Indians asked why the Yankees were mapping the land, they boldly answered that so many hundred families from New England would come and settle there. "This is our land," said the Indians settled on it. "No," answered the others, "the land is none of yours; it belongs to the Mingoes (Iroquois). You are only their tenants—slaves—dogs."

The Delawares protested this apparent sale of their lands and said that if the Mohawks (the alleged sellers and one of the nations of the Iroquois Confederacy) did not prevent the New England people from settling on the Susquehanna, they (the Delawares), would go to Ohio to the French. The Mohawks officially denied the sale and said they would never sell any land on the Susquehanna. Furthermore, under the terms of the Iroquois Confederacy, no member nation could make an independent land transaction. The Iroquois could recognize such a transaction as valid only through the approval of the Confederacy as a whole.

On April 22, 1755, Teedyuscung led a delegation of Indians from Wyoming to Philadelphia for a conference with Governor James Morris. The delegation was assured of Pennsylvania's support for their habitation of Wyoming, and in fact they were asked to stay there to hold off the Connecticut settlers. Morris promised to send further instructions for action. However, the instructions did not arrive, and the conflict rapidly worsened.

Teedyuscung was caught in a complex situation. The Western Delawares, the Lenapes, resettled in the Ohio Territory—including at least one of his sons—were now waging war against the British. The French and Indian War (Seven Years War) against England for control of the North American colonies was under way, and the French and Indians were allied in their common interest in ousting the British farming settlements. These settlements constituted a very serious threat to the fur trade.

The Western Delawares mounted a sustained series of raids, forcing the British back from their frontier settlements. Then the French and the Western Delawares combined in an attack on Gnadenhutten, the Moravian Indian town on the Lehigh River. Refugees from Gnadenhutten arrived in Wyoming Valley, and feelings ran high against the "false promises" of the English, who after all had promised over and over again to protect them. Teedyuscung and his followers abandoned their loyalty to Pennsylvania. They joined forces with their relatives, and raided the settlements in the area that is now Monroe County.

In 1756, in order to avoid a retaliatory raid from New Jersey, the Wyoming Valley Indians fled to Tioga, close to the New York border. From there, Teedyuscung journeyed to Fort Niagara to meet the French. But the French, since they were in great need themselves, could not help him with the provisions necessary for the Eastern Delawares to maintain hostilities. This left Teedyuscung with no choice but to make peace with the English authorities of Pennsylvania. A series of peace councils ensued.

In July 1756, Teedyuscung and Governor Morris met at Easton, only to decide that another meeting would be necessary. Meetings between Teedyuscung and Pennsylvania's next governor, William Denny, concluded in November 1756. Teedyuscung raised the sore issue of the Walking Purchase, and the Pennsylvania government promised an investigation. Teedyuscung was shown the original documents in which the Lenapes had supposedly given up their title to the land. He accepted their validity and asked for compensation for the loss. The third council, held in August 1757, concluded with peace established between Pennsylvania and the Wyoming Valley Indians.

Teedyuscung followed up the 1757 agreement by making overtures for peace to the Western Delawares and Shawnees. His initiative was successfully pursued by the Moravian missionary, Christian Frederick Post, and a fourth peace conference was held at Easton in October 1758.

The fourth council settled several land disputes among the Indians and colonists, including a formal denial of fraud for the terms of the Walking Purchase, seemingly accepted by Teedyuscung. He was finally forced to withdraw his charges permanently at a 1762 conference in Easton. The resolution of the conflicts between the Lenape, the Iroquois, and the proprietorship of Pennsylvania opened the way for a coordinated effort to deal with their common enemy, now the most serious threat to the territory.

The Connecticut settlers were continuing to move ahead with their plans for invading Wyoming Valley. They established a staging area at Coshecton (Coshitunk) on the Upper Delaware River in 1760. In 1761 Teedyuscung, the Pennsylvania authorities, and the Iroquois all met at Easton to develop their strategy for blocking the Yankees.

Teedyuscung's life exemplified the conflicts engendered by the cultural cross-currents of the Europeans and the Native Americans. When Swedes, Dutch, and then English usurped the Lenapes' ancestral lands in New Jersey, Teedyuscung sought new territory—first in Pennsylvania's Kittatinny Mountains and later in Wyoming Valley. Teedyuscung, the diplomat reaching across the cultural gap, wore English clothing on state occasions in Philadelphia. His biographer A. F. C. Wallace says, in *King of the Delawares: Teedyuscung 1700–1763,* "Think of Teedyuscung and remember him well: he is a man who tried to bridge in one lifetime the cleft between two worlds—the white man's world and the Indian's world." ILLUSTRATION BY WM. SAUTS NETAMUX'WE BOCK, LENAPE ARTIST AND WOLF CLAN CHIEF OF THE HOMELAND BAND

In September 1762, the Connecticut Yankees widened the route to Wyoming Valley sufficiently to accommodate wagons, and about 150 men moved in to begin constructing their settlement near Mill Creek, not far from the present site of Wilkes-Barre General Hospital. Pennsylvania's governor failed to respond in time to Teedyuscung's appeal for a support force. However, a delegation of Indians from the Iroquois Confederacy did respond. They confronted the settlers and protested their intrusion. After considerable discussion, and an agreement to meet in Albany for a formal conference in the spring, most of the settlers withdrew. Twenty-five stayed on to sow some wheat.

In describing the disputes occurring between himself and these settlers to Pennsylvania's next governor, James Hamilton, Teedyuscung closed his report by saying that should the settlers come back, the Indians would take up the invitation of the Western Delawares and move to the Allegheny area. But he never had the opportunity to plan for or follow up on a course of action.

On April 19, 1763, Teedyuscung died in his bed as his house burned down. He was in a drunken stupor, a condition not unknown to him. Major

William Parsons wrote in 1756 about Teedyuscung, "He can drink three quarts or one gallon of rum a day without being drunk." Alcohol, like smallpox, was a European import that caused the Indians grave problems. In *Valley of Opportunity* Peter C. Mancall cites the growing dependence on it as a major factor in the cultural breakdown that was destroying the Indian communities.

Witnesses reported that Teedyuscung's house had been fired from the outside. The same fire wiped out a number of other Indian homes in the village. Many Indian families left the valley, some for the Moravian settlements along the Lehigh River and others for the Ohio Territory, although a few stayed until after the arrival of the Connecticut settlers on May 15.

Having eliminated the opposition, the Connecticut settlers put in a productive summer. But on October 15, 1763, Indian warriors swept down on the small community and destroyed it. Captain Thomas Bull, Teedyuscung's son, who had settled with the Western Delawares in Ohio, is thought to have led the attack on the Connecticut settlement to avenge his father's death.

Wyoming Valley was again an empty buffer zone. No permanent Indian settlement was ever made here again, and the next homes to be built would be the work of the Yankee and Pennamite settlers, who still had a conflict to resolve over this desirable land.

Harvey quotes from Stone's *Poetry and History of Wyoming,*

> *This chieftain was an able man, who played a distinguished but subtle part during the border troubles of the French War, particularly toward the close of his life. He was charged with treachery toward the English, and perhaps justly; and yet candor demands the acknowledgement that he did not take up the hatchet against them without something more than a plausible reason; while by so doing he was the means of restoring to his people something of the dignity characteristic of his race, but which had almost disappeared under the oppression of the Six Nations. . . . He did not long continue upon the war-path but . . . became an early advocate and ambassador of peace.*

Teedyuscung had succeeded in staving off death and destruction while working to restore his tribe's dignity until he himself was destroyed.

The Five Settling Townships

Wilkes-Barre, Kingston, Hanover, Pittston, and Plymouth

"WE CAN ONLY wish that King Charles had been a little more careful when he was handing out charters!" was the comment of U.S. Senator Harrison A. Williams on a 1959 dispute between New Jersey and Connecticut. In northeastern Pennsylvania, we can sympathize with that comment.

The most generous interpretation of William Penn's famous charter from King Charles II would put Pennsylvania's northern boundary on a line north of Buffalo, Syracuse, and Albany, at the forty-third parallel of latitude. The least generous interpretation would place the northern third of this state under the government of Connecticut. The conflict between Pennsylvania and Connecticut over ownership shaped the culture and politics of Wyoming Valley's white settlement from its moment of birth.

Connecticut's 1662 charter predated Penn's 1681 charter. It stated that the forty-first parallel was Connecticut's southern boundary—running from sea to sea—with the exception of any land "then possessed by other Christian prince or State." This exception forced Connecticut's westward-bound citizens to leap over New York, which already had an established white settlement in the Hudson River Valley. Evidences of Connecticut's claim to the western lands (its Western Reserve) may still be found today not only in Wyoming Valley, but on across northern Pennsylvania and into Ohio.

Pennsylvania, of course, did not recognize the prior claim of Connecticut's charter from King Charles. Nor did Pennsylvania recognize any validity in the transaction with the Indians on which the Connecticut Yankees based their right of ownership of Wyoming Valley. Nor was Pennsylvania the only entity objecting to the settlement of Wyoming Valley by the Connecticut Yankees of the Susquehannah Company.

The British and French both opposed any colonial settlement beyond the Appalachian Mountains. The French knew that farming would disrupt the economic base of their lucrative fur trade. And the British did not want the responsibility of protecting settlers in the mountains. Following their victory in the French and Indian War, the British formally enacted their position into law as the Proclamation Line of 1763. This line followed the crest of the Appalachian Mountains, and colonists were forbidden to settle beyond it. Those who had already entered the forbidden territory were ordered to return. The British believed that the colonies would be both less expensive to protect and easier to control if the colonists were confined to the coastal and riverine areas.

The Iroquois also objected strongly to the white settlement of Wyoming Valley. They knew the value of this land. As we have seen, in order to keep it as a buffer territory between themselves and the white settlers, they invited a number of displaced Indians to live there, tribes whose own home territories had been along the seaboard. This is how the Nanticokes, the Shawnees, the Mahicans, and the Lenni Lenape came to live briefly in Wyoming Valley.

The Lenni Lenape (or Delawares) in particular saw Wyoming Valley as their hope for the future. Defeated in battle by the Iroquois and subsequently displaced from their ancestral lands by the white settlements to the southeast, they were pleased to accept the powerful Iroquois' invitation to move here. In the previous chapter, we learned how Teedyuscung, who had become a Christian convert of the Moravians, left the Christian Indian community at Gnadenhutten to accept the position of chief of his tribe and leader of the Indian settlement here.

So it was in the face of opposition from the Pennsylvanians, the French, the British, the Iroquois, and the Delawares that the Connecticut settlers decided to move westward into the mountains, away from towns whose location on harbors and rivers made them accessible by boat. On steep, narrow trails designed for feet, not wheels, they made their way to this valley.

These settlers were acting in opposition to every powerful force in their world except the one that most affected their own futures. The incredibly high rate of survival among children in New England had created a population that was bursting out of bounds. It was a population of farmers. And New England is a rocky area. Between 1620, when the Plymouth Plantation was established, and 1763, when the British government proclaimed a line to contain colonial settlement, all the good farm land in New England had been claimed. So this beautiful valley, with its flood-enriched, arable soil, was a powerful magnet.

The Susquehannah Company was organized in Connecticut in 1753. The French and Indian War prevented any attempt to cross the mountains for almost ten years. But in 1762 the Susquehannah Company sent in a group of men to begin a settlement. They built three small blockhouses at Mill Creek, near Wilkes-Barre General Hospital's present location, cleared land, and planted crops before returning to Connecticut. They planned to return in the spring.

The Great Road—now Wyoming Avenue—was laid out in 1770. It has followed the same route through Wyoming Valley's west side communities to the present day. This view is from a stereopticon slide showing the section near Swetland Homestead in Wyoming in the mid-nineteenth century. WHGS

Teedyuscung warned them not to return. As king of the Delawares he was responsible to the Iroquois for keeping the valley free of white settlers. Early that next spring, however, the chief was killed when his cabin caught fire, and most of the Indians in Wyoming Valley moved on. In 1763, the settlers came back to an almost unoccupied valley.

Pennsylvania responded to reports of this Connecticut settlement by sending a company of militia to drive them off. When the soldiers reached Wyoming Valley, however, nothing remained of the settlement but burned fields and cabins and massacred bodies. From the evidence, it seemed clear that Teedyuscung's son, Captain Bull, chief of the Western Delawares, had wiped out the settlement to avenge his father's death.

Major John Durkee, Susquehannah Company president and town planner, gave Wilkes-Barre its unusual name. Born at Windham, Connecticut, on December 11, 1728, he married Martha Wood of Norwich, Connecticut, in 1753. His military career, which began in 1756 with the French and Indian War, included the British invasion of Cuba in 1762. He was a soldier, a merchant, and an innkeeper, active in the Sons of Liberty, and deputy to the Connecticut General Assembly. On September 22, 1770, he was captured by a force of Pennamites and imprisoned in the Philadelphia City Jail until August 1772, when he was discharged without prosecution in view of his long incarceration. He returned home to Norwich, Connecticut, making only brief visits to Wyoming Valley in 1773 and 1774, where he was still president of the company of settlers. During the American Revolution, he served as colonel of one of Connecticut's eight regiments until his death on May 29, 1782 at age 54. WHGS

In 1765, Captain Amos Ogden of New Jersey got permission from the Pennsylvania authorities to operate a trading post at Wyoming. He built a "substantial log building for use as a store- and dwelling-house" near the site of Teedyuscung's former town, which had been an Indian trading center. Otherwise, the valley remained largely unoccupied until almost the end of the decade. Then, in 1768–69, the momentum for settlement—and further conflict—got fully under way again.

Late in 1768, before the ink was dry on the agreement with the Iroquois Confederacy ceding Wyoming Valley to Pennsylvania (the Treaty of Fort Stanwix), Governor John Penn ordered surveys of the disputed land. One was for a tract of 20,000 acres on the west side of the Susquehanna River, in and adjoining Wyoming Valley, to be known as the Manor of Sunbury. Another was for a tract of 9,800 acres on the east side of the river to be known as the Manor of Stoke.

In January 1769, Charles Stewart and John Jennings joined Captain Ogden in Wyoming Valley with a number of men from Northampton County in Pennsylvania and from New Jersey. Each man was to have "a lease for seven years of 100 acres of bottom-land, with wood-land sufficient to support their plantation, upon paying the acknowledgement of an ear of Indian corn per annum." In exchange they were to do their "utmost . . . to exclude and re-

Timothy Pickering (1745–1829) successfully maneuvered the new county of Luzerne through its early years of integration into the Commonwealth of Pennsylvania. He lived in Wilkes-Barre from 1786 to 1792, first on River Street in a house owned by John Hollenback, and later in the house he built on South Main Street. The latter, having been home to several generations of the Ross family, was torn down in 1931. WHGS

move . . . unlawful intruders . . . from off the land." In January this group of forty or fifty Pennamites and Jerseyites built their own cabins and a blockhouse at Mill Creek.

The First Yankee-Pennamite War began a month later. In February 1769, a company of forty Connecticut settlers, who had been sent by the Susquehannah Company, reached the north end of the valley. Their reward for undertaking the dangerous reestablishment of the settlement was to get first choice of the land in the valley. Because the bottom lands on the west side of the river were by far the best farm land, the forty settlers chose that site.

Before the men could cross the river, however, they received notice from John Jennings, sheriff of Northampton County (the Pennsylvania county which then had authority over Wyoming Valley), to desist from their undertaking. Three were arrested, and the rest retreated.

The forty returned in March and, probably because they could not then get across the river, built cabins near the mouth of the Lackawanna River in what is now the Pittston area. They were again arrested. Some escaped, and the rest were released on bail.

In May, more than 300 Connecticut settlers arrived, not including those out on bail. They built Fort Durkee near the river, southwest of what is now the intersection of West Ross and West River Streets in Wilkes-Barre, and began farming on both sides of the Susquehanna. In June, the Pennsylvania militia attempted to force them off but failed.

During the summer of 1769, David Mead surveyed the five settling townships, called Wilkes-Barre, Nanticoke (later renamed Hanover), Pittston, Plymouth, and Forty (later renamed Kingston). Then, on November 14, a successful expedition of the Pennamites drove the settlers out and took over Fort Durkee. The whole valley was vacated and left under a small guard of Pennamites.

In February 1770, Lazarus Stewart and the Paxtang Boys, allies of the Yankees, reoccupied Fort Durkee. The Connecticut settlers returned to the valley and resumed building cabins and planting crops.

Surveying within the townships proceeded during 1770. Major John Durkee developed the town plan for Wilkes-Barre. The neat rectangle of central Wilkes-Barre—between North and South streets, River and Back streets (later Canal Street and now Pennsylvania Avenue), with its central Public Square and reserved River Common—is the work of Major Durkee. Lots were drawn on June 29. Incidentally, it was also Major Durkee who named the new town for John Wilkes (1727–1797) and Col. Isaac Barré (1726–1802), defenders of the American colonists' rights in Great Britain's Parliament.

At the same time (June 1770) lots in the Forty (Kingston) Township were being laid out. On the choice west side, David Mead laid out town lots at the bend of the river, meadow lots on the flats, and back lots in the hills. The line of the Great Road, now Wyoming Avenue, was laid out in 1770 and has continued intact until the present day. On June 28, 1770, a list of the forty original settlers was certified to Major John Durkee, president of the Susquehannah Company. Lots on the west side lands were drawn the next week. Each of the forty settlers received a town lot, a meadow lot, and a back lot; and the names of the freeholders were recorded in the township records. The mountain lots were not divided for a number of years, continuing to be owned in their entirety by the forty settlers.

Originally known as the Forty Township, the first recorded use of the name "Kingstown" can be found in the minutes of the meeting of Tuesday, July 3, 1770. It is said that Ezra Dean "proposed to furnish a quart of good Connecticut whisky for the privilege of naming the town." He called it Kingston in honor of his wife, a native of Kingston, Rhode Island.

It is nevertheless noteworthy that the five names finally adopted for the townships all contained direct allusions to Great Britain. Kingston is obvious. The English port city of Plymouth was the principal departure point for settlers leaving for the British Colonies. Hanover was the name of the British royal house from the accession of George I in 1714. John Wilkes and Isaac

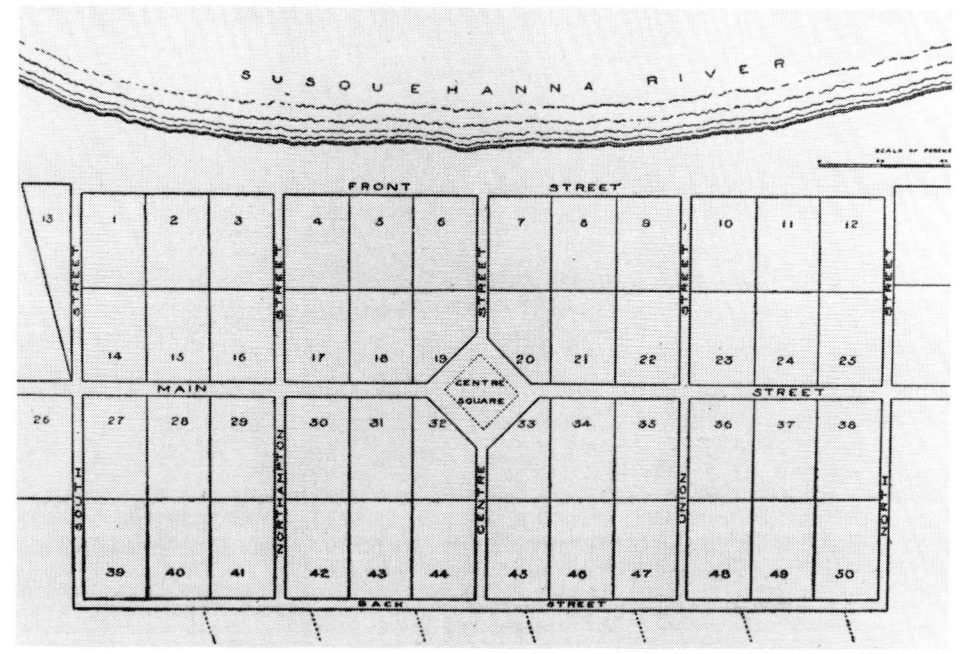

The original town plot of Wilkes-Barre as developed by Major John Durkee. His spacious layout allowed for both Public Square and the River Common. The subdivisions clearly were intended for small family farms. Paths along the backs of these properties probably encouraged the development of Franklin and Washington streets. FROM OSCAR J. HARVEY, *History of Wilkes-Barre*

Barré both took notice of what was happening in the colonies, and William Pitt was prime minister. The Connecticut settlers may have believed that if their conflicting claim with Pennsylvania ever reached a British court these names would work in their favor.

The first specific mention of the name "Forty Fort" occurs in the 1773 minutes of the Kingston Town Meeting in the context of allowing Timothy Rose of Kingston to keep a ferry "opposite the Forty Fort." Both Miner and Reynolds, early local historians, contend that the Forty Fort had existed since 1770, since its existence is implied in the July 3, 1770, minutes referring to "the House building on the bank of the River near the Great Spring."

> *In the meantime, [says Oscar J. Harvey] the number of settlers was being rapidly increased—many of the proprietors who had been in the valley on previous occasions returning to make another effort to establish themselves in the rich and attractive region; while a score or more of men from southern Northampton County, southern Pennsylvania, the Minisinks, New York and New England, who were not proprietors in The Susquehanna [sic] Company—drawn to the valley by the surprising accounts which they had heard and read concerning the*

Pennamite-Yankee contest, so unusual and vigorous in its character—were persuaded, without much difficulty, to buy rights and half-rights in the Susquehanna [sic] Purchase from Major Durkee, Captain Butler and others at Wilkes-Barre who composed the "committee appointed to admit settlers."

In January 1771, the Pennamites, under Captain Amos Ogden's leadership, returned to the Wyoming Valley and immediately began constructing Fort Wyoming on the River Common in Wilkes-Barre. According to Harvey's calculations, Fort Wyoming stood about four-tenths of a mile north of Fort Durkee, and less than fifty yards southwest of the present intersection of Northampton and River streets. There are historical markers for Fort Durkee and Fort Wyoming on Wilkes-Barre's River Common—much closer together than the forts themselves were. The river has eroded its east bank considerably in these 220 years, and the common is much narrower than it once was. Also, Fort Durkee, according to Harvey's careful calculations, was not only further west but at least a block farther south than the marker.

On January 21, after a brief altercation with the Pennamites, the Paxtang Boys slipped out of Fort Durkee and the valley. The Pennamites enlarged Fort Wyoming. Fort Durkee was abandoned and probably demolished. In August 1771, the combined forces of the Yankees and Paxtang Boys returned. They drove out the Pennamites and took over Fort Wyoming.

After three years of hard work and quiet growth in all five of the settling townships, the Connecticut General Assembly, heavily lobbied by the settlers and their representatives, officially attached the valley to Connecticut as the Town of Westmoreland in the county of Litchfield. Legally, this created some confusion since this new "town" already contained five organized townships. Conflict over where the center of their "town" should be—on the east or the west side of the river—was finally resolved by an agreement to meet alternately on each side.

The settlements grew steadily, thanks to the early establishment of the open land system described in the introductory chapter. It is estimated that by the beginning of the American Revolution in 1775, somewhere between two and three thousand people were living here. The farm land was rich, but the labor required was very hard. Living was at the subsistence level, supplemented by the shad harvest from the river in the spring and game from the woods.

Both the restored cabin of Colonel Nathan Denison and his family in Forty Fort and the original cabin of Luke Swetland and his family, still standing at the rear of Swetland Homestead in Wyoming, illustrate the living style of that harsh early period.

In December 1775, the Connecticut settlers responded to a new attempt by Pennsylvania to assert its claim. The Battle of Rampart Rocks, which took place where Tilbury Terrace in West Nanticoke is located, was a decisive

Fort Wyoming was constructed by the Pennamites in 1771 about 50 yards southwest of the point where West Northampton Street joins South River Street in Wilkes-Barre. After changing hands three times in the First Yankee-Pennamite War, it was reactivated as Fort Dickinson at the beginning of the Second Yankee-Pennamite War. The Yankees demolished it in 1784.
COURTESY THE BOOKMAKERS, INCORPORATED

victory for the Connecticut faction. As a result of this battle, the Town of Westmoreland finally became the Connecticut County of Westmoreland, and the townships could function again as they had originally been designed to do.

Ironically, this last battle of the First Yankee-Pennamite War (1769–1775) was fought just days after the Continental Congress of the newly formed United States called for a cessation of hostilities between the Yankees and Pennamites during the conflict with Great Britain.

In 1778, the Battle of Wyoming put both Forty Fort and Wyoming Valley on the national and world maps of the day. The Battle of Wyoming, a Revolutionary War battle and not a Yankee-Pennamite battle, rearranged the sides for the duration of the war. It was Americans, rather than Yankees or Pennamites, who fought against the combined forces of British, Tories, and Indians.

Forty Fort was the site of the decision to do battle, and the surrender of Forty Fort following the battle marked the temporary loss of Wyoming Valley to the British forces. The fame of Wyoming Valley spread through the stories and myth-building following the battle, drawing sympathy and support at home and abroad for the American cause.

After the Revolutionary War, the conflict between Pennsylvania and Connecticut over the Wyoming territory was referred to the court at Trenton, as constituted under the new United States Articles of Confederation. The Decree of Trenton (1782), however, rather than resolving the conflict between the settlers, led directly to the Second Yankee-Pennamite War. The court failed to deal with any of the issues concerning title to the land.

The Second Yankee-Pennamite War began when Pennsylvania denied citizenship and land titles to the Connecticut settlers. In 1783 Pennsylvania troops garrisoned Fort Wyoming, changing its name to Fort Dickinson. In May 1784, they drove the Connecticut settlers out of the valley. The Yankees returned in force. In November 1784, they forced the Pennamites to withdraw and demolished Fort Dickinson.

Colonel John Franklin led an abortive attempt to establish the separate state of Westmoreland, which would be answerable to neither Pennsylvania nor Connecticut, but this endeavor failed. (John Franklin gave his name to Franklin Street in Wilkes-Barre, although this is not widely known.) But the Pennsylvania legislature finally understood that a different approach was necessary if the Yankee-Pennamite disputes were to be ended. Consequently, the Pennsylvania General Assembly created the separate county of Luzerne on September 25, 1786. Colonel Timothy Pickering was appointed to oversee the establishment of the new county (see "The New County of Luzerne"). Harvey quotes Pickering's description of his part in resolving the conflict:

> *Having received some information of the mischievous dispute relative to the Wyoming lands, I embraced every opportunity, while passing among the settlers to learn their feelings and ascertain the footing on which their peaceable submission to Pennsylvania might be effected.*
>
> *On my return to Philadelphia . . . I informed [Mr. James Wilson] that they were entirely satisfied with the Constitution of Pennsylvania, and were ready to submit to its government, provided they could be quieted in the possession of their farms. They had settled them, they said, in the fullest confidence that they were covered by the Charter of Connecticut; they had made very valuable improvements, built houses and barns, and raised good stocks of cattle and abundance of the necessaries of life—when the whole were laid waste and destroyed by the common enemy in 1778. And, more than all these things, a great number of their brethren had perished in battle. That from these calamities they had not recovered—they were poor, and incapable of removing and seeking new settlements.*

To Wyoming Valley's settlers, Colonel John Franklin (1749–1831) was a deeply loved hero. While Pickering was attempting to resolve the disputed land titles, with much less support and cooperation from Pennsylvania's General Assembly than originally promised, Franklin continued to explore the possibility of the new state of Westmoreland as the solution of the Yankee-Pennamite conflict. He recruited supporters through the distribution of additional Susquehannah Company land grants—land which Pennsylvania believed the company no longer had a right to grant. Arrested by the Pennsylvania authorities, he was held in close confinement for six months in Philadelphia. No bail was allowed and no trial scheduled. His followers retaliated by abducting Timothy Pickering. This led the United States Congress to resolve that troops should be sent into Luzerne County. Before the army marched, however, word came that Pickering had been released.

After almost a year in prison, and with his pledge that he would return to Wyoming and use his influence in quelling the disturbances, John Franklin was finally scheduled for trial. Instead he was moved to a jail in Easton and eventually released. Franklin settled in Athens, still a part of Luzerne County. Finally pardoned in 1792, he was appointed High Sheriff of Luzerne County. Between 1794 and 1804, he served several terms as the county's elected representative to the Pennsylvania General Assembly, where he was influential in shaping the Compromise Act of 1799, the legal resolution of the Yankee-Pennamite land disputes. WHGS

The next news I heard on this subject was from my friend Dr. Benjamin Rush. He told me that the General Assembly . . . had just passed a law erecting the Wyoming settlement, and a large extent of country above and below it, into a new County, by the name of Luzerne; that the usual county offices would be created, all of which would be conferred on me if I would accept them. That, being a New England man, the Connecticut settlers would place a confidence in my information and advice, which they would be inclined to withhold from a Pennsylvanian; and thus I might be the happy instrument of putting an end to an inveterate and disastrous controversy.

The establishment of the new county of Luzerne meant that local citizens could now be elected to represent the area at the state level and to handle authority at the local level. Colonel Pickering arrived in Wilkes-Barre early in January 1787 and began the process of administering the oath of allegiance to Pennsylvania, overseeing the election of county officials and state representatives, and sorting out the conflicting land claims. Those that could not be decided at the county level eventually were resolved in the Pennsylvania General Assembly and the courts, and this very complex conflict was finally settled by the Compromise Act of 1799.

With eighteen years of struggle behind it, Wyoming Valley no longer needed to rely on its frontier blockhouses, stockades, and forts: the Mill Creek Blockhouses (1762 and 1768), Fort Durkee (1769), Fort Wyoming (1771), Stewart Blockhouse (1771), Forty Fort (1772), Plymouth Blockhouse (built in 1772 and expanded to Shawnee Fort in 1776), Lackawanna Fort (1772), Wintermute's Fort (1773), Fort Wilkes-Barre (1776), Gaylord's Stockade (1776), Fort Brown (1776), the second Fort Wyoming (built in 1776, renamed Fort Dickinson in 1783), Rosencrants' Blockhouse (1777), and Jenkins' Fort (1777). Wyoming Valley was no longer the frontier. It could begin the process of becoming a community.

What was the significance of the Yankee-Pennamite Wars? Did they have any effect on the communities that emerged? Dr. William Price has theorized that the growth and development of the area was enhanced by the conflicts between the two cultures as they struggled for control. By contrast, other areas settled during the same decade by only Pennsylvania settlers or only Connecticut settlers grew relatively slowly. Instead, in Wyoming Valley, the differences between these two groups of settlers began a process of social and cultural homogenization that not only made growth and development possible but may actually have stimulated it.

Captain Lazarus Stewart and the Battle of Wyoming

On July 3, 1778, the American defenders of Forty Fort decided to march forth to meet the British forces, the Tory Rangers, and the Indians in what would come to be called the Battle of Wyoming. Considerable controversy surrounded that decision, but there is no doubt that Captain Lazarus Stewart took the position that a "prompt and speedy conflict in the open field" was the better course. Stewart Pearce, in his *Annals of Luzerne County,* tells us that

> *Stewart contended that the enemy were increasing in number; that they would plunder the settlements of all their property; that they would burn the dwellings and destroy the crops and leave nothing for subsistence during the coming Winter; that there was no hope of reinforcements on their own side and that if the savages should carry the fort by storm, when they were wasted by fatigue and famine, they would all, together with their women and children, perish in an indiscriminate slaughter.*

Ironically, this is actually a very good description of the result of the decision to march into battle, the chief difference being that the British and Indian forces honored their promise following the battle that no women and children would be killed.

What was Lazarus Stewart, a Scots-Irish Presbyterian, doing among the Connecticut Yankees of Puritan descent at Forty Fort? His presence and that of the other "Paxtang Boys" demonstrate the split personality of Pennsylvania first as colony and later as commonwealth. Having vowed to deal honorably with the Indians, Penn and his successors wished to maintain treaty agreements with them. Unsettled land, however, was useless to the proprietors. Posters and handbills were distributed throughout Europe and the British Isles to attract colonists. But the newly arrived immigrants found little opportunity in the already settled Philadelphia area and rapidly moved westward into the hills and valleys of the Appalachian mountain chain—into land still claimed by the Indians which the provincial government felt no responsibility to defend.

Lazarus Stewart's parents had emigrated with their families from Northern Ireland in 1729. In 1734 Stewart was born on the Pennsylvania frontier in what is now Lancaster County. In 1755 he raised and commanded a company of volunteers that accompanied General Braddock on his ill-fated expedition against the French and Indians on the Ohio River. After Braddock's defeat, settlements on the lower Susquehanna within thirty miles of Harris's Ferry (Harrisburg) were destroyed by the Western Delawares and Shawnees; but the Provincial Assembly (almost entirely made up of Quakers) refused to vote any funds for the defense of the province. After three years of retreat and devastation, the British government took over the management of the frontier war; and from 1758 to 1762 Lazarus Stewart commanded a company of rangers guarding the settlements on the Juniata River.

The French and Indian War (called the Seven Years' War in Europe) officially ended on January 26, 1763. Within months, however, the chief of the Ottawas organized the uprising known as Pontiac's War, again devastating the homes and families of the settlers in the Pennsylvania mountains and valleys. The Scots-Irish and Germans on the frontier immediately responded by forming volunteer companies. A company of the Paxtang Rangers from the Paxtang region of Lancaster County was led by Captain Lazarus Stewart.

Two incidents during this conflict led Pennsylvania Governor John Penn to promise a reward to anyone bringing in and prosecuting the leaders of the "Paxtang Boys," of whom Lazarus Stewart was the most important. Believing that the Conestoga Indians (latter day Susquehannocks) were harboring leaders of the war parties who had murdered and mutilated the settlers, the Paxtang Rangers attacked the Conestoga village, killing six and burning the town. Afterwards, believing that the remaining Indians—who had taken refuge in the workhouse in Lancaster—were still sheltering the murderer of a Paxtang family, Stewart and his men went after him to hold him for trial. In the melee that ensued, in which the rangers fought both the Lancaster County officials at the workhouse and the Indians themselves, all fourteen Indians were killed. Was this the slaughter of innocents or the punishment of butchers? The viewpoints of Lancaster and Philadelphia were diametrically opposed.

Ill will between the Lancastrians and the Philadelphians continued to escalate. The frontiersmen were denounced as "riotous and murderous Irish Presbyterians." Stewart and his friends wanted what they believed would be a fair hearing—to be tried at Lancaster, near the scenes of the butcheries committed by the Indians. Instead, if taken, they were to be tried in Philadelphia, "that [we] may be tried, convicted, sentenced and hung without delay," Stewart wrote. Stewart and his friends began to think about relocating in another territory whose government was more supportive of its frontier settlements.

The Reverend John Elder, Stewart's colonel and commanding officer wrote, "[Lazarus Stewart] and his friends talk of leaving. If they do, the Province will lose some of its best friends, and that by the fault of others—not their own."

Some of the Paxtang Rangers had formed part of the 1763 Pennsylvania expedition to Wyoming Valley. Although their purpose was to warn the Connecticut settlers to move out of Wyoming, they had found only the tortured remains of nine men and one woman left behind by the Indians who had wiped out that small settlement.

When the Paxtang Rangers learned six years later that the Connecticut settlement was to be renewed, "they proposed that they associate themselves with the New England settlers in improving and holding possession of the [Susquehannah] Company's lands at Wyoming." In May 1769, a meeting was arranged at Paxtang with the company's representatives; and by that summer, at least five men from Paxtang and Hanover in Lancaster County had joined the settlers in Wyoming Valley. The First Yankee-Pennamite War was under way; and in November, the Yankees were forced to surrender Fort Durkee to the Pennamites. The Yankees were driven from the valley. In February 1770, Captain Lazarus Stewart and the Paxtang Boys joined the Yankees in regaining possession of the fort. As agreed, they then took possession of "a good township of land six miles square . . . to become parcel of our said settlers and under the same regulations with our settlers."

In August 1770, Lazarus Stewart and a number of the Lancastrians left Wyoming intending to return in November with their families. However, in mid-September, while in Lebanon, Pennsylvania, Stewart was arrested by the sheriff of York County and three deputies for his part in driving the Pennamites out of Wyoming. He escaped from his captors with the aid of an ax handle shortly before twenty armed men arrived in the town with the goal of rescuing him. Another reward was posted, and he was again arrested, this time as he crossed the Susquehanna on his way to York.

When the Paxtang Boys heard, they again rode to the rescue. But the sheriff, with Stewart in custody, was already a day ahead of them on the road to Philadelphia. The governor had now declared that Stewart was, "the most dangerous man in the province." Somehow Stewart managed to loosen the rope that tied him to his sleeping guard. Handcuffed and without coat, hat, or shoes, he traveled through the woods to Paxtang. (Later depositions suggest that this frontier hero had some cooperation from his captors, who collected the reward despite his escape.)

Meanwhile, back in Wyoming Valley, the Pennamites had recaptured Fort

The map shows settlements and events in the Wyoming Valley from about 1700 to the end of the Revolutionary War. It is important to remember that the items were by no means concurrent. For example, the Shawnees left before the Nanticokes arrived; the Nanticokes in turn left before the Delawares arrived. Fort Wyoming and Fort Durkee (which figured in the First Yankee-Pennamite War) were destroyed before Fort Wilkes Barre was built to protect the settlers during the Revolution. MAP DRAWN BY JOHN BECK FOR HANLON'S *The Wyoming Valley: An American Portrait,* REVISED AND AUGMENTED FOR THIS BOOK.

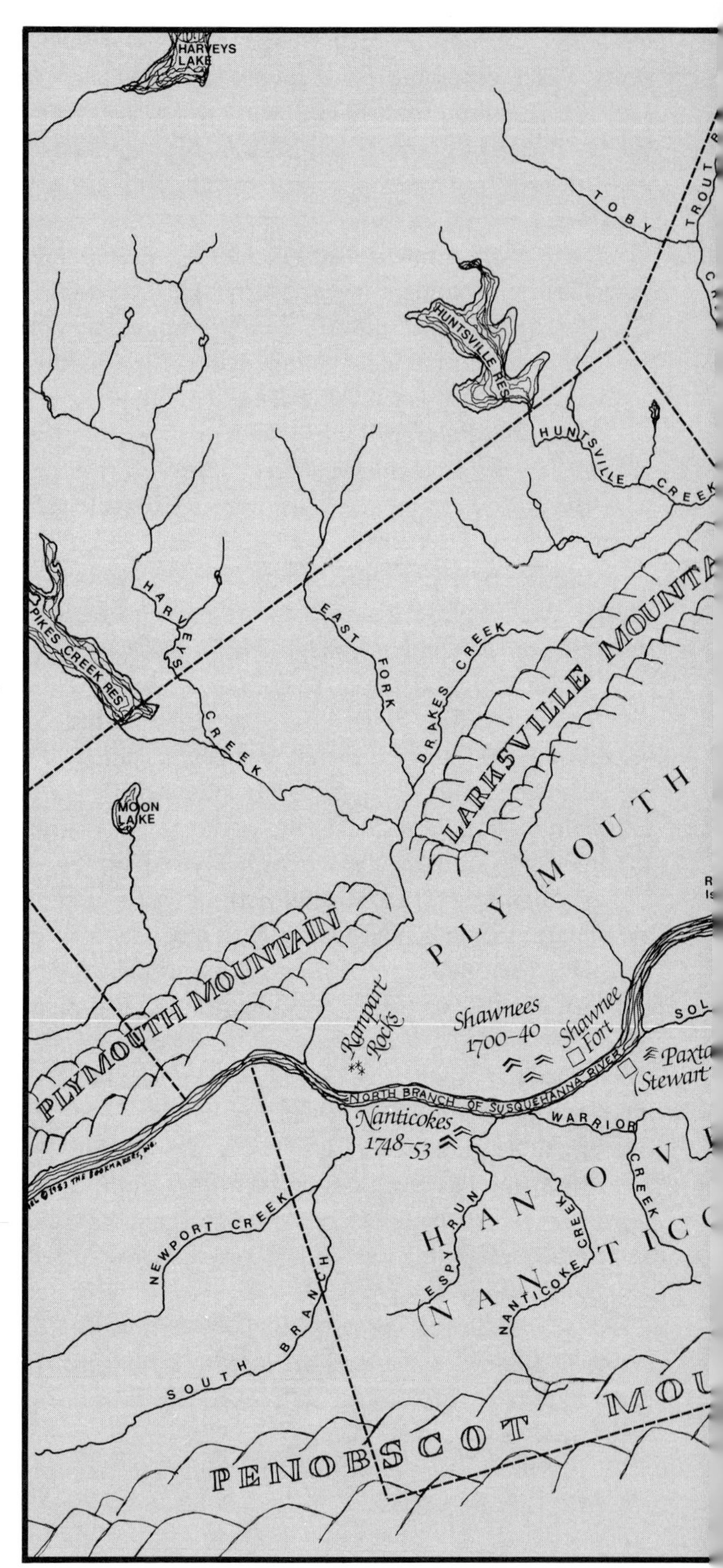

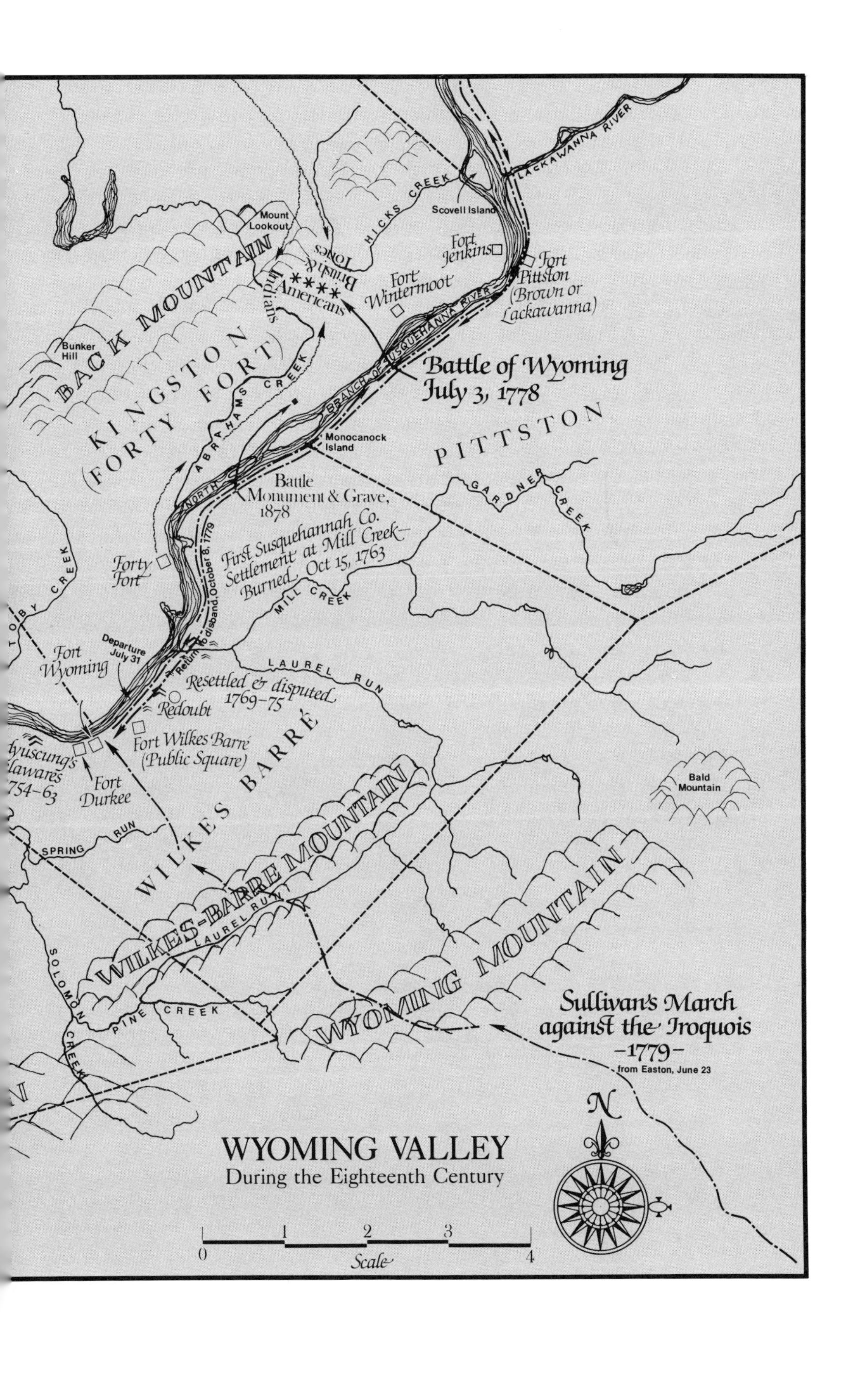
WYOMING VALLEY
During the Eighteenth Century
Back Mountain
Mount Lookout
Bunker Hill
Kingston (Forty Fort)
Indians
British Tories
Americans
Hicks Creek
Scovell Island
Lackawanna River
Fort Jenkins
Fort Pittston (Brown or Lackawanna)
Fort Wintermoot
North Branch of Susquehanna River
Battle of Wyoming July 3, 1778
Abrahams Creek
Monocanock Island
Pittston
Gardner Creek
Battle Monument & Grave, 1878
First Susquehannah Co. Settlement at Mill Creek Burned Oct 15, 1763
Mill Creek
Forty Fort
Toby Creek
Return to disband, October 8, 1779
Departure July 31
Fort Wyoming
Laurel Run
Resettled & disputed 1769–75
Redoubt
Fort Wilkes Barré (Public Square)
Fort Durkee
Wilkes Barré
Bald Mountain
Spring Run
Wilkes-Barre Mountain
Laurel Run
Wyoming Mountain
Solomon Creek
Pine Creek
Sullivan's March against the Iroquois -1779-
from Easton, June 23
N
Scale
0
1
2
3
4

Durkee. In December, Stewart and the Paxtang Boys left Hanover, Lancaster County. Arriving in Wyoming, they retook the fort by simply going in the north gate—opened by the brother of one of their party already inside the fort—and driving out the Pennamites. And in January 1771 it was voted, as had earlier been agreed, that Stewart and his associates were entitled to all the Susquehannah Company's rights in the township they had chosen. Formerly known as Nanticoke it was now to be called Hanover in honor of their former home, Hanover Township in Lancaster County.

On January 18, 1772, the sheriff of Northampton County and a posse of about one hundred men arrived with a writ for the arrest of both Lazarus Stewart and a number of others in the fort. For three or four days, the sheriff and his deputies approached the fort singly and in small numbers requesting that the inhabitants submit themselves to arrest. Stewart responded that he had sent his own messenger to the governor and was awaiting a response. Finally, Nathan Ogden, brother of Captain Amos Ogden, was fired upon from the fort, almost surely by Stewart, and killed. Soon thirty or more guns were fired from the fort and wounded three other Pennamites. That night, Stewart and his party left Fort Durkee and took refuge in the woods, about six of them eventually making their way to Connecticut; the rest returned to Lancaster County. Once again, the Pennamites occupied Fort Durkee.

By midsummer, the Yankees were ready to move back again. Lazarus Stewart journeyed secretly to Lancaster, reassembled those Paxtang Boys who had fled with him from Fort Durkee and joined forces with the Yankees to march on the valley. First, they took possession of the newly built blockhouse on Mill Creek, then they built and occupied four redoubts on a hill about a half-mile down river. From these redoubts the Yankees controlled all ingress and egress to the new Pennamite Fort Wyoming. On August 15, 1771, the Pennamites capitulated, and the Yankees once again took control of Wyoming Valley.

The settlement of Hanover Township began with preparations for its defense. Harvey tells us that

> *In the fall of 1771 Captain Stewart began the erection of a block-house in Hanover Township. This was the first building erected in the township by a settler under the Susquehanna [sic] Company, and it stood on a slight rise of ground a few rods from the bank of the river, a short distance below the Wilkes-Barre/Hanover Township boundary line. It was built of logs, was one and a-half stories high, and contained four rooms on the ground floor with ample space on the floor above for the convenience of its occupants. The part of the building above the second floor projected beyond the walls of the first story—this "overshoot," as it was called, enabling the defenders of the house to protect the walls from assaults by attacking parties.*

Lazarus Stewart's blockhouse—a combined home and fort—stood in Hanover Township. There is no known picture of the legendary firebrand. FROM HARVEY'S *History of Wilkes-Barre*

In the spring of 1772, the Yankees and Lancastrians began to bring in their wives and children. Although the First Yankee-Pennamite War continued for three more years, the Yankees were not again dislodged from the valley. In 1775 the Yankees and Pennamites suspended hostilities in response to the appeal to both parties by the Continental Congress to focus their efforts on the war against Great Britain.

By the third of July 1778, the morning of the Battle of Wyoming, the Yankees and Lancastrians had become a community. The Yankee Colonel Nathan Denison had named his eldest son Lazarus Denison after Captain Lazarus Stewart, and there was a strong friendship between them. In that group at Forty Fort, Stewart was respected for his experience, particularly in Indian warfare, and he had the greatest familiarity with the depredations associated with it. Unfortunately, the decision makers in the fort, with inadequate information about the invading force, seriously underestimated its size. In fact, it was even argued that if they did not attack at once the raiding force would loot and burn the upper valley farms and rapidly retreat northward with their booty.

Stewart believed there was no other choice. He did not trust the promise of good terms of capitulation for the inhabitants in exchange for surrender without bloodshed. In fact, he believed that if no stand were made the result would be exactly the same bad outcome the settlers faced when the battle was lost. His arguments carried the day, over the objections of both Zebulon Butler and Nathan Denison. Denison later told John Franklin that he said as much against it as he could without being called a coward.

Miner states, "Every captain that led a company into action was slain, and in every instance fell on or near the line." Captain William M'Kerachan was the first officer of the Hanover Company, but because he lacked experience at war, he resigned his post to the greater experience of Captain Lazarus Stewart. They fell together in the Battle of Wyoming.

The Bloody Rock

On Susquehanna Avenue in Wyoming is a rather ordinary, rather large rock, not far from the sidewalk. This so-called Bloody Rock, also called "Queen Esther's Rock," was the setting for a story widely circulated following the Battle of Wyoming and carefully recorded in the nineteenth-century histories of the area. This is the story of the gruesome aftermath that supposedly followed that battle. How much of the story is true, and how much is the result of the wartime propaganda machine that develops in every conflict? Let the reader be the judge.

The Battle of Wyoming took place on July 3, 1778. It was a small battle, lasting barely half an hour, but it had major significance in the American Revolution. Great Britain's goal in invading the Wyoming Valley and attacking the settlers was to destroy this important settlement, scare other, smaller settlements out of the mountains, and dominate the western frontier. This was key to the British strategy for containing the colonists and ending the American rebellion.

Britain's Indian allies included four of the Six Nations of the Iroquois. Of these, the Senecas in particular were anxious to reclaim the valley. They did not regard the Connecticut settlers' claim as valid, and they believed the land had been unfairly acquired. The Seneca war chief Sakayengwaraghton was the leader of the approximately 460 Indians who formed the war party.

The British and Indian alliance also included 110 Tories, or Loyalists. These were American colonists who maintained their loyalty to Great Britain. The British and Tory force under Major John Butler's leadership was called Butler's Rangers.

The invading body of British, Tories, and Indians numbered somewhere around six to seven hundred. Opposing Butler's Rangers and the Indians was a force made up of about 350 men and boys who, for the most part, were still in Wyoming Valley because they were either too young or too old to be fighting in one of the companies under George Washington's command. The threat to Wyoming Valley had led Washington to release the Wyoming com-

Evidence of the wide recognition given the Battle of Wyoming and its aftermath is found in this engraving of the *Disastro di Vioming* from an Italian book on the history of the United States. The same engraving also found its way into a French history from the same period. WHGS

panies, but most of them arrived back in the valley too late for the battle. Veteran commander Colonel Zebulon Butler did arrive in time to take charge of Fort Wilkes-Barre. He then joined Colonel Nathan Denison and the men gathered at Forty Fort, including a few other veterans on leave. Butler advised against moving out of the fort. Nevertheless, when the decision to march was made, over his objections, he led the Americans into battle.

The battle took place near Fourth Street in Wyoming on July 3, 1778. Within thirty or forty minutes, the Americans were soundly defeated. In addition to their superior numbers and more seasoned soldiers, the British forces also successfully used a flanking move, carried out by their Indian allies, which caught the settlers by surprise and cut them off from the river.

The battle became a retreat, which became a rout. With the British Rangers and Indians on their heels, about two hundred of the settlers were caught and killed on the spot. Others were captured and dragged back across the flats and up to the plain. After Forty Fort's surrender on July 4, however, there is no record of any additional killing, despite the looting and destruction of most of the farms in the valley and the massive retreat of the inhabitants.

Sixteen or eighteen of the captives, we are told, were held down by warriors in a circle around the Bloody Rock that night of July 3 while a woman

Forty Fort, built in 1772, stood at the bend of the west bank of the Susquehanna River. The town that bears its name today grew around it. This drawing by Edmund L. Dana, which first appeared in Pearce's *Annals of Luzerne County* (1860), has reappeared in almost every local historical work since. WHGS.

identified as Queen Esther alternately dashed out their brains with a maul or sank a tomahawk into their heads, "singing or as if counting with a cadence" as she moved around the circle. Two of the captives, Lebeus Hammond and Joseph Elliott, "seeing their end approaching" suddenly shook off the Indians who held them and made their escape. The bodies of fourteen or fifteen others were later found around the rock where they had died. Nine other bodies were found in a similar circle some distance above.

Who was this Queen Esther, for whom the Bloody Rock is now named? She is believed to have been Esther Montour, who was known at the time to travelers along the Susquehanna as Queen Esther.

Esther Montour was born about 1720 and belonged to the Seneca nation. Her great-grandfather was French, but whether he was the Count de Frontenac or a French gentleman and adventurer is not clear. Esther was married at an early age to Eghobund (Eghohowin), a chief of the Munsees whose village was Sheshequin (now Ulster), on the Susquehanna River in what is now Bradford County. After a visit to Sheshequin by the Moravian missionaries John and Mary Rothe, seventeen inhabitants left to join the Moravian Indians. Eghobund and the remainder of his clan moved five miles up the river to the village later known as Esthertown. Eghobund died, and Esther took over the management of the affairs of the village—seventy log and plank houses, with five miles of cornfields, orchards, and pasture lands opposite Tioga Point.

In 1777, James Sutton and John Jenkins traveled to Esthertown to recover a captive, Daniel Ingersoll. Queen Esther treated the visitors courteously, and said that she was opposed to war and believed that the settlers and Indians could live together in peace. During the evening they spent with her, a company of Indians seated themselves on a log in front of the house and began to sing the "war song." Oscar Jewell Harvey quotes Dr. Peck's account: "When she came in she frankly told her guests that the Indians were determined to waylay and kill them, adding, with great emphasis, 'I can do nothing with them. Now you lie down until I call you.' They did so, and when all was still in the town she called them and said, 'You must go down the river. Go down the bank, take my canoe and paddle it without noise.' They slipped off and found their way home in safety."

In early June 1778, a young girl, Jane Strope, who had often seen Queen Esther at her father's house, was taken captive with her family. Harvey quotes from a letter written in 1853 that gives details of Jane Strope Whittaker's account of her captivity:

> *During the preparation for the attack upon Wyoming, the family of Mr. [Sebastion] Strope were detained at Tioga Point. . . . At this time they were visited by their old friend Queen Esther, who showed them many marks of kindness. On one occasion when about to return home she desired to have the little captive accompany her to her castle for a visit. . . . In company with her mother, Mrs. Whittaker crossed the river and rambled over the premises of the Queen.*

Esther Montour is described by Jane Strope Whittaker as "tall but rather slight in form, hair black but soft and fine. Her form was erect and commanding, and her appearance and manners agreeable. . . . Her costume was rich and showy and comported well with her claims to deference and queenly dignity." Her home, called both castle and palace, was "a long low edifice, irregular in shape . . . with a porch at the doorway of some architectural pretension, and surrounded by quite a number of other buildings."

Since this portrait of kindness to visitors, friendship toward white settlers, and a spoken desire to live at peace is at such odds with the bloody rock incident, some authors have seriously doubted that Queen Esther was "the Hecate of that fell night." Paul Wallace suggests that Esther's sister Catharine Montour, wife of the Seneca chief Telenemut, was more likely to have been the woman at the bloody rock. In fact, Wallace tells us that Catharine's name appears in several early accounts of the massacre as that of the "priestess" who presided at it. On the other hand, Queen Esther was known to a number of the Wyoming Valley settlers and was clearly identified by them on July 3 and again on July 4.

Charles Miner, writing about these events in 1845, comments:

ABOVE: The marker placed at Queen Esther's Rock by the D.A.R. a century ago is quite specific about her deed. LEFT: The current historic marker is less certain. The rock itself—enclosed in brick walls and covered with an iron grille—is impossible to photograph. PHOTOS BY THE AUTHOR

It is the opinion of Mr. [Joseph] Elliott [one of the two who escaped from the ring at the bloody rock] that her exasperation of passion was partly owing to this: Several Indian spies had been arrested, and were held prisoner at Forty Fort. Queen Esther had been down from her palace to obtain their release, which Colonel Nathan Denison had deemed it proper to refuse.

Far more important, on July 1, as the settlers prepared to meet the enemy advance, a squad went upriver from Forty Fort to Exeter. It came upon the bodies of the Harding brothers, Stukely and Benjamin. They had been part of a party of eight who had left Jenkins' Fort the day before to work their corn, not realizing that the rangers and Indians were already in the area. Seated near the Hardings' scalped and cut up bodies were two Indians. One they shot where he sat, the other as he fled into the river. One of these Indians was believed to be Queen Esther's son.

Only two days later, during the evening and night of July 3, Queen Esther was supposed to have led the almost ritualistic slaughter of the captive settlers. And on July 4, she entered Forty Fort at the head of the Indian column to accept the fort's surrender. According to John Franklin's account, she said to Colonel Denison as he came out of the fort to meet them, "Well, then, Colonel Denison, you made me promise to bring more Indians. Here, see, I bring you all these."

In the autumn of 1778, Queen Esther took her people and their livestock into hiding when she was warned of the approach of Colonel Hartley's raiders. They then abandoned Esthertown altogether. The following summer, Lieutenant Colonel Adam Hubley, one of General Sullivan's officers on the march to eliminate the Indian "threat" in the area, wrote in his journal on August 11, 1779, that, "We then entered the place on which Queen Esther's palace stood and was destroyed by Col. Hartley's detachment last fall." Another officer records that Sullivan's force then fired the entire town, "a glorious bonfire of upwards of thirty buildings at once."

Esther Montour was later married to a Tuscarora chief named Steel Trap and moved north with him to Cayuga Lake. Our last glimpse of her comes from Hannah Gore Durkee in 1790. Mrs. Durkee was living at Scipio, New York, when Queen Esther and her sister stopped at the Durkee home one evening on their way to Onondaga. They asked for shelter for the night, which was furnished them. Esther Montour is believed to have died at Canoga, New York, about 1800.

Was Esther Montour the savage dancer of the bloody rock? William Kashatus, III, who has done extensive research in the original materials relating to the Battle of Wyoming, stated in the Wilkes-Barre *Sunday Independent* on July 3, 1988, that his research did not reveal any primary-source evidence to substantiate Queen Esther's savage dance. Is the bloody rock just a story? Did it grow from a real incident, acquiring names and details as it was repeated over the years? Or was it the conscious or unconscious work of a propaganda war making the most of a real battle? Perhaps primary evidence will eventually come to light that verifies or contradicts the accounts of Lebeus Hammond and Joseph Elliot. Meanwhile we must each decide for ourselves how much to believe.

The New County of Luzerne

On September 25, 1786, the General Assembly of the Commonwealth of Pennsylvania created a new county out of the region known as Wyoming. The new county encompassed the territory now comprising Luzerne, Lackawanna, Bradford, Susquehanna, and Wyoming counties, as well as parts of what are now Carbon and Lycoming counties. It was larger than the combined states of Delaware and Rhode Island, and three-fourths the size of Connecticut.

Between 1782 and 1786, the Wyoming territory had been in continuous turmoil. The conflicting land claims of Pennsylvania and Connecticut had led to the First Yankee-Pennamite War. But that war had resolved nothing. In fact, it ended only because the interests of both colonies in the Revolutionary War had temporarily superseded the claims of the two colonies against each other. When the Revolution ended, the conflict between the two states still needed to be resolved.

A Court of Commissioners, specially charged by the Continental Congress to meet at Trenton, New Jersey, determined the "claims, rights, and possessions" of Pennsylvania and Connecticut in and to the Wyoming lands. On December 30, 1782, the court decreed, "We are unanimously of the Opinion that the State of Connecticut has no right to the Lands in Controversy."

The issues of title to the land and rights to the soil—not resolved by the Trenton decree—were naturally of grave concern to the settlers living in the territory. During the next four years, those inhabitants of Wyoming whose title to their land was held only under Connecticut's authority tried to find a way to keep that land and to validate their titles, or even to find other land that they could occupy without additional expense. After all, the Connecticut titles to their land represented not only years of hard work and sacrifice, but also, in most cases, their only assets.

Among the settlers who wanted to validate their Connecticut titles were Pennsylvanians who had moved into the area at the invitation of the Yankees and held their titles solely under Connecticut law. Some lucky Pennsylvanians who had come to Wyoming Valley because of tenancy holdings under Penn-

Chateau de Beuzeville in Veys, District of Caventau, was the ancestral home of the Viscounts of Luzerne. WHGS

sylvania land claims had also acquired Connecticut titles to the same land, since they preferred the Connecticut system of freeholding to Pennsylvania's tenancy and quitrents. Having acquired both, they were the only settlers assured of keeping their land no matter which way the dispute was resolved.

Complicating the issue of valid titles even further were the changes made in Pennsylvania's landholding laws as Pennsylvania made the transition from colony to commonwealth. Because the colony had been a proprietorship, land had not been sold outright. Instead, the colonial Pennsylvania pattern of settlement was one of manors with tenants who paid quitrents. Now that Pennsylvania was an independent commonwealth, land in Pennsylvania could be owned outright.

The Wyoming settlers vigorously protested the decision of a Pennsylvania commission that allowed them the use of one-half their cleared and settled land for just one more year (two years for widows and orphans). This decision would mean their complete impoverishment by the end of the year. They then watched with apprehension as Pennsylvania reorganized the entire area into two new townships under Northumberland County rule. These replaced all former township lines and eliminated all self-government. The settlers endured misgovernment and persecution at the hands of the newly arrived and strangely elected officials, who were empowered by the Northumberland County author-

Anne Caesar de la Luzerne (1741–1791) was Minister Plenipotentiary to the new United States capital at Philadelphia. To the Americans he symbolized French support for their cause. WHGS

ities to oust them. They suffered mass imprisonment, witnessed their houses being burned, and fought and won the Second Yankee-Pennamite War. They also petitioned New York State for unoccupied land further north along the Susquehanna River.

The settlers even invited General Ethan Allen of the Green Mountain Boys from the newly created state of Vermont to aid them against the Pennamites, and they secretly discussed the creation of their own new state. This was Colonel John Franklin's favorite resolution of the conflict, since it would allow the valley people to be independent of both Pennsylvania and Connecticut. And in the midst of this political and military turmoil, they endured the disastrous March 1784 ice flood.

It is no wonder that by 1786, when Colonel Timothy Pickering made his first visit to Wyoming, he described it as showing the vestiges of ruin these years had wrought. The settlers' log hovels were wretched beyond description, he said, many not even having chimneys but only "a hole left in the roof through which the smoke escapes."

Finally, the settlers elected a committee of five directors to form their own government. They then petitioned the Commonwealth of Pennsylvania to create a separate county encompassing the territory of Wyoming. John Franklin and John Jenkins carried this petition to Philadelphia, where they were eventually heard, whereupon the "Bill for erecting the Wyoming District into a separate County" was read, considered, and passed, forty-four to fourteen.

The new county was named Luzerne. Anne Caesar de la Luzerne had been appointed by King Louis XVI of France to be Minister Plenipotentiary

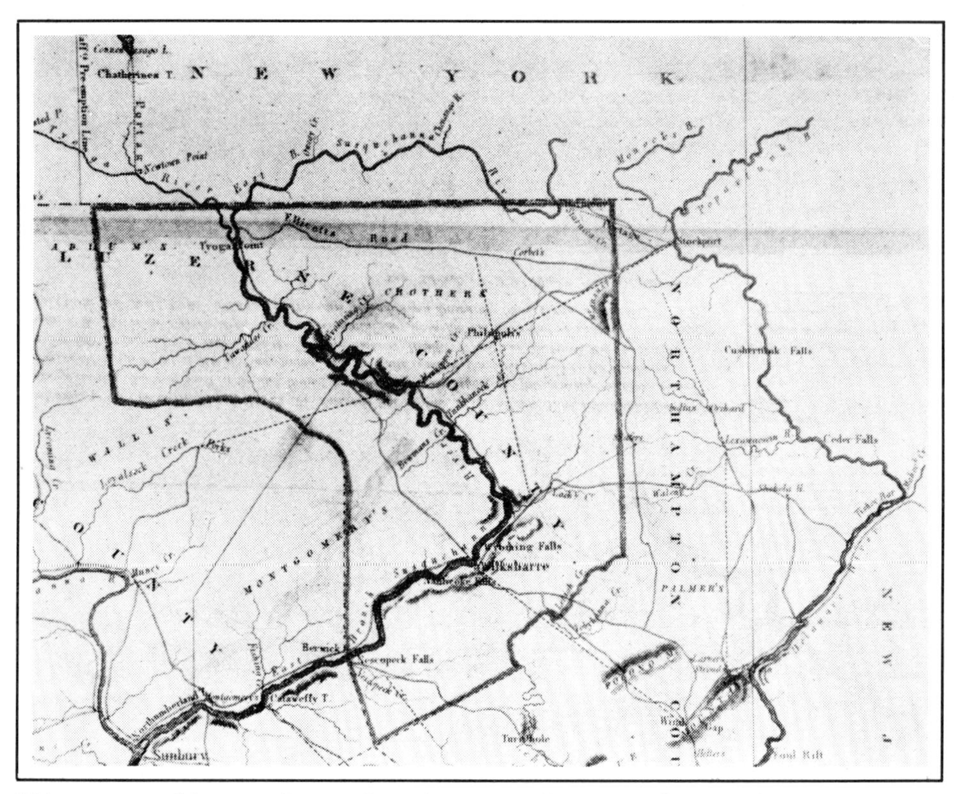

This 1791 map of Luzerne County shows how Pennsylvania's northeast quadrant was once divided into Northampton, Northumberland, and Luzerne counties. FROM HARVEY'S *History of Wilkes-Barre*

to the United States. In November 1779 he arrived in Philadelphia, then the capital of both the United States and Pennsylvania. He had traveled by way of Boston and West Point, where he visited with General George Washington.

The Chevalier de la Luzerne was welcomed in Philadelphia as the savior of the new nation, and with good reason. Without France's support, the American experiment might easily have failed. Luzerne, representing the power of France, particularly its ability to offset the might of Great Britain, embodied America's best hope of winning the Revolutionary War.

In addition to symbolizing French strength and support, the Chevalier de la Luzerne was both respected and liked by the Americans in Philadelphia. He held such a grand entertainment to celebrate the birth of the Dauphin of France (Louis XVI's son and heir) that Dr. Benjamin Rush felt compelled to describe it in elaborate detail, commenting, "How new the phenomenon for all republicans and freemen to rejoice in the birth of a prince who must one day be the support of monarchy!"

Luzerne was recalled to France in 1784. Two years later the following was sent to him via the French chargé d'affaires: "The Assembly of Pennsylvania, wishing to hand down to posterity a testimonial of its gratitude for the services which M. le Chevalier de la Luzerne rendered to the Union, has just given his name to a new County." Luzerne responded to this honor with praise for the state of Pennsylvania and added, "I have had the further advantage of a personal knowledge of the different members of your government and the opportunity of judging with what wisdom, prudence and firmness they have succeeded in establishing one of the best Governments in the world."

This praise was particularly merited by the creation of a new county for the territory of Wyoming. How easy it would have been for the Pennsylvania Assembly to ignore John Franklin and John Jenkins and their petition and to continue to look to the sheriff of Northumberland County and the use of force to resolve the conflicting claims to the land—regardless of the cost to the settlers who had cleared and cultivated it. The creation of the new county removed the Wyoming territory from the political control of Northumberland County. It allowed the settlers to be governed by county officials they themselves elected. And it opened the way for the fair and just resolution of the conflicting land claims on an individual basis.

The Chevalier de la Luzerne was next appointed as Louis XVI's Ambassador to the Court of St. James in London. He died in 1791 at the age of fifty while France was in the throes of its own violent revolution. But the county named in his honor had finally reached a political equilibrium that would allow its great potential to develop.

This rock shelter, called Indian Rock Cabin, is located on Abraham's Creek. It may be the one in which Frances Slocum and Nathan Kingsley stayed on the first night of their captivity. The possibility led to giving Frances Slocum's name to the state park now located in that area. Archeologist Max Schrabisch, who is pictured here, found evidence of infrequent use of the shelter by hunters. FROM *Proceedings and Collections,* WHGS

The Wonderful Story of Frances Slocum

FRANCES SLOCUM WAS a little girl kidnapped by Indians in November 1778—and rediscovered by her family in September 1837, almost sixty years later. The story of Frances Slocum sounds like a legend, but the historical evidence is unusually complete. And, unlike Martha Espy Stewart, wife of Lazarus Stewart, and Esther Montour, who represent two sides of the bitter struggle for possession of Wyoming Valley, the story of Frances Slocum demonstrates a life that bridges both cultures.

The Slocum farm occupied what was then the outermost edge of the settlement at Wilkes-Barre, at about the corner of East North Street and what is now Pennsylvania Avenue. Jonathan Slocum, Frances's father, was a Quaker, a conscientious member of the Society of Friends; and as such, he did not take part in the Battle of Wyoming on July 3, 1778. He probably did not move his family into Fort Wilkes-Barre; and in fact, he was slow to leave Wyoming Valley after the battle. The family also returned to the valley very quickly, at the end of August that same summer, when they found their farm and home undisturbed.

On November 2, 1778, the family were going about their work as usual when a small party of Indians attacked. Mrs. Slocum heard a shot, opened the front door, and saw the lifeless body of Nathan Kingsley, who had been living with the Slocums along with his mother and brother after their father's death in the Battle of Wyoming. Leaving the younger Kingsley boy and the five-year-old Frances hidden under the staircase in the cabin together with Ebenezer Slocum, age thirteen, who had a lame foot and could not run, the rest of the household ran out the back. The ten-year-old Mary carried the toddler Joseph toward Fort Wilkes-Barre, and Mrs. Slocum took her newborn infant Jonathan to hide at the edge of the swamp. When she saw the Indians taking the three children out of the cabin, she ran back from the swamp and persuaded them to leave Ebenezer, whom she was sure they would kill because of his lameness.

Maconaqua's moccasins, blouse, and blanket are in the William Penn Museum in Harrisburg. The exquisite needlework in the decorative trim on this moccasin was probably done by Maconaqua herself. PHOTO BY JOHN WITTHOFT, PENNSYLVANIA STATE MUSEUM, HARRISBURG

She then tried to persuade them to leave Frances and the young Kingsley boy. But with Frances over one man's shoulder, young Kingsley over another's, and a bag of plunder from the cabin over the shoulder of the third, the Indians mounted their horses and rode off.

The men from the fort heard the shot, it is thought, because before young Mary reached the fort, she was met by a squad of soldiers who rode to the Slocum house. From there they attempted unsuccessfully to follow the three Indians.

Years later, Frances Slocum said she and Kingsley had been carried over a mountain and a long way down on the other side to a cave, where the Indians had left their blankets and other articles and where they stayed that night. The location of that cave or rock shelter is one of our local mysteries. The Frances Slocum State Park in Kingston Township was so named because folklore maintains that the rock shelter there was the one used by the Indians that night. There are other theories, however, and very little evidence.

After several days of travel, the small band came to an Indian village, probably Chemung in southern New York. After staying there for some days, they resumed their journey and eventually came to the village of the group's leader, a Delaware chief named Tuck Horse. This village may well have been Fort Niagara, where the British had gathered the remnants of several Indian nations to fight for them in the Revolution.

At this point, Tuck Horse dressed Frances in the Indian way with beautiful beads, which pleased the five-year-old very much, and painted her face. Frances

This portrait of Maconaqua was painted by George Winter after she and her original family were reunited in 1839. The original is in the William Penn Museum and a copy in the collection of the Wyoming Historical and Geological Society. WHGS

said, many years later, "He took me by the hand and led me down to the river side to a house where lived an old man and woman of the Delaware nation. They had once several children but now they were all gone—either killed in battle or having died very young. I was brought to these old people to have them adopt me, if they would. . . . After Tuck Horse had talked with them awhile, they agreed to it, and this was my home. They gave me the name of Weletawash."

The Delawares, or Lenni Lenape, were displaced persons at that time, having been pushed from the homes of their ancestors by the white settlements at Philadelphia and southern New Jersey, then uprooted once again by the settlements at "the forks of the Delaware"—Easton, Bethlehem, and Allentown—and displaced yet again by the settlement in Wyoming Valley. The Delawares were a subject nation of the Iroquois at this time, and many lived among the Senecas, one of the Iroquois nations. A large number of Delawares had also gone directly west from the Philadelphia area and settled in what is now Ohio.

About 1790, Frances was married to a young Delaware brave named Little Turtle, who left her a few years later to go further west with the main remnant of Delawares. She refused to go with him and stayed with the old man and woman who had adopted her.

Early in 1795, while her adoptive parents were moving downstream in a canoe and Frances was accompanying them along the riverbank on horseback, she came upon a wounded Indian lying in the path. After Frances dressed his wounds, they carried him in the canoe and cared for him until he recovered. He remained with them for some time and kept them well supplied with game.

Eventually Frances became the wife of this Miami brave, Shepoconah. After her foster parents died, they moved to the area of the Ohio Territory, later the state of Indiana, along the Mississineva River. There Frances was formally admitted into the Miami tribe and given the name Maconaqua, meaning young bear. Shepoconah was chosen war chief and served until about 1815, when his deafness forced him to retire. He and Maconaqua then moved a few miles upstream to what became known as Deaf Man's Village. Of their four children, the two boys died at a young age. The two girls continued to live with Frances in this village, and there her family finally discovered her.

That discovery is another dramatic story. Ruth Tripp Slocum, Frances's mother, remained convinced that Frances was alive. The persistence of the family search, the wide territory they covered, the rewards they offered, and the contacts they made, demonstrate this conviction. Nevertheless, not until January 1835 did the events that led to her discovery begin. One night that month, Col. George W. Ewing happened to ask for overnight accommodation at Maconaqua's home on the Mississineva River. He had known Maconaqua for several years and had stayed there before. But on that evening, because she was feeling ill and believed she could not die in peace without doing so, she told him the story of her early life.

Col. Ewing wrote a letter to *The Intelligencer,* a newspaper in Lancaster, Pennsylvania, telling Maconaqua's story. He chose a central Pennsylvania newspaper since Maconaqua could recall only that she came from Pennsylvania. It sat in the newspaper office for two years before it was printed; but once it appeared, it was brought to the attention of the Slocums. Jonathan Slocum (Frances's baby brother, not her father) immediately wrote to Col. Ewing, who assured him that Maconaqua was still alive.

Isaac Slocum, the first of Maconaqua's family to visit her, recognized her by the scar on her hand. Joseph Slocum and Mary Slocum Towne were next to make the arduous trip to Indiana. But despite all their persuasions, her white relatives could not get Maconaqua to leave the village where her husband and sons were buried and her daughters and their husbands lived. Two years later, there was a second happy reunion, and Maconaqua tried to get Joseph to live with her. Although she was unsuccessful in this, they stayed in touch for the rest of their lives.

When the federal government forced the Miami tribe to leave its home along the Wabash in 1845, Maconaqua successfully appealed to Congress through her Wilkes-Barre relatives, and with the support of their representative, Benjamin Bidlack, was allowed to remain in her home. When the influx of white settlers began to harass her and her tribal relatives, she asked that George R. Slocum, Isaac's son, be adopted into her family. He and his wife and children moved

The Frances Slocum Playground is located at the corner of North Street and Pennsylvania Avenue in Wilkes-Barre where the Slocum farm stood at the time of Frances's kidnapping. The building shown in this postcard from about 1910 was intended as a [very unauthentic] replica of the Slocum house. F. CHARLES PETRILLO

into the area where he not only resolved the conflicts with the new neighbors but converted Peter Bondy and Jean Baptiste Brouillette, Maconaqua's sons-in-law, to Christianity.

Frances Slocum was born in Warwick, Rhode Island, on March 4, 1773. She was carried into captivity from her home in Wilkes-Barre, Pennsylvania, on November 2, 1778, and adopted first by the Delawares, then by the Miamis to whom she was known as Maconaqua. She died on March 9, 1847, and was buried near Reserve, Indiana, where she had lived for thirty-two years.

This story can still move us today. A brave and resourceful woman demonstrated intense loyalty to her adoptive culture but was also able to reestablish, in her old age, a relationship with her original family that helped her adoptive family as well. Maconaqua's story symbolizes a bridge between two conflicting cultures. She herself crossed the gulf between these cultures to help provide a secure place for her descendants in the community of aliens who had taken over their territory.

Two Postscripts

Maconaqua's Grave. In 1966, because a new dam on the Mississineva would inundate the cemetery where Maconaqua and her husband were buried, their bodies were moved. Maconaqua's remains demonstrated her cross-cultural life. She was buried in a coffin, as dictated by white custom. In the coffin, in accordance with Indian custom, were a gold coin and a pipe full of tobacco, as well as food and water for her journey indicated by a blue plate and bowl, a silver spoon, and a water glass. Also surviving the ravages of time were her silver head band, ankle bands, beads, and fragments of a scarf, as well as a gold ring.

Maconaqua's Will. In 1985 a woman in Kokomo, Indiana, bought a box of books at a rummage sale. Her daughter-in-law, Laura Chadwell, found two documents in the box. In 1991, Laura and her husband Jim Chadwell donated the documents to the tribal secretary for the Miami Indians, Lora Siders. Between 1985 and 1991, the Chadwells had read about Frances Slocum, visited the sites in the area that related to her life, learned more about the Miami Indians, and determined that the documents should be returned to them. One document, dated 1849 and signed by President Zachary Taylor, grants 640 acres to the daughter of Frances Slocum. The other is Maconaqua's will in which she leaves lands owned by her to her daughters.

Medicine on the Wyoming Frontier

When the Wyoming Valley was first settled in the 1770s, medicine in America bore little resemblance to our present day concept of highly trained doctors, technically advanced hospitals, scientific research, and professional standards. Although the era of enlightening discoveries in medicine had begun in Europe, its influence was just beginning to reach the distant cities of Philadelphia and New York. American medicine was also absorbing information from another rich source. According to M. B. Gordon's history of medicine in the colonies, the native American knowledge of herbs and plants definitely added fifty-nine drugs to our modern pharmacopeia, and the Indian knowledge of anatomy was "unquestionably better than that of their colonial contemporaries. They universally employed suction at the site of snakebite . . . and handled their wounds, empyemas, fractures, and dislocations as well [as] if not better than the 18th century white physicians."

In 1751 the Pennsylvania Hospital opened its doors in Philadelphia. It was the first large-scale hospital in colonial America, a result of the efforts of Benjamin Franklin and Dr. Thomas Bond. In 1765 the first American medical school, forerunner of the University of Pennsylvania, began the systematic education of physicians; and in 1767 a second medical school was established as part of King's College (now Columbia University) in New York City. Harvard followed suit in 1782.

The physicians who found their way to the frontier stockades of Wyoming, however, had never seen the inside of a medical school. They had acquired their knowledge of the medical arts through the ancient practice of apprenticeship—grinding powders, mixing pills, and riding with their masters on rounds—holding the basin for a patient to be bled, adjusting plasters, and learning to sew up wounds by watching the doctor at work.

These frontier doctors rode long and wearisome distances to set limbs, bind up injuries, and fight smallpox, pneumonia, and diphtheria. The cures were blunt. The doctor slit the throat of a child choking with diphtheria—a primitive tracheotomy to open the windpipe. Fishhooks were used to keep the aperture from closing. Cures were vigorous, too. Seizing a patient sick with fever, the doctor opened a vein and drew blood until unconsciousness was near. This lowered the heart action. The patient broke into perspiration. The fever and delirium vanished. The doctor next administered tartar as an emetic and followed it with a calomel purge, finally administering opium to "lock the bowels." When the doctor paid a return visit, the patient—if he survived—was usually "well, if a little weak," a response that may have been inspired by the desire to prevent additional treatment. Richard Dunlop, describing these methods in *Doctors of the American Frontier,* points out that many seem curious today, not just because the doctors were improvising but because they were prisoners of the medical thought of the time.

The first physician to arrive in Wyoming was Dr. Joseph Sprague. He was definitely here for a town meeting on September 30, 1771, when he was granted a settling right, but Miner believes he may have come as early as 1770. In any case, he and his family occupied a home in the stockade at Mill Creek, adding to their scant income by opening a boarding house, the largest in the settlement. Dr. Sprague was a stonemason by trade who practiced the healing arts on the side. Harvey quotes from a 1787 letter of Timothy Pickering to his wife, "Enjoin it upon Dr. Sprague to dig [the well] as low as possible and stove it well." Sprague engaged in a great deal of buying and selling of land. The site where Wilkes-Barre's City Hall now stands was once his, along with numerous other lots throughout the valley.

Two legal actions were filed against Dr. Joseph Sprague. In 1788 he was fined five shillings for each of seven profane oaths. The justice levying the fine was Dr. William Hooker Smith, described later in this chapter. Also in 1788, his wife Eunice Chapman Poyner Sprague filed an action against him for divorce, the first such action in Luzerne County. The divorce was granted. This had been a second marriage for both partners. Dr. Joseph Sprague had at least two children from his first marriage: one fell at the Battle of Wyoming; the other, Joseph Sprague, Jr., became executor of his father's estate in 1800.

Eunice Chapman Poyner Sprague was born in 1732 and in 1749 was first married to Poyner, a Huguenot, at Sharon, New York. Poyner died of smallpox at Albany, leaving his wife with two or three children, one of whom, Phoebe Poyner Young, died in Wilkes-Barre at age 89 in 1845, the last survivor of the original settlement in the stockade at Mill Creek.

Eunice Chapman Poyner Sprague was undoubtedly the first woman to practice medicine in Wyoming Valley. F. C. Johnson tells us that following the expulsion of the Pennamites, she returned to Wilkes-Barre, and "thrown upon her own resources, she engaged in midwifery and practice among children."

Wesley Johnson writes in the *Historical Record:*

Eighteenth-century medicine bore little resemblance to the medicine of the twentieth century to which we have become accustomed. Favorite nostrums and quick cures, however, always have an appeal. HARVEY'S *History of Wilkes-Barre*

I do not remember her, but often, when I was a small boy, heard the old people speak of "Granny Sprague" as a successful practitioner of midwifery and of the healing art among children. Mrs. Dr. Sprague's residence and office, which I well remember, was a one-story log house on the corner of Main and Union Streets, then known as Granny Sprague's corner.

Dr. Hollister wrote of Eunice Sprague:

> *She was a worthy old lady, prompt, cheerful and successful, and at this time the sole accoucheur [midwife] in all the wide domain now embraced by Luzerne, Lackawanna, and Wyoming counties. Although of great age, her obstetrical practice as late as 1810 surpassed that of any [other] physician in this portion of Pennsylvania. For attending a confinement case—no matter how distant the journey, how long or how fatiguing the detention—this sturdy and faithful woman invariably charged one dollar for services rendered, although a larger fee was never refused if anyone was able or rash enough to offer it.*

Eunice Sprague died in Wilkes-Barre on April 12, 1814, aged 82 years.

Many of the earliest practitioners in the colonies were clergy. Dr. William Hooker Smith developed his medical knowledge in that tradition. He arrived in Wyoming in 1772 to join his daughter Sarah Smith and her husband James Sutton. Smith's father was the Reverend John Smith, ordained minister of the Presbyterian congregation at Rye, New York, later also at White Plains. The Reverend John Smith probably practiced medicine at both places, for he was commonly called Dr. Smith. And Dr. William Hooker Smith states, "After I came to Rye, I studied Physick under my father, who was a practical physician." On March 2, 1769, he placed the following advertisement in the *New York Journal:*

> *Whereas the Rev. John Smith, Minister of the Gospel in Rye and White Plains, is possessed of a Piece of Skill for the help of distracted Persons, and has been for many years successful in the cure of them—but being advanced in years and very infirm—has therefore communicated his skill to his son, WILLIAM HOOKER SMITH, who hereby informs the public that he lives at White Plains, and is ready to serve in such cases, on reasonable terms; any Persons whose Friends or Relatives may stand in need of his Relief and Help . . . . I would further inform the Public that I can almost infallibly determine the curable Persons by an examination of the Age, Inclination, Constitution, Shape and Make of the head.*

Smith and his son-in-law James Sutton acquired lands in Exeter, Plains, and Kingston townships. Sutton operated a saw mill and grist mill in Exeter Township, while Dr. Smith practiced medicine and eventually became the first justice of the Fifth District of the newly formed Luzerne County in 1787.

Dr. William Hooker Smith practiced according to the popular medical theory of the day. Smith is described in Hollister's *History of Lackawanna Valley* as

The Osterhout Free Library in Wilkes-Barre was founded by Issac Smith Osterhout, the grandson of one of Wyoming Valley's earliest physicians, William Hooker Smith. The Historical Society's Museum is visible to the rear. F. CHARLES PETRILLO

an unwavering phlebotomist. Armed with huge saddlebags, rattling with gallipots and vials and thirsty lance, he sallied forth on horseback over the rough country calling for his services and many were the cures issuing from the unloosed vein. No matter what the nature or location of the disease, bleeding promptly and largely, with a system of diet, drink and rest, was enforced on the patient with an earnestness and a success that gave him a widespread reputation as a physician.

In 1789, Dr. Smith and his son-in-law erected a forge above Pittston, now Old Forge, and for several years produced iron to float down the Susquehanna to market. Dr. Smith was the first person to recognize the area's potential mineral wealth. As early as 1791 he bought the right to dig iron ore and mine stone coal from a Mr. Scott of Pittston for five shillings, and he continued purchasing these mineral rights until 1798, despite local ridicule.

Another example of his wide-ranging interests is his tract on "Alchymy Explained and made Familiar; or a Drop of Honey for a Despairing Alchymist; collected from the Alchymist's Rock or Philosopher's Stone," written in 1809 and printed in 1811. Although alchemy, the search for the transmutation of base metals into gold, seems absurd from today's sophisticated viewpoint, Smith shared this interest with those whom we now recognize as the originators of modern chemistry. These papers were left in the care of his youngest daughter, Susannah Smith Osterhout, for his grandson, Isaac Smith Osterhout. Osterhout was not only the founder of the Osterhout Free Library in Wilkes-Barre but made provision for the housing of the collections of the Wyoming Historical and Geological Society in the museum behind the library at 69 South Franklin Street, Wilkes-Barre.

Dr. Lemuel Gustin came to Wyoming in 1773 or 1774, studied medicine with Dr. William Hooker Smith, and married his third daughter. In March 1778, he bought a lot in Kingston. On June 12, 1778, his wife died. On July 3 of that year, the Battle of Wyoming occurred. Dr. Gustin and his father-in-law attended to the wounded and then escaped down the Susquehanna with their families. Dr. Gustin did not return to Wyoming Valley but practiced medicine in Carlisle until his death in 1805.

There was one other physician during this very early period, Dr. John Calkins. He visited Wyoming in 1773, and acquired land in Wilkes-Barre by a deed dated 1775. He seems to have had his home at Cochecton on the Delaware but to have been in this area on at least the six or seven occasions for which entries are made against his name in Elisha Blackman's account books.

In "Pioneer Physicians of Wyoming Valley," Frederick C. Johnson lists an additional forty-five doctors who practiced here, many for only a short time, at the end of the eighteenth and during the first half of the nineteenth century. The career of one of these, Dr. Edward Covell, demonstrates the dramatic changes taking place in American medical education.

Edward Covell was the son of Dr. Matthew Covell, who had settled in Wilkes-Barre as a young man (date unknown) and practiced here until his death in 1813. Edward was born in Wilkes-Barre in 1792 and graduated from Princeton in 1812. "After having received an early and liberal education, he was prepared under the instructions of the celebrated Dr. Benjamin Rush of Philadelphia and others of his school [the University of Pennsylvania] for the practice of medicine."

Dr. Edward Covell was the first physician known to have a formal medical education to practice in Wyoming Valley. He brought to the community his greatly increased knowledge of the rapidly expanding fields of anatomy, physiology, pathology, and pharmacology. George B. Kulp tells us in *Families of the Wyoming Valley* that when Dr. Edward Covell died in 1826 he was held in the highest esteem as a physician and as a person, being "greatly loved and respected."

George Catlin

Frontier Artist

ON JULY 26, 1796, the village of Wilkes-Barre ("fifty houses, a court house, and a jail") witnessed the birth of a baby whose unusual life work was to be the preservation of "a record of the American Indian that is unsurpassed in accuracy, scope, and detail." The baby was George Catlin, son of Putnam Catlin, a lawyer, and Polly Sutton Catlin. Polly, at age seven, had been among those in Forty Fort at the time of the Battle of Wyoming.

Catlin's parents moved from Wilkes-Barre to the Onaquagua Valley in New York when he was one year old, but his ties with Wyoming Valley were strong, and Catlin returned to attend the Wilkes-Barre Academy: "with books reluctantly held in one hand and a rifle or fishing pole, firmly and affectionately grasped in the other. At the urgent request of my father . . . I was prevailed upon to abandon these favorite themes, and also my occasional dablings with the brush, which had secured already a corner in my affections; and I commenced reading the law for a profession."

In 1823 Catlin left the practice of law in Wilkes-Barre and moved to Philadelphia where the great artists of the early nation—Thomas Sully, Charles Wilson Peale, and Rembrandt Peale—formed the nucleus of the Pennsylvania Academy of Fine Arts. In a fascinating article, "Indian-Loving Catlin," found in *The Proceedings and Collections of the Wyoming Historical and Geological Society,* Volume 21, 1930, Marion Annette Evans adds, "He was fast becoming a popular portrait painter of fashionable Philadelphia, and would no doubt have faded into comparative obscurity in a generation, had not chance fixed for him 'a whole life-time of enthusiasm.'" In Catlin's own words,

> *A delegation of some ten or fifteen noble and dignified looking Indians, from the wilds of the "Far West," suddenly arrived in [Philadelphia], arrayed and equipped in all their classic beauty,—with shield and helmet—with tunic and manteau—tinted and tasselled off, exactly for the painter's palette. In silent and stoic*

George Catlin sketched himself painting a Mandan chief. This picture is the frontispiece of Catlin's *Letters and Notes,* published in 1841. FROM *Proceedings and Collections.* WHGS

> *dignity, these lords of the forest strutted about the city for a few days, wrapped in their pictured robes, with their brows plumed with quills of the war-eagle, attracting the gaze and admiration of all who beheld them.*

Catlin resolved that "the history and customs of such a people, preserved by picturial [sic] illustrations, are themes worthy of the lifetime of one man, and nothing short of the loss of my life shall prevent me from visiting their country and becoming their historian."

W. J. Linton's engraving of George Catlin provides a portrait that fits Mayne Reid's description: "[Catlin] was about five feet eight inches tall, sturdy, one of the most graceful specimens of humanity one ever encountered. He was of a fine healthy bronze, well proportioned, while in every gesture he was graceful." FROM M. A. EVANS, *Proceedings and Collections,* WHGS

In 1829, Catlin began a series of visits to Indian tribes, especially in the plains. In 1832, already perceiving that the bison were an endangered species, he initiated the idea of protecting them in a national park in the Yellowstone area. By 1837, he had visited forty-eight tribes who were still relatively untouched by European culture in an area stretching from Ohio to Oregon and extending south to Florida and Alabama. Evans comments, "It is interesting to think of them [Catlin's wife, Clara B. Gregory, traveled with him during the last three years of this period], dressed in the complicated fashion of the period, wandering in the unbroken wilderness, with no 'civilized' protection at their command, carrying freshly painted portraits in a tin box on Catlin's back, the dry paintings unstretched, rolled up in knapsacks." More than three hundred portraits in oil and two hundred scenes of villages, dances, games, ceremonies, and hunting groups—together with an extensive collection of artifacts—formed "Catlin's North American Indian Gallery."

From 1837 until 1845, Catlin exhibited this collection to many thousands of Americans and Europeans, first in the United States (in New York, Philadelphia, Washington, and Boston); then in Europe (in London, Liverpool, Manchester, cities in Scotland, and finally in Paris, with a side expedition to Brussels). During these years, he compiled his materials, resulting in the 1841 publication of *Letters and Notes of the Manners, Customs and Condition of the North American Indian* illustrated with many engravings.

While in England and France, Catlin had attached groups of Indians who were visiting Europe to his gallery. The first group of nine Ojibbeways he made welcome in return for the hospitality and kindness he had received in the wilderness of North America. He and the Ojibbeway were formally presented to Queen Victoria, and Catlin's interest in this group's reaction to the 'civilization' of Europe led to two more volumes on his travels with them and other Indian groups through Europe. The Indians, for example, commented unfavorably on the "so vast many poor people" filling London and Paris, and the "poor prisoner buffalo" at the zoo.

Of special interest to Wyoming Valley is Catlin's description of his conversation with Louis-Philippe, then king of France. Evans writes, "Catlin was invited to the royal breakfast table at the palace of St. Cloud, at which time the King discussed his early travels in America, mentioning his journey by canoe to a small town called Wilkes-Barre in the Valley of Wyoming. 'I here surprised his Majesty,' writes Catlin, ". . . by informing him that I was a native of Wilkes-Barre and that while his Majesty was there I was an infant in my mother's arms.'"

Between 1852 and 1857, Catlin traveled in the Far West and in Central and South America, creating a less voluminous but nevertheless important record of the Indians of these regions, which he also exhibited and wrote about in detail. "Art may mourn," he concluded, "when these people are swept from the earth."

Catlin tended to be somewhat apologetic about the quality of his paintings: "Every painting has been made from nature, and that too, when I have been paddling my canoe, or leading my pack horse over and through tractless wilds." However, Catlin has recorded for all times the "individual life and historical fact" of a disappearing world. What he lacked from the mid-nineteenth-century critic's view—the grandiose style that aimed for dramatic effect—is an artistic as well as scientific asset in the twentieth century.

In 1918 Edwin Balch wrote, "Almost all [Catlin's] pictures are about 19 inches by 25 inches in size, lengthwise, often oval. The paper is light grayish brown, the register is usually middle, bright colors are used sparingly and only in accents. The paint is laid on thin and smooth, almost like tinted drawing, rather than painting. Catlin made every speck go as far as possible in the wilderness. Detail is perfectly carried out; perspective is good; sense of proportion is splendid; light and shade are well managed. His dramatic instinct shows in his ability to place a scene on a canvas in such a way as to make a picture of it. He can create an appearance of a crowd, a multitude of animated beings . . . as few painters have done. . . . Everywhere there is a sincere rendering of what he saw, a faithful rendition of the forms and colors of nature." Today, the great bulk of Catlin's work is housed in the Smithsonian Institution although individual paintings owned by many museums are often part of their permanent exhibits.

When George Catlin died in New Jersey in 1872, two years after his final return from Europe, he had fulfilled his early purpose. He left a record "unique and imperishable for the benefit of future ages."

Old Fell House

ON OCTOBER 22, 1986, the old brick building at the corner of South Washington and East Northampton streets in Wilkes-Barre was demolished. As almost every older resident of Wyoming Valley knows, it was on this site that Judge Jesse Fell successfully burned anthracite in a grate of his own design without a forced draft. Blacksmiths Obadiah and Daniel Gore had been experimenting with hard coal as a substitute for charcoal almost from the time of their arrival in Wyoming Valley in 1769. In a few months, they had succeeded in both igniting it and keeping it burning with the aid of forced air from a bellows and found it generated an intense heat. From that beginning, its use by blacksmiths spread throughout this area; and during the Revolutionary War at least two boat loads of anthracite went down the Susquehanna for use in casting cannon near the present site of Carlisle. But local entrepreneurs were unable to develop a commercial market for the black stone outside Wyoming Valley.

Judge Fell's idea was to set a natural air current in motion by the heat of the fire itself. According to Ernest G. Smith, he seems to have experimented with several different arrangements, possibly including one made of green hickory. When he was finally ready, on February 11, 1808, for a public demonstration of the iron grate he had developed in his nephew's blacksmith shop, only two of his friends showed enough faith in him to respond to his invitation. Eighteen years later, he wrote to his cousin Jonathan Fell, "Such was the effect of this pleasing discovery that in a few days there were a number of grates put in operation."

Actually, hard coal experiments had already been successfully performed by two Philadelphians, Oliver Evans in 1803 and Frederick Graff in 1805, both using "Lehi" coal. But Fell's independent discovery, "being made [as Smith notes], in a locality where it could quickly and generally be brought into use, and the fact that he made no pretext of deriving personal benefit from the introduction of his device for the common good, mark him as a benefactor."

The Fell House underwent many transformations between 1787, when it opened as the Sign of the Buck and 1905 when Anton Weiss built the Fell House, but the fireplace remained intact until 1986. TOP LEFT: The Sign of the Buck, as it was supposed to have looked in 1795, in a drawing made a hundred years later by George W. Leach, Jr., whose portrayals of early Wilkes-Barre tend to emphasize the pretty and the picturesque. TOP RIGHT: The building shown in this stereopticon photograph by C. F. Cook from the 1860s or 1870s is recognizably the right hand section of the same structure (it's possible that it was one of Leach's sources), but

the wing to the left has been replaced with a brick building. BOTTOM LEFT: By the 1890s or so, the brick building, suffering badly from neglect, was for sale, as shown in this photo from a glass negative by John Jennings. (Note that the building to the right seems to stand on the foundation being laid in the top right photo.) BOTTOM RIGHT: It is believed that Weiss's hotel incorporated beams and doors saved from the earlier buildings as well as preserving the fireplace intact. It stood essentially unchanged until 1986. This photo was taken a few years before its demolition. JENNINGS PHOTO COURTESY F. CHARLES PETRILLO; OTHERS WHGS

Jesse Fell (1751–1830) moved to Wyoming Valley in 1785 with his wife Hannah Welding and their four children. In 1787 he opened a store and tavern on the corner of South Washington and East Northampton streets. He became sheriff of Luzerne County in 1789. Despite being a Quaker and a professed non-combatant, he served as brigade inspector of the Luzerne Militia from 1793 to 1798 when he was succeeded by Putnam Catlin, George Catlin's father. In 1798 Fell was appointed associate judge for Luzerne County and served until his death thirty-two years later. He became the first burgess of the new borough of Wilkes-Barre (1806) and later sat on Wilkes-Barre's borough council for several years. In 1845 Fell Township was organized and named in his honor. It became Lackawanna County in 1878. This silhouette, from Harvey's "History of Lodge No. 61's F. & A. M.," is the only known likeness of Judge Fell. WHGS

Jesse Fell and Hannah Welding Fell, Quakers from Bucks County, Pennsylvania, moved to the Wyoming Valley late in 1785. On December 21, 1787, they purchased the property at what would become the corner of Washington and Northampton streets for forty pounds, "one acre with dwelling house, barn and well on same." The house was enlarged and a small portion used as a store for some time, the remainder devoted to an inn, "the first [in Wilkes-Barre] of which we have any tradition." By 1799 the property was described as "'The Sign of the Buck,' a two-story log and frame building with an addition one story high. Has ten rooms, six fireplaces, three entries, a garret, a good cellar and an excellent well of never failing water at the kitchen door. On the premises a good frame barn, 38 x 28 feet; shed, stable, 30 x 20 feet, and near at hand a wood lot."

This is the Hon. Stanley Woodward's more romantic description:

The old Fell tavern was after the fashion of an English inn. The county of Luzerne had just been organized, a court established, and Wilkes-Barre was beginning to assume the honorable and important position of the county town.

The judges and lawyers and jurymen, the parties and their witnesses, all the people who came to court must have a place to "put up," as the phrase was. [The court house was then located on Public Square.] Lines of stages were being established and occasionally a traveler from a distance would want accommodation. I have had, from a former resident of this city, now deceased, and who upon his first visit to Wilkes-Barre, was for a short time a guest of the Fell tavern, a description of the customs of that day.

The living or sitting room was big and well furnished with old-fashioned high back, split wood chairs; a large fireplace in which great logs of hickory wood were burning so brightly as to furnish both light and heat, made a winter's evening cheery and attractive to all comers; at one end a modest assortment of decanters containing the various beverages with which our ancestors were wont to sterilize their water; a barrel of cider on tap in the corner; the atmosphere redolent of tobacco; the ornaments on the walls consisting chiefly of rifles and powder horns and antlers, interspersed with relics of the Wyoming Massacre, and of the Indian sway in the valley, with here and there a rough portrait of some revolutionary hero.

There were less than five hundred people in Wilkes-Barre then [two thousand in all of Luzerne County], but a large percentage of the men folk gathered nightly in winter in the big room of the tavern, and sat around the wood fire and discussed the affairs of the time, crops, prices, politics, religion, the luck of the hunter who had just come home to get a wagon to haul in his game, the prospect of a good spring for shad in the Susquehanna, the coming lawsuit to be tried at the next term of the court, and the merits of the opposing counsel [there were then but four lawyers at the bar]—all these and many other such themes the stranger heard the settlers talking about, as they sipped their hot sling on a winter's evening in the old Fell tavern, in the year of our Lord 1800.

But the old tavern had other attractions. The upper floor was so constructed that the whole space could be transformed into a ballroom, and here, during the sessions of court and on other grand occasions, the girls and the matrons as well as the men paced through the stately minuet or threaded the maze of the cotillion.

Fifty years after Judge Fell's experiment, on February 11, 1858, a meeting was called at the old Fell tavern, still a public house. An old grate—said to be the original—was set up in the fireplace, a fire lit, and a plan for a permanent organization was adopted, which became the foundation of the Wyoming Historical and Geological Society.

In April 1886, a Swiss innkeeper named Anton Weiss purchased the original Fell tavern for $18,000 from the heirs of Philip Banker. Banker had acquired it from Marvin Long, who in turn had purchased it from Jesse Fell. According to a 1926 newspaper article, brick additions had been made to the original log building from time to time. In 1905 the ancient structure was razed except

The Fell Tavern's fireplace held the grate devised by Judge Jesse Fell for burning anthracite without forced air. Since Fell immediately made a number of duplicates of his successful design for his friends and neighbors, the question of which grate is actually the original is one of our local mysteries. The grate pictured here was the scene of repeated ceremonial coal burnings for many years on the anniversary of Fell's successful experiment on February 11, 1808. PHOTOGRAPH BY JOHN JENNINGS. COURTESY F. CHARLES PETRILLO

for the massive brick and stone chimney. Around this a new Old Fell House was erected. Portions of the great wooden beams and joists and the wooden pins taken from the original inn adorned the space that had been the long room of the old tavern and now became the bar of the new. The hinged wooden room divider which had been used to section off the back portion of the long room when the court was in session was again suspended from the ceiling. Of this reconstructed long room, however, only the fireplace and grate survived the 1972 Agnes Flood.

In 1963, the *Sunday Independent* interviewed Anton Weiss's sons, Phillip and Tony Weiss. Not only had the old inn been the site of the founding, in 1794, of Lodge No. 61, Free and Accepted Masons of Wilkes-Barre, and of the Wyoming Historical and Geological Society on February 11, 1858, but the two men recalled that the Planters Nut and Chocolate Company had been organized there. Phil Weiss could recall the meeting and the men who encouraged Mr. Obici to get it going.

"Before prohibition," the Weiss brothers said, "we were kept busy day and night (six days a week, twenty-four hours a day), and the bar business was so flourishing that we didn't care if we rented any of the rooms. We also gained a reputation for good food." The inn had been a main stop for travelers since the days of horses and wagons, and its location was convenient to the railroad station on Pennsylvania Avenue.

Following the 1972 flood, George Mrochko, then owner of the building, reopened the restaurant and the bar as "The Tavern." In 1977 the buildings on three sides of the Old Fell House were demolished by the Wilkes-Barre Redevelopment Authority. At that time the Old Fell House was preserved in its entirety because of its historic status. Since the closing of several more businesses on East Northampton Street, however, that section of downtown Wilkes-Barre dwindled commercially, and prior to its sale, the restaurant's hours had been shortened considerably.

In 1986 Wilkes-Barre General Hospital Corporation purchased the building and site on which the Old Fell House stood. The hospital announced at the time of its acquisition that the original fireplace would be preserved and incorporated into the new building planned for the site. The fireplace, however, was demolished along with the rest of the building. The hospital also announced in November 1986 that it would erect a historical marker, but as of this writing in 1992 the site is bare. The planned marker is to commemorate the old tavern and the events that took place on that corner. Certainly, Judge Jesse Fell's successful experiment with stone coal was one key event in changing our community from a rural village into a thriving urban center.

This pastoral scene shows Wyoming Valley as it may have looked in the last years of the shad runs, before dams and pollution made the river uninhabitable for the fish. The viewer in the foreground is on a mythical high point somewhere on the east side of the Susquehanna River where the view of the village of Wilkes-Barre is almost directly downstream. Even allowing a great deal for the river's changing course and for the results of strip mining and erosion, the point from which the artist worked seems more fanciful than possible. WHGS

When Shad Were Plenty

LATE APRIL AND EARLY MAY were most remarkable in the early days of Wyoming Valley for the wonderful migration of shad. They made their way upstream against the current, swimming in vast shoals of thousands, moving together at the same speed and maintaining the same distance apart with almost military precision.

The males came first, about two to three years old, younger and smaller than the females. Eight or nine days later, the females followed, four to five years old and bearing the eggs or roe. Their goal was the headwaters of the Susquehanna, where they deposited their eggs, to return downstream old and weak in June and July. The fry hatched in one to two weeks and over the summer made their way back to the Chesapeake Bay, already fingerlings and ready to enter the ocean by fall.

The name *shad,* which comes from the Old English *sceadd,* is almost unknown now in England except among those who study or catch fish. But the word was brought to North America by the English settlers and applied to several related American fish and to some unrelated ones as well. In addition we have, in the United States, the shad berry, the shad bush, the shad fly, and the shad frog, plants and animals whose appearance on the scene coincides with the annual appearance of the migrating shad.

American shad *(Alosa sapidissima)* are beautiful fish. The belly forms a keel, widely considered to be an adaptation for removing the sharp shadow that would be created below the central part of the body by top lighting. Seen from below, the keel and the glossy silver sides cause the fish to disappear in the mirror-like reflection of the water's surface. Viewed from above, the fish is a dark bluish color, which looks like the color of deep water. Shad are plankton feeders, with a remarkable series of sieves in their throats called gill rakers which screen their food. Also called the common or white or Potomac shad, these fish have special adaptations to regulate the osmotic pressure of the blood that permit their migration from salt ocean into freshwater rivers. The conversion requires some time, so shad migrating out of salt water tend to

The Nanticoke Dam was constructed in 1830 to provide slackwater for the North Branch Canal. TOP: The channel to the West Nanticoke lock is visible to the left. BOTTOM: In the lower right corner the "chute" can be seen (also visible in the top picture) that permitted lumber rafts and other river vessels to bypass the dam. West Nanticoke and Tilbury's Knob are on the opposite bank. Construction of the dams that made the canal system possible marked the end of the shad runs in the Susquehanna. TOP: WHGS; BOTTOM: F. CHARLES PETRILLO

form large aggregations in brackish estuaries while the changeover in their osmotic regulating systems takes place. Then they begin their upstream journey.

A 1769 traveler among the Indian villages of the upper reaches of the Susquehanna, Richard Smith, notes in his journal,

At the last named Place [Tuscarora Town] there is a Shad Fishery common to the People of Ahquhaga also; they tie Bushes together so as to reach over the River, sink them with stones, and haul them round by Canoes; all persons present, including strangers, such is their laudable Hospitality, have an equal division of the Fish. They reckon the Distance from Ahquhaga to Wialoosin [Wyalusing] 100 Miles and from thence to Wywomec 60, which last is the same as Wyoming.

Wyoming Valley was a favored place for the Indians to harvest the shad runs. The take was preserved for winter by slow and careful smoking. The shad fishing in the Susquehanna was known to the Moravians, and the journal of the Sullivan Expedition mentions the shad at Wilkes-Barre. In 1772 a seine or net for catching shad was brought by the Connecticut settlers to Wyoming and was held as common property. The settlers preferred salting to smoking as the means of preservation. Salt, however, was scarce. It had to come by wagon and river from New York State or be worked up river in boats. Ernest G. Smith mentions that on one occasion the entire supply of the river villages was exhausted and an emergency delegation was sent to Philadelphia in the hope that they could return with the essential salt supply before the fishing season ended.

Organized shad fisheries developed. About ten men would form a company, knitting twine from homespun flax into sections of a seine sixty to eighty yards long. The catch was divided by separating the fish into as many piles as there were rights in the seine. One man would turn his back to the piles and while a second pointed to one pile, the first would call the name of the man to whom the pile would go.

In an account of a later period quoted by Smith it's noted that the shad fisheries were no longer common property. "The owner of the soil was the owner of the fishery, and no one was allowed to fish without a permit. The owners of the fisheries also had the seines and when not using them would hire them out to others and take their pay in shad; the seiner's share was always one-half the catch." Another writer, however, mentions that his father, who was the owner of the seine, drew one-fifth of the catch.

The most vivid description comes from Charles Miner in the *Record of the Times* of May 9, 1855, again quoted by Smith:

But our business is with the capitol old Kingston fishery ground, just above the bar, opposite the mouth of Mill Creek. On a fine day, the village of Wilkes-

Barre would be half depopulated. Lawyers ripe for fun, Printers, Justices, Doctors, Mechanics, Merchants—indeed everybody who loved shad and relished a frolic, who could get a skiff, canoe, or any craft to take them over. . . . The vast canoe, half as big as Columbus' first ship, with the long seine on board is just starting up hugging the western shore. . . . Coming to the falls [the present riff above the North Street Bridge at Wilkes-Barre] the canoe is laid straight across to the eastern land with all possible swiftness, the seine being cast in as she goes; Now the canoe, hugging the eastern shore, descends slowly, carefully—while the party on the Kingston side march down with the rope flapping on the water to keep the fish in the middle of the stream. Suddenly you hear . . . "pull away"—the canoe darts over to the landing place—the boys jump into the water to take the rope ashore—"Haul in steadily"— . . . "Mind the lead line"—"Haul in"—Presently the shad fins begin to appear as the semi-circle of the seine contracts and approaches. "See, See!" The water is alive with them! A shout goes up! Hurrah! [All] are in in an instant, some on their knees, some to their armpits in the river holding down or hauling in the lead line. . . . The beach is lined with the beautiful flapping things. Haul after haul is made. Evening approaches . . . the shares are allotted. All divided; some from our village purchased with money. Lawyers and Doctors received willing portions for fees due; the Printer for his paper. The widow and the poor were never forgotten. Half a century ago every family calculated on putting up a barrel of shad—many with great care; and so fat and rich were they, that an epicure might regard them a luxury!

The quantities of shad caught were immense. A draught of 9,290 taken at Nanticoke is mentioned in a Philadelphia paper on May 6, 1800. In addition, "a few days previous to that, 6,963 were taken at a draught and frequently in the course of a season from 1,500 to 4,000 are taken daily at the same fishery." Pearce, in his *Annals of Luzerne County,* mentions one haul of 10,000, the seine being so heavy it could not be drawn ashore. Hendrick B. Wright describes three of the fisheries at Nanticoke, Plymouth, and Wilkes-Barre and estimates their combined annual yield at not less than 200,000 shad.

These great harvests meant that the price stayed low, at two, three, or four cents, probably never higher than ten cents per fish. At one point, a hundred fish were sold in the outlying villages for six dollars. Or a bushel of salt could buy a hundred shad. Most important, a family could put up a year's supply for no more than a week's wages.

Year after year as the shad swam upstream they were being pulled out of the river by huge nets all day long, day after day. Fisheries are mentioned at Berwick, at Nescopeck, at Nanticoke, three at Plymouth, at Fish Island (opposite Wilkes-Barre), on the Wilkes-Barre Common, at Kingston, at Forty Fort, not to mention all the other towns and villages up and down the Susquehanna. It seems a miracle that any shad at all made it through to the headwaters in order to spawn the next generation.

It was not overfishing, however, that eliminated the great annual migration of shad in the Susquehanna. It was the building of the canals along the river, starting in 1825. This inland navigation system required the construction of dams across the river to supply water to the canals. And although the canals have long since been superseded by the railroads and highways, many dams serving flood control, recreational, and hydroelectric purposes are still intact. Charles E. Myers, in *The History of Shad Fishing on the Susquehanna River and Current Efforts to Restore the Species,* gives us hope that shad restoration will be a success. The shad restoration program was initiated in 1970 by fishery agencies from New York, Maryland, and Pennsylvania and the U.S. Fish and Wildlife Service. An experimental fish trap and lift was installed in 1971 at the Conowingo Dam, but the migration stayed at about two hundred per year until 1981. The Pennsylvania Fish Commission, however, is now stocking shad fry and fingerlings, and in addition put thirty thousand adult shad from the Hudson into the Susquehanna between 1982 and 1987. As a result both of the stocking and of a moratorium on shad harvesting by Maryland, fifty-two hundred shad were collected at Conowingo in 1986, and forty-two hundred of them were transported above all dams. By 1990 the number exceeded fifteen thousand. The goal is to establish a self-sustaining river population of two million shad.

Whether the section of the North Branch of the Susquehanna between Nanticoke and Pittston can support shad is questionable. This twenty-mile strip where the acid mine water has drained into the river for many years may not now support these fish. But there is great hope that as the surface-coal refuse dumps and culm banks are either eliminated or successfully planted with trees and shrubs, the surface erosion that creates acidic runoff will be sufficiently reduced. In addition, the flooding of the mines has reduced the rate of acid breakdown there. Dr. Myers concludes his paper by stating that, "The evidence reviewed here supports an opinion that shad will survive and will be able to migrate upstream beyond Wyoming Valley for spawning." This is good news indeed. May tomorrow echo yesterday:

"Ah!" cried the old People, still chewing on the past, "What times when we were young and shad were plenty."

Old Ship Zion was planned in 1791, but not completed until 1811. It served as the place of worship for Congregationalists, Episcopalians, Methodists, and Baptists until 1817 when a falling out over Christmas decorations led the Episcopalians to sell their rights in the building. Eventually each congregation built a separate church: St. Stephen's Episcopal on the site it occupies today in 1824; First Presbyterian, reorganized from its Congregational affiliation, to a building on the present site of the Osterhout Free Library in 1833; First Methodist to its present location on North Franklin Street in 1849; and First Baptist to quarters on West Northampton Street in 1847. Old Ship Zion was torn down in 1857.

The building to the rear was the Wilkes-Barre Academy. Originally Luzerne County's first courthouse and jail, it became a school in 1807 and was demolished about 1843. George W. Leach, Jr., based his 1896 drawing on a photo from the early 1850s. To compensate for Leach's practice of making his drawings prettier than their subjects, Don Keenan has, for this book, brought it closer to the reality shown in the faded photo. WHGS

Prosperity and Its Problems

The valley had lumber, farm produce, and—above all—anthracite. To reach coastal markets, valley residents built bridges and the valley became part of an elaborate system of canals—quickly built but replaced by railroads in a few decades. With prosperity came more immigrants—from a rich variety of ethnic and religious backgrounds—to work the mines. As they built their churches and their schools, conflicts and misunderstandings were inevitable. Exploitation of workers was also a problem—especially the abusive practices of child labor. Citizens of the valley lived through all this in the course of the nineteenth century—all part of the process of becoming America.

The Market Street Bridge, pictured here at its official opening in 1929, has survived two major floods. Restored in 1986 to its original beauty as a result of extensive cleaning and reconstruction by the Pennsylvania Department of Transportation, it has also recovered its architectural integrity through the removal of the intrusive overhead lane markers and the replacement of the modernistic light fixtures of the fifties with replicas of the original lamp posts. WHGS

Bridging the Susquehanna

As we sat fuming one hot summer day in 1986, sitting in a snarl of backed up traffic from the reconstruction work on the Market Street Bridge between Wilkes-Barre and Kingston, we remembered a time when the only way to cross the river was by ferry.

There was only one ferry. In May 1806, the village of Wilkes-Barre was officially incorporated as a borough, and one of the first problems the council addressed was the more stringent regulation of the ferry. The exclusive right to keep, maintain, and let a ferry went each year to the highest bidder. This was a lucrative enterprise. Ernest G. Smith quotes Stephen Wilson:

> *In the Spring of 1811, father [Elnathan Wilson] leased the old ferry house, with its equipment of flats and skiffs and about five acres of land for $100 a year. It was on the West bank of the Susquehanna opposite the foot of Northampton Street.... The first year father built two flats and a skiff and put $3000 in the bank. He often took in thirty or forty dollars a day, though in winter when the river was frozen over his income stopped, except what he took in from his tavern, for the ferry house was a hotel in those primitive days.*

In exchange for this exclusive right, the ferryman was to keep a sufficient number of boats in good repair at his own expense, and no person wishing to cross was to experience any unnecessary delay. In fact, the lessee was subject to a fine of twelve and a half cents for each person who was detained ten minutes during operating hours (half an hour after sunrise to one hour after sunset). Any unauthorized competitor was to be fined two dollars for transporting any person across the Susquehanna. Nevertheless, John Meyers set up a rival ferry at the foot of North Street—obeying the letter of the ordinance by charging nothing and depending on tips for his reimbursement.

The town council, however, could not regulate the high water or the ice buildups in the river, and a ferry by its very nature occasioned delays in traffic. In addition, the road leading from the ferry landing on the river bank up to

This tollhouse controlled access to the covered bridge until 1908 when the county bought the bridge for $165,000. In a photograph taken during an ice jam the sign above the bridge itself is legible. It reads, "FIVE DOLLARS FINE FOR RIDING OR DRIVING FASTER THAN A WALK OR CARRYING FIRE BY SMOKING OR OTHERWISE OVER THIS BRIDGE." WHGS

This drawing is the oldest representation of the Market Street Bridge in the Wyoming Historical and Geological Society Collection. It is the 1818 bridge, which was rebuilt in 1819 and lasted until 1824. Matthias Hollenback's warehouse is in the foreground. The next bridge, which opened in 1826, appears in the sketch of Wilkes-Barre on page 2. That covered bridge served the community until 1892. WHGS

This steel structure served as the link between Wilkes-Barre and Kingston from 1892 to 1929. Note the trolley car crossing on the tracks on its south side, balanced by the pedestrian walkway along the north side. PHOTOGRAPH ABOUT 1915 BY JOHN JENNINGS. COLLECTION F. CHARLES PETRILLO

River Street was undermined almost every year by high water. The repeated rebuilding of the road was steadily diminishing the River Common. The demand for a bridge increased, and in 1807 the state legislature authorized the governor to form a bridge company.

Toll bridges were considered a good investment, as were toll roads, during this period of expanding commerce; but the sale of shares for the Wilkes-Barre bridge went slowly, and years passed before a sufficient sum was subscribed. Meanwhile the location of the bridge—Northampton, Market, or North street—was disputed at length, with the ferrymen, naturally, opposing the bridge altogether. Market Street was finally selected. In June 1817, a newspaper reported that "two abutments are nearly completed, and the piers ready to be sunk as soon as the present swell of water has subsided." The bridge was floored and opened for traffic in December of 1818, but the high water of April 1819 destroyed the Wilkes-Barre half, and it did not reopen for wagons until December.

According to Smith, five years later—on Friday, February 18, 1824—the entire superstructure of the bridge was swept away by a windstorm. An eyewitness, writing to the *Record of the Times* in 1858, stated:

> *My father and myself happened to be crossing on the ice a few rods below the bridge that evening, loaded with a fine lot of bass that we had taken with*

This fascinating view shows the river in flood during the construction of the present Market Street Bridge. The southern half of the new bridge was finished and opened before the old bridge was dismantled. Notice the trolley car tracks being laid across the northern edge of the new section. A pair of tracks that ran in the center of the 1929 bridge were paved over in the late 1940s and finally removed as part of the recent reconstruction. Floodwater is visible far up Market Street in Kingston, and through the industrial haze, some current landmarks, such as the former trolley car barn (most recently a car dealership) and several church steeples, are visible. Before the construction of the levee system—the dikes—in the late 1930s, the Susquehanna flooded at twenty-two feet. PHOTOGRAPH BY ACE HOFFMAN STUDIOS. COLLECTION F. CHARLES PETRILLO

hook and line at Toby's Eddy. . . . The wind was blowing almost a gale from the southwest, which seemed to be stronger along the river than anywhere else. It took the bridge bodily from the piers, and it fell with a tremendous crash on the thick blue ice below, and broke into atoms. The ice broke up next day towards sundown, and carried downstream with it most of the broken timbers and iron. . . . I afterwards saw what purported to be a log house, standing on the bank of the river not far from Columbia [near Lancaster] which was built of the smooth pine timbers from the bridge, that had been taken up whilst floating down the stream.

This time the bridge was rebuilt by calling in debts to the Commonwealth of Pennsylvania on lands in Luzerne County. These were old liens and mortgages from the original settlement of conflicting land claims after the Second Yankee-Pennamite War. The knowledge that the state meant business and that the money would be spent on the bridge rather than for the general operating expenses of the commonwealth led to prompt payment. By October 1824, the managers were ready to let a contract; and on December 6, 1825, the completed structure was dedicated. In 1826, the sides and roof of the bridge and the tollhouse were completed.

The "old covered bridge" continued in service to the community until 1892 when it was replaced by a steel structure. Since a steel bridge connecting North and Pierce streets had been completed in 1888, the Market Street Bridge could be simply closed down while the replacement structure was built. This 1892 steel bridge, in turn, was replaced in 1929 by the grand granite design of Carrere and Hastings—a beautiful bridge, reflecting the city-beautiful movement of the early twentieth century. And as PennDOT completed its reconstruction and traffic flowed smoothly once more, we gave thanks not only for our restored monumental bridge but also for not having to wait for the ferry.

This aqueduct carried the Wyoming Division of the North Branch Canal across the mouth of Mill Creek at the northern edge of Wilkes-Barre. This picture, taken from an 1873 photo, shows the water falling through the aqueduct into the creek. The aqueduct piers are still standing, having been converted into use as a railroad bridge. PHOTO SCHURCH & CO., SCRANTON. COURTESY F. CHARLES PETRILLO

The Canal System and the Coming of Prosperity

FOR ONE EVENTFUL generation canals dominated American transportation by linking the great eastern rivers with the Great Lakes and the Atlantic Ocean. In the thirty-three years between 1825, when the Erie Canal was completed, and 1857–1858, when the Commonwealth of Pennsylvania abandoned canal construction and sold its canal system to private companies, a vast inland transportation system was created, flourished, and declined. Those three decades, however, dramatically affected the shape of development in America and in Wyoming Valley.

The Erie Canal opened the west, linking the Hudson River and the Great Lakes. It made available cheap, easy, and relatively rapid access to international markets out of New York Harbor. Because of their currents, the rivers alone could provide only one-way transport. Arks and rafts shipping goods downriver had to be dismantled and sold for lumber at their destination, since there was no practical means of hauling the craft upriver for reuse.

Prior to the Erie, canals had been built chiefly to ease passage around difficult areas of otherwise navigable rivers, to shortcut long bends, or to create small links in natural waterways. But the Canal Era meant the application of incredible ingenuity to the creation of an entire transportation system of large, water-filled ditches, with dams on rivers and creeks creating the water reserves that would keep the ditches full.

The Canal Network

THE CANAL ERA in Pennsylvania began with the 1826 bill to authorize construction of "The Pennsylvania Canal," passed two months after the Erie opened for operation. Although slow getting started—construction of the Erie Canal had begun in 1817—Pennsylvanians were well aware of the commercial potential of these two-way waterways in bringing the produce of the hinterlands to their major markets. As a result, the state eventually had more than twelve hundred miles of state and privately built canals in use.

The engineering feats of the state-built Pennsylvania Main Line Canal, connecting Philadelphia to Pittsburgh by water, included the first tunnel in the western hemisphere and a series of inclined planes for hauling canal boats over the Allegheny Mountains.

The Schuykill Canal, built between 1816 and 1825, connected Port Carbon with Philadelphia. It was conventional in design, and by contrast, the Lehigh waterway was truly ingenious. The Lehigh system was constructed between 1818 and 1823, improved in 1829 and extended between 1835 and 1837. It incorporated Josiah White's "bear trap" lock in a dam and slackwater system. Water released from the dams created artificial "floods" that floated coal barges to the next slackwater pool with its canal dam and lock system. Some of the canal locks on the upper Lehigh River were the highest in the world.

At Easton, the Lehigh Canal connected with a New Jersey canal system reached by crossing the Delaware River to Phillipsburg. Also at Easton, the Lehigh Canal linked with the Delaware Canal, which ran from Easton to Bristol. These canal systems, built by private corporations, opened up the southern and middle coal fields of Pennsylvania to the Lehigh Valley and Philadelphia markets.

The North Branch Canal

WYOMING VALLEY'S CITIZENS devoted years to working with other canal interests throughout the state and finally achieved the legislation necessary for expanding state-subsidized canal construction northward. This was essential if Wyoming Valley were to become a part of this increasingly intricate canal system. The link between Wyoming Valley and the growing network of canals was to be the North Branch Canal. In 1828 construction began. The canal followed the North Branch of the Susquehanna River from Northumberland to Wyoming Valley, reaching West Nanticoke in 1830. The Wyoming Division, connecting West Nanticoke with Pittston, was completed in 1834. At last the northern coal fields, particularly Wyoming Valley's high-quality anthracite, could have access to major markets.

With a canal along the upper Susquehanna, Wyoming Valley coal could reach the lower Susquehanna and the Chesapeake Bay. In addition, the canal greatly increased access to the West Branch of the Susquehanna, which had its own canal system. And with the Union Canal (also built in 1828) connecting the Susquehanna River near Harrisburg with the Schuylkill River, the people and products of Wyoming Valley could reach the Philadelphia market far more cheaply and smoothly than ever before.

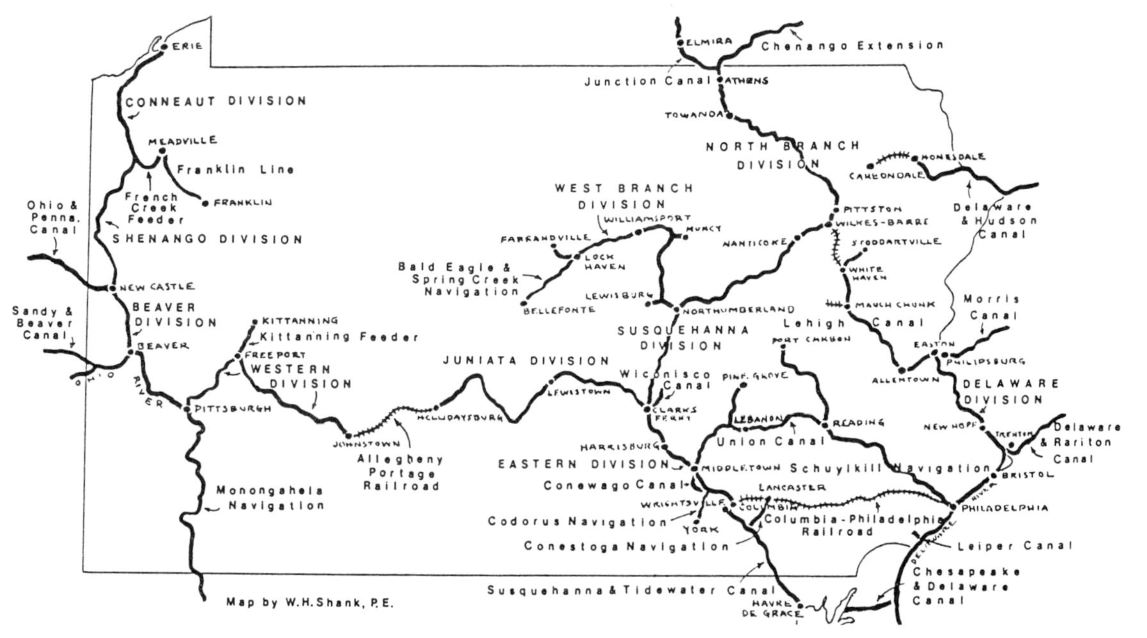

This map, reproduced from *The Amazing Pennsylvania Canals,* was drawn by William H. Shank, P.E. of York, Pennsylvania. It shows all 1243 miles of canals operated—not necessarily concurrently—in Pennsylvania over a period of 135 years. Railroads that formed a part of the canal system are also shown, as are connectors to the six surrounding states. WILLIAM H. SHANK

By 1840, the Susquehanna and Tidewater Canal, running along the west side of the river from below Harrisburg to the Chesapeake Bay, provided a more direct route to Baltimore for both Wyoming Valley's coal and north central Pennsylvania's lumber.

Just as the canals were once used merely to provide shortcuts for river transportation, some early rail systems were constructed to provide more direct routes between canals. During the early 1840s, coal from Wyoming Valley was pulled over the mountains from Ashley on a stationary inclined rail system (the Ashley Planes), then carried by conventional railroad to White Haven. From White Haven, the coal was transported to Philadelphia by way of the Lehigh and Delaware canals. After a massive flood in 1862, the stretch of the canal from White Haven to Mauch Chunk (now Jim Thorpe) was converted to a railroad. (Plans are currently under way to develop a national heritage corridor along this route. The corridor would run from Ashley to Bristol, near Philadelphia, tracing the course of this old railroad-canal system.)

The North Branch Extension of the North Branch Canal continued the waterway further north along the Susquehanna from Pittston to Athens. Constructed between 1849 and 1856, it linked Wyoming Valley's coal industry with Elmira, the Finger Lakes, the Erie Canal, and the Great Lakes.

Finally, even New York City's harbor could be reached from Wyoming Valley over gravity railroads in the Pittston-Scranton area and the Delaware and Hudson Canal. This canal went from Honesdale in Wayne County to Roundout, New York, on the upper Hudson River.

How would Wyoming Valley have developed if there had been no North Branch Canal? What if its interested citizens and legislators, banding together with those of the other towns of the Susquehanna's North Branch, had not succeeded in persuading the Pennsylvania General Assembly to act? Miller and Sharpless in *The Kingdom of Coal* tell us that in the 1820s, the mountainous area of northeastern Pennsylvania was "a sparsely populated wilderness of forests and mountains. In the entire region only Wyoming Valley had a settlement—Wilkes-Barre—of any size and it was little more than an overgrown trading village clinging to the banks of the Susquehanna River." If there had been no coal, there would have been no reason to invest so much money in digging canals. But if there had been no canals, there would have been no market, and therefore no reason for digging coal.

The Wyoming Division

THIS SECTION OF the North Branch Canal was constructed between West Nanticoke and Pittston. It required two decisions that would shape the future of the valley: Should the canal continue along the west side of the river or should the canal boats be towed across the slackwater to the east side? And if the east side was used, what route should the canal take through Wilkes-Barre?

The controversy brought the canal commissioners to Wyoming Valley to examine personally the two routes and to hear the proponents of each. Although still a village of about 1200, Wilkes-Barre was already the largest town in the valley. However, the decision was ultimately determined, not by the size of the competing municipalities but by the fact that the Lackawanna River, which empties into the Susquehanna on the east side, could provide a reliable source of water for the canal. In addition, the estimated construction cost on the east side was slightly cheaper. So from Nanticoke northward the canal ports were on the east bank, and Wilkes-Barre consolidated its position as the commercial center of the area.

The second decision, the path of the canal through Wilkes-Barre, affected the shape of the city for future generations. In most riverside towns, the canals ran along the river. When the canal beds were closed in later years, they created an ideal site for the railroads and railroad yards, which today in many cities have given way to heavy riverside highway construction, thus precluding scenic or recreational use of the riverfront.

The canal route through Wilkes-Barre was unusual. According to Leroy K. Bugbee in *The North Branch Canal:*

This photo of the original South Street Bridge, probably taken in the late 1860s or 1870s, shows the canal running under the bridge side by side with a few of the railroad lines that eventually replaced the canal. Careful study reveals a canal boat in the middle distance just to the right of the bridge, near the piled lumber that sits on the space now occupied by the parking lot of Bishop Hoban High School. The river is visible in the far distance. The Good Shepherd Lutheran Church at the corner of West South and South Main streets (upper right) is the only recognizable building standing in 1992. WHGS

There were three possible routes that could be followed through Wilkes-Barre: one was along the River; the other two routes ran through to the rear of the town, one along Back Street [now Pennsylvania Avenue] and the other even further east. The latter proved impractical. Col. G. M. Hollenback, the wealthiest man in northeastern Pennsylvania, was involved in the final route because it passed along his property, which was on the east side of Back Street. He insisted the Canal should be 150 feet east of Back Street "on the border of the marsh." . . . He further assured the Canal Commissioners he would build a basin at his own expense.

Hollenback won his case, and as a result grew richer still.

The route of the North Branch Canal followed the west side of the Susquehanna River as far north as West Nanticoke. It officially reached West Nanticoke with the completion of the Nanticoke Dam in 1830, the canal becoming more fully operational in 1831. The dam created slackwater—the slowed, raised river level behind the dam—for five miles upstream.

The Wyoming Division of the canal was built between 1831 and 1834. It began above the Nanticoke Dam, with the area of slackwater through which the canal boats could be poled. About a mile of tow path was constructed along the western edge of the river. At the end of the western tow path, canal boats were poled across the river, or used the rope ferry spanning the river. In later years, small steamboats were used to tow the canal boats across the pool.

The canal boats were then towed along the towpath on the eastern bank of the river to the basin at Buttonwood. There the tow path bridged the mouth of Solomon's Creek in Hanover Township. Immediately beyond the creek, an outlet lock with a twelve-foot lift drew the canal boats from the river into the canal. The canal paralleled Solomon's Creek for a short distance, with the towpath running along its east side. A short distance above the outlet lock, there was a second lock with a ten-foot lift. The canal then ran in a northeasterly direction, away from the river and Solomon's Creek, through Hanover Township into South Wilkes-Barre.

Just south of Hanover Street in Wilkes-Barre the canal crossed South Main Street. A third lock, with a ten-foot lift, was located just below Hazle Street. The canal then curved slightly east to run parallel to Back Street (now Pennsylvania Avenue), along what later became the route of the Pennsylvania Railroad tracks. After running several blocks through what was then the rear of the town, the canal turned northwest a few yards above Union Street to avoid rocky bluffs. It ran between Union and Jackson streets for four blocks to River Street. This part of the canal bed, once part of the Laurel Line route, is now used chiefly for parking lots.

At River Street, the canal entered the southern end of the Redoubt Basin, which was 850 feet long and 175 feet wide. Filled in, the basin is now the site of the Luzerne County Court House. (The Redoubt Basin was named for the redoubts that were built on the hill, now terraced for parking, that once rose above it and were used by the Yankees to lay siege to Fort Wyoming, successfully ousting the Pennamites.) This public basin was open to commercial interests for loading and unloading cargoes. At the North Street end of the basin, the canal returned to its course along the east side of the Susquehanna River. The towpath now ran along the river bank to the west of the canal.

Above the Redoubt Basin an aqueduct with stone piers carried the canal over the steep chasm of Mill Creek. This structure was later converted into a

This view of the Redoubt Basin shows the canal continuing northward at its far end. The basin served as a public docking site for canal boats to load and unload. The Luzerne County Jail is dimly visible in the center at the top. F. CHARLES PETRILLO

railroad bridge. Still standing, this bridge and the West Nanticoke lock at Harvey's Creek are the only two structural remnants of the actual canal in the valley. The bridge, which can be seen from the northwest corner of the Hollenback Cemetery, is one of the oldest bits of construction in Wilkes-Barre. Some traces of the canal bed and tow path can still be seeen in the area just to the south of the bridge between the Hollenback and Wilkes-Barre cemeteries and the river.

Above Mill Creek, some stretches of the canal were cut a short distance from the river. There was a lock in Plains Township with a six-foot lift and a final lock at Port Blanchard with a seven-foot lift. In Pittston, the canal terminated 3,100 feet above the mouth of the Lackawanna River. From a dam further upstream on the Lackawanna, a 3,700 foot feeder canal drew water from the river to feed the Wyoming canal line.

This photograph, circa 1920, shows the change in Wilkes-Barre's landscape. The canal ran along the near side of the Lehigh Valley Coal Company Building, now the Administration Building of King's College. It crossed under River Street and behind the old Palm House on the River Common, along the lane that now provides access to the rear of the Court House. Then it swung to the north into the Redoubt Basin. The Court House is located on the filled-in basin, its size dwarfing the old Redoubt Hill. The houses in the background to the right are on North Street, on lots terraced out of the hillside that once dominated this area.
F. CHARLES PETRILLO

The Wyoming Division, including the towpaths along the Nanticoke slackwater and the Lackawanna feeder, was seventeen miles long. (This detailed description of the route of the canal from Nanticoke to Pittston is based on F. Charles Petrillo's precise delineation in *Anthracite and Slackwater: The North Branch Canal 1828–1901.)*

Before the Civil War, the North Branch Canal was the primary means of hauling Wyoming Valley coal to mid-Atlantic markets, particularly to Philadelphia and Baltimore. Markets to the north in the Great Lakes region were opened after the North Branch Extension was completed in 1858. After the Civil War, however, the use of railroads for hauling coal increased, and by the 1880s the Susquehanna canal system was struggling to compete with the railroads.

The North Branch Extension Canal from Pittston to New York State was nearly destroyed by a flood in March 1865. Although reopened, it was finally closed in 1872, and the Lehigh Valley Railroad constructed a line over it. The Wyoming Division through the valley closed in 1882. The original line from Northumberland to West Nanticoke served the Nanticoke mines (Susquehanna Coal Company) until December 1900. That canal was closed in April 1901, along with nearly all the remaining canals in the state.

The canal is long gone. With it have gone the packets, which could deliver passengers from Wilkes-Barre to Philadelphia (via Harrisburg and Reading), in only forty-eight hours. Gone are the 130-ton double-linked barges of coal that made the anthracite industry possible before the advent of the railroads. Gone also are the canalers who lived aboard their boats and transported goods from April to November, from before sunrise until after sunset. Gone are the mulewhackers, boys of nine or ten who walked the towpaths with the mules all day. The ditches were abandoned or filled in, and the boats were sold to their captains to be anchored permanently as homes for their families. The coal was loaded onto trains, which were much less susceptible to ice, drought, and flood, and traveled on routes that were not limited to sources of large quantities of water.

The Impact of the Canal

WYOMING VALLEY was changed forever by the North Branch Canal. With its successor, the railroad, it enabled Wyoming Valley to become the world's largest producer of anthracite by the time World War I began. The coal mines were the magnet that drew the people, and the people transformed the village into a city with its surrounding communities. The canal put Wilkes-Barre on the commercial and industrial map of America and made it part of the national transportation network. The Northeast Extension of the Pennsylvania Turnpike and Interstates 80, 81, and 84 are the canal's current heirs, providing the nationwide linkages for the valley's present diversified economy.

The North Branch Canal literally laid the groundwork for a beautiful city. The filled Redoubt Basin became the perfect site for the new Luzerne County Court House, leaving an open Public Square at the city's center. Warehouses were constructed in the area of Back Street, now Pennsylvania Avenue, rather than on the river. And the common grazing land along the river was kept intact. Canal politics of the 1830s can be credited with the preservation of Wilkes-Barre's lovely River Common, now transformed from grazing land to park.

The Baltimore Coal Mine was the refuge of one escapee while the slave-hunters scoured Wilkes-Barre for him. This picture, from about 1870, shows an area both more exposed and more heavily worked than would have been the case thirty years earlier. L. W. AND E. A. HEERMANS, PHOTOGRAPHERS. COLLECTION OF F. CHARLES PETRILLO, FROM AN ORIGINAL PHOTOGRAPH IN THE WHGS COLLECTION

William C. Gildersleeve

The Despised Hero

FOR AT LEAST forty years prior to the Civil War, Wilkes-Barre was a station on the underground railroad. Pennsylvania was the hub of this nationwide escape network for slaves, combining the relative safety of its mountains with major rivers, canals, and roads that led north. The Susquehanna River links northeastern Pennsylvania to the Chesapeake Bay into which many southern rivers flow. After the construction of the Union Canal between the Susquehanna and Schuylkill Rivers, one could also reach Wyoming Valley by water from Philadelphia's harbor.

The person whose efforts tied Wilkes-Barre to this underground network of safe stations along both water and overland routes was an ardent abolitionist. William C. Gildersleeve was born in McIntosh, Liberty County, Georgia, on December 6, 1795. His father, the Reverend Cyrus Gildersleeve, was minister of the Midway Presbyterian Church in McIntosh. His mother, who had been married before, brought her plantation into the marriage, and Gildersleeve became a slave-holder and cotton grower as well as a minister. Mrs. Renchie Elliott Gildersleeve, née Norman, died in 1807.

In 1810 the family moved to Bloomfield, New Jersey, and in 1821 settled in Wilkes-Barre where the Reverend Gildersleeve became minister of the Congregational Society (now First Presbyterian Church of Wilkes-Barre) and the Presbyterian Church of Kingston. He also served congregations in Pittston, Providence, Plymouth, Hanover, and Newport. According to George B. Kulp, Cyrus Gildersleeve brought a slave with him to Wilkes-Barre: "known as 'Mam Helen,' [she] lived to an advanced old age—something over a hundred years—and spoke with confidence of being 'assisher' to entertain General Washington in the home of her old master in Georgia."

William C. Gildersleeve finished school in New Jersey, went to work for Israel Crane's store in Newark, and married Nancy Riggs of Mendham, New Jersey. After the move to Wilkes-Barre, he established his own store on the north side of Northampton Street near River Street, less than two blocks from his home on North Franklin Street. At some time after 1839, the family moved to South Main Street. (The lane which runs through the block where they lived, from East South Street to East Ross Street, between South Main and South Washington streets, is named Gildersleeve Street in his honor.)

According to Kulp,

> *W. C. Gildersleeve was a decided anti-slavery man. He knew something of it from personal observation on his father's plantation and other plantations in Georgia, and did not hesitate to denounce it as unrighteous and an abomination, although by so doing he became alienated from all his kindred in Georgia. He was a pronounced abolitionist, as much so as Garrison or Wendell Phillips, at a time when it cost something to take such a position, and as such he stood almost alone in this city.*

Both Gildersleeve's home and his business contained hiding places for fugitives from slavery, and he saw them safely to the next stations at Providence (now part of Scranton), Abington, and Montrose. Mary C. Sayre, Mr. Gildersleeve's daughter, recollects several incidents in *A Bit of the Gildersleeve Family,* such as the arrival late one evening of fourteen fugitives who, despite many cloudy nights, had tried to follow the north star from Kentucky. They were nearly starved. The Gildersleeves managed to find food for them and get them on their way that same night, hidden in a hay wagon.

Sayre describes another incident:

> *Once, my father took a group of slaves by night to Abington, but the wagon broke down in Pittston. A Mr. Benedict brought his lantern out at midnight to see what was wrong and when he understood what father was doing, he directed father to take the slaves into his back yard where he had a big wagon. The slaves were transferred to the new wagon and they drove off.*

Mr. Gildersleeve recruited friends when help was needed. Mr. Emmons, a painter, took food and water to a man who stayed hidden for three weeks in the Baltimore Coal Mine in the East End section of Wilkes-Barre while his owner combed the town looking for him. The owner finally gave up and left town. Although others in Wilkes-Barre, like Charles Miner, supported abolition, there is no record that they regularly participated in the underground railroad.

The slave-catchers also found their way to Wilkes-Barre, hunting down the fugitive slaves. Although Pennsylvania was a free state, federal law allowed the recapture of slaves everywhere in the United States. Only Canada was truly

Sinton's Store, site of a fugitive slave's capture, once occupied the southwest corner of the intersection of Market and Franklin streets now the site of Merchants Bank North, once the Wyoming National Bank Building. The store had been moved from River Street—the original commercial section of the village. It was operated by two Quakers, Jacob and Joseph Sinton, until they died in 1836 and 1837. The store continued under their name until 1860 when the building was torn down. SKETCH BY GEORGE LEACH, JR., 1879, COPIED FROM AN EARLIER DRAWING DATED 1819. WHGS

safe. Nevertheless, a number of fugitives did find permanent refuge in Wilkes-Barre, settling in the free black community and getting jobs in the growing town.

One very unlucky fugitive was recaptured in Sinton's Store, at the corner of West Market and South Franklin streets, while doing an errand for his employer. According to Mary Sayre, the man was seized, handcuffed, bound, and thrown on the floor of a lumber wagon "as if he were a dead hog"—all done so quickly there was no time to send for help.

Another story, or perhaps another version of the same incident described above, is recounted in *African-Americans in the Wyoming Valley* as told in *The Union Leader* in 1885. It tells how Hansen, a runaway slave from Virginia, was hired by Jamison Harvey. Emerson I. Moss says, "Hansen was discovered . . . and locked himself in the Harvey house. Harvey was subsequently indicted by a federal grand jury for harboring a fugitive slave. The federal court, sitting in Williamsport, did not appear sympathetic to Harvey, and he was certain of conviction and a heavy fine. Harvey sought to buy Hansen's freedom, but the offer was refused. In order to avoid certain prosecution,

Harvey paid the slave owner a settlement fee, and the slave was returned to his Virginia master."

Mary Sayre also describes a more fortunate fugitive, probably William Thomas, who was

> *employed as a waiter in Gilchrist's Hotel. . . . After the boarders had all left the dinner table, four men entered and called for dinner. . . . While carving some meat, two sprang at him with handcuffs and succeeded in getting [them] on one hand. This was a great help to him in fighting. He got away from them but lost a great deal of blood. He ran like a deer and jumped into the river. As the strangers fired, he would dodge under the water. One ball took a bit of his ear off. He tired them out. After they turned away, he crawled out and lying in the stones pretended to be dead. They kicked him and rolled him over and finally left him. A few friends got him safely to a corn field and spirited him away after dark. He said they would never have taken him back alive.*

A detailed account of this incident, different in several respects but almost surely the same event, is given in *African–Americans in the Wyoming Valley 1778–1990.* Moss cites the description found in Attorney George R. Bedford's memoirs, including Bedford's belief that the brutality of the attack on Thomas changed the attitude of several local citizens who became active abolitionists.

Most of the people in Wilkes-Barre regarded the abolitionists as lawbreakers, as indeed they were. Twice, when abolitionist speakers came to town, they were beset by mobs. In 1837, Mr. Gildersleeve was unable to find a public place where the Reverend John Cross could speak, so he held the meeting in his home. The mob removed pictures, trampled plants, and took away the fence and shrubbery; but Mr. Cross, in spite of threats of personal violence, continued his speech.

In 1839, Mr. C. C. Burleigh of Boston was invited to speak in Wilkes-Barre. He was only ten minutes into his talk when a crowd of young men entered, shouting that the tar and feathers were ready. Mr. Burleigh was smuggled to Judge Dana's home. From there he went under guard to the stage and was safely removed from the town. The mob then got Mr. Gildersleeve to come to Gilchrist's Hotel in response to a note purporting to be from Mr. Burleigh. They poured black dye on him and rode him on a rail to his house. He was probably saved from further violence by the presence of his daughter who forced her way through the mob to take a determined position at his side. When they reached his house, the mob smashed windows and furniture. They did not disperse until Mr. James Nesbitt and Mr. Norton, the harness-maker, threatened them with horse pistols.

Mr. Gildersleeve, this despised hero, afterwards told his family that when he was lifted onto the rail he told himself that it is only conquerors who ride

William C. Gildersleeve built this house on South Main Street in Wilkes-Barre about 1840. The Wilkes-Barre Chamber of Commerce Journal published this photograph shortly after the house was demolished to make room for the Tabernacle, site of a successful revival meeting conducted by evangelist Billy Sunday in 1913. St. Nicholas' church tower is visible in the background. WHGS

on the necks of their enemies. He survived the hazards of the many night journeys and continued with his work, although he was forced to withdraw from his position as an elder of his church. This was a very painful separation since he had also served for many years as superintendent of the Sunday School. As a result, Gildersleeve transferred his association to the Presbyterian Church in Montrose.

Gildersleeve was one of the main agitators for, and founders of, the Home for Friendless Children in Wilkes-Barre. He helped it get started with the rent-free loan of a small frame house he owned on South Street. Later he donated $10,000 toward an endowment fund. Known as the Soldiers' Orphanage after the Civil War, the home is now the Children's Service Center at 335 South Franklin Street in Wilkes-Barre.

William C. Gildersleeve lived to see popular feelings turn against slavery and abolition become the dominant point of view in Wilkes-Barre. Before he died on October 7, 1871, the Thirteenth Amendment to the Constitution had outlawed slavery in the United States.

St. John's Academy of Pittston opened in a double brick dwelling next door to St. John the Evangelist Roman Catholic Church in 1864. In 1880 the school moved into this three-story building whose cornerstone reads "1864 + 1898"—the official founding dates of the academy and the high school. The new quarters provided for thirteen classrooms and living space for faculty and boarding students. The building is now called Gabriel House. Operated by Catholic Social Services, it provides living quarters for single women, the first single room occupancy program of its kind in Pennsylvania. SISTERS OF THE IMMACULATE HEART OF MARY

St. John's Academy

Luzerne County's First Catholic Secondary School

ON SEPTEMBER 14, 1864, St. John's Academy, Pittston, formally opened. This first Catholic secondary school in Luzerne County developed with the great surge in the Roman Catholic population of Wyoming Valley, families drawn by the jobs created by the growing coal-mining industry. In fact, the whole parochial school movement in America was one result of the increasing Roman Catholic population nationwide. But it was also related to America's increasing interest in education. All education in America was transformed in the nineteenth century.

Before 1800, formal education of children outside the family took place, for the most part, in the homes of the teachers, individuals who would take in a few pupils to earn extra income and impart special skills. Although early public schools, like the Wilkes-Barre Academy founded in 1807, were "public" in the sense that they were open to all who could pay the tuition charges, the emergence of the common school dominated mid-nineteenth-century educational reform. In Pennsylvania this era began with the passage of the Free School Act in 1834. A common school was supported by taxation, operated by an elected committee or board at no charge to the student, and intended for the education of all children in a community.

The common school movement, however, was so deeply rooted in the white, Anglo-Saxon Protestant ideology from which it emerged that it accepted as an absolute good the attributes of that culture—its Protestant hymns, Protestant prayers, and King James Bible readings—regardless of how they might be viewed by Americans with different religious and cultural backgrounds. Although there is almost universal agreement among Americans that religious values need to be taught, the question of when, where, and how this is to be accomplished in an open society is still being discussed a century and a half later.

Jay P. Dolan, historian of *The American Catholic Experience,* tells us that since this great public school movement had such a strong Protestant slant, American Catholics were left with few choices. In some areas of the nation, particularly New England, they worked to effect sufficient change in the system to make public education compatible with Catholicism, or at least reasonably palatable to Catholics. In areas where Catholics were the dominant religious group, public schools were sometimes operated by Catholic institutions. Ultimately, the long-term focus of American Catholics became the establishment of a Catholic school system parallel to the public school system. At the meeting of the Second Plenary Council in 1852 in Baltimore, the nation's Roman Catholic bishops recommended that in every diocese a school be built next to every church.

By 1852, the Roman Catholic Church was well established in the United States. In 1788, Monsignor John Carroll had been elected Bishop of Baltimore, with jurisdiction over all American Catholic churches. In 1808, the Philadelphia Diocese was organized, with jurisdiction over Pennsylvania, Delaware, and western New Jersey. This huge geographic area was gradually reduced by the partitioning off of new dioceses; and in 1868 the Scranton Diocese was created, with a Catholic population of sixty thousand.

Even before the establishment of the Scranton Diocese, however, the first Catholic secondary school in Luzerne County had been founded. By 1841, there were at least ten Catholic families in the Pittston area—sufficient for Father Henry Fitzsimmons of Carbondale to call upon them regularly as he rode a circuit from Slocum Hollow (now Scranton) to Wilkes-Barre and back three or four times a year. St. Mary's was built on Chapel Hill in Pittston as a mission church in 1851, but the Catholic population in Pittston was increasing so rapidly that a lot on the corner of William Street was acquired in 1853 for a second church. St. John the Evangelist was dedicated on October 17, 1858. Father John Finnen, who had served briefly as assistant at St. John's and had also been in charge of St. Mary's, became rector in 1861.

In 1863, Father Finnen paid a visit to the motherhouse of the Sisters, Servants of the Immaculate Heart of Mary, in Reading, to negotiate for their services in opening a convent school in Pittston. Two of the IHM Sisters traveled by stagecoach from Reading to Wilkes-Barre, where they were met by Mary O'Donnell and Belinda Reap. In Pittston they inspected the large brick dwelling house adjoining the church on William Street. With the nuns' agreement to the undertaking, Father Finnen purchased the building and oversaw its conversion into classrooms, with a portion set aside for living quarters for the teachers. Six sisters arrived in August, and in September 1864 St. John's Academy was opened. The day it opened, 150 girls were signed up as prospective students despite its relatively high tuition of one dollar per month.

In 1899 St. John's Parochial School and St. John's Academy were chartered as St. John's High School. The school moved into its new building, under construction in this picture, in 1922. The building, on William Street in Pittston, now houses Seton Catholic High School. *Sisters of the Immaculate Heart of Mary*

St. John's Academy could not have been established without Finnen's energy and initiative, but it was the willingness and dedication of the IHM Sisters that made the school possible. The order had been founded in 1845 on the banks of the Raisin River in Monroe, Michigan, its first convent a log cabin. The founder, Mother M. Theresa Maxis Duchemin, was born in Baltimore in 1810. Her mother was a French-African refugee from the slave revolt in Hispaniola, the Caribbean island that is now divided between Haiti and the Dominican Republic. Her father was an Englishman visiting Baltimore.

Mother Theresa first became a member—in fact, one of the founders—of the Oblate Sisters of Providence, a black order in Baltimore. Father Louis Florent Gillet, a Belgian Redemptorist, urged her to leave the Oblate Sisters and start a new teaching order. Father Gillet was eager to establish a school in his newly assigned mission field in Michigan, and Mother Theresa accepted the challenge. The new order struggled through an austere beginning, but it survived to become a prosperous congregation.

From its foundation, the education of youth was a major objective of the IHM congregation. In fact, even before St. John's Academy was founded, there were IHM Sisters at work in the future Scranton Diocese in what is now Susquehanna County. Father John P. Gallagher, in *A Century of History,* describes the successful establishment in 1860 of St. Alphonsus Academy at Susquehanna Depot: "After a shaky start, resolved very quickly by an adept change of name [to Laurel Hill Academy] to suit Protestant sensitivities, enrollment climbed steadily upward." The revenue from Laurel Hill was sufficient by 1862 to fund an ungraded elementary free school for boys and girls in a nearby converted church building.

The presence of female religious orders was vital to the church's educational work. According to Dolan, "One of the first things a frontier bishop did was to recruit a religious order of women for the diocese." It was just three years after Pope Pius IX created the Scranton Diocese that Bishop William O'Hara made his successful appeal to a group of fifteen IHM Sisters following a retreat at Susquehanna Depot. Twelve of those present agreed to organize the Scranton Province of the Sisters, Servants of the Immaculate Heart of Mary, under Mother Superior Mary Joseph. By 1872 they were in residence in their new motherhouse across the street from the Scranton Cathedral's Rectory.

Those first six teaching nuns in Luzerne County, whose arrival at St. John's Academy in Pittston predated both the creation of the Scranton Diocese and the establishment of the IHM motherhouse in Scranton, were Sister M. Cephas, Superior; Sister M. Antoinette; Sister M. Elizabeth; Sister M. Regina; Sister M. Gabriel; and Sister M. Agatha, all IHM.

St. John's Academy was open to both boys and girls, but very few families could get along without their sons' wages, so relatively few boys were enrolled and almost none stayed to complete the requirements. Sister M. Egidious, IHM, who had been a principal in the New York City schools before entering the order, worked with the boys of the parish during night school sessions. She also organized a uniformed cadet corps and a junior drum corps in 1871 from her "miner boys." Charles McCarthy, in a series of articles published in 1954 in the *Pittston Sunday Dispatch,* states that "These organizations marked the real commencement of the Catholic Temperance Movement in this region."

In 1878, Father John Finnen appealed for funds for a new free parochial school to be built adjacent to St. John's Academy. Michael Reap's $2000 gift began a community response that was so positive that the school was able to open in 1880 debt free. It had primary, intermediate, and grammar grades taught by seven IHM sisters. On opening day, 550 pupils registered at this first tuition-free parochial school in northeastern Pennsylvania.

Mother M. Theresa Maxis Duchemin (1810–1892) was the founder of the congregation of the Sisters, Servants of the Immaculate Heart of Mary. FROM *Mother M. Theresa Maxis Duchemin* BY SISTER M. IMMACULATA, IHM

St. John's Academy continued to operate on a tuition-paid basis until the academy and the parochial school were combined under the direction of Reverend Eugene Garvey, Father Finnen's successor. The merged institution, St. John's High School, was officially chartered on March 17, 1899. On February 19, 1906, fire destroyed the library and science facilities. All students were evacuated without injury, and the school was rebuilt on the same site with an additional wing and a new youth center added. Adam Drayer, in his *History of Catholic Secondary Education in the Diocese of Scranton,* notes that the high school was granted a first-class rating by the Pennsylvania Department of Public Instruction in 1914, and in 1916 it became affiliated with The Catholic University of America.

In 1917, Father Coroner, then pastor, requested funds for a new school building. Although $200,000 was needed, the funds were oversubscribed within a week; and in 1922, the new facility opened. St. John the Evangelist High School became Seton Catholic High School in 1976. No longer a single parish responsibility but a diocesan high school, Seton Catholic serves twenty-three parishes in the Greater Pittston Area.

What happened to the anti-Catholic sentiment that flared when St. John's Academy first opened its doors? Dr. Drayer points out that

> *Since public school facilities in Pittston were limited at that time, children of all denominations attended St. John's. This relieved some of the religious prejudice. Father Finnen, too, helped lessen bigotry, because his . . . attitude toward the pas-*

tors of the various sects was always friendly and not a few Protestant ministers were his lifelong friends.

Other factors were also at work. Father John Finnen was a man of exemplary character and determination. Between 1861 and his death in 1899, he created an outstanding parish church and school complex. In this endeavor, he was participating in two of the major forces shaping America as we know it today. First as a church leader during the period when Roman Catholicism was becoming America's largest religious denomination, he transformed the domain of a circuit-riding priest with a mission chapel into an impressive establishment.

Second, Father Finnen and the Sisters, Servants of the Immaculate Heart of Mary, were part of another vast swell of change and growth taking place across the United States. While we make clear the distinction between the common or public school and the private, parochial, or independent school, we want to remember that they are two parts of one great movement—the education of America.

The Luzerne County Medical Society

DURING THE NINETEENTH CENTURY, medicine in America and Europe emerged from the mixture of nostrums and superstitions upon which people had relied from time immemorial. The concept of highly trained and well disciplined physicians providing for the health care of a whole society had its American roots in the establishment of a medical school at the College of Philadelphia in 1765. Philadelphia became the center of medical activity in America; and by the mid-nineteenth century, surgery, obstetrics, and pharmacy had also acquired professional respectability.

In 1847, with the founding of the American Medical Society in Philadelphia, the idea of physicians joining forces to reinforce professional standards began to spread. An attempt in 1855 to draw together the physicians of Luzerne County lasted only three years, but a second attempt on March 4, 1861, laid the foundation for the Luzerne County Medical Society, which has endured to this day.

That first meeting was held in the Luzerne County Court House, which stood in the middle of Public Square in Wilkes-Barre. The second meeting in that year and in subsequent years was held in Scranton. (Lackawanna County was part of Luzerne County until 1878; in 1879, the bylaws were amended to discontinue the Scranton meeting.) A third meeting each year, to be held in Pittston, was added to the rotation schedule in 1864. Summer meetings were held at Glen Summit, Dallas, or Harvey's Lake. The first woman was elected to membership in 1877. (No name is given in Dr. Lewis Buckman's history and the original minutes are lost. The first woman listed in the membership roster is Sarah J. Coe, M.D., a graduate of the University of Michigan.) In 1911 the Hazleton Branch was mentioned, but it was not formally organized as a Branch Society until 1923. In 1932 the Women's Auxiliary to the Luzerne County Medical Society was founded.

After meeting for several years in the rooms of the Wyoming Historical and Geological Society, then moving to the Royal Arcanum Hall, and finally

In 1866, Dr. E. R. Mayer became the first recorded presenter of a scientific paper before the Luzerne County Medical Society. In 1870 he served as president of the society. His picture was found in a composite showing the medical staff of the Wilkes-Barre City Hospital (now General) from 1872 to 1900.
PHOTO BY IMPERIAL ART PUB. CO. COURTESY LUZERNE COUNTY MEDICAL SOCIETY

to the Young Men's Hebrew Association, the society leased the sixth floor of the Coal Exchange Building for seven consecutive years. The move into this location led to the addition of a curator to the society's officers, "to have charge of all medical books and periodicals, and to preserve, take care of, duly register and label all pathological specimens."

The subsequent move, in 1897, to the Anthracite Building, coincided with the formal establishment of a medical reference library and the employment of an assistant librarian. The ultimate move, in 1915, was to the newly constructed fireproof home for this collection and to a fixed place of meeting—the Medical Society's present building at the rear of 132 South Franklin Street in Wilkes-Barre.

On May 9, 1866, a resolution was adopted "requesting Dr. Mayer to report his experience in the application of ice and hot water according to Dr. Chapman's method." This is the first record of a scientific paper presented to the society. Other topics covered included crytogamic poisons, inherited diseases, urticaria, puerperal fever, and treatment of dysentery—"the disease was not fatal in Carbondale." Papers were presented by society members on scalds and burns, gonorrhea, and the use of cocaine as an anaesthesia. The first guest lecture on record was presented in 1894 by Dr. H. W. Frauenthal of New York City who spoke on "Lateral Curvature of the Spine". Among other guests, Dr. Jay F. Schamberg presented "Cutaneous Manifestations of Small-Pox and Scarlatina and the Diseases with which they are apt to be confounded, illustrated by a large number of Lantern Slides."

The Hospital for the Insane at Retreat, Pennsylvania, faced the Susquehanna River. This view from the rear shows the railroad depot and the entrance to the grounds. The Almshouse was already located at Retreat when the hospital was constructed. Both were under the direction of the board of the Central Poor District of Luzerne County. In 1911 the tax levy for the Poor District was 2 mills. The eight directors anticipated reducing it by one-half in 1913. In the 1970s, Retreat was rebuilt as a state penitentiary. FROM *Annual Report of the Central Poor District* 1912. WHGS

Among the ethical issues discussed, one of the most important concerned requiring the registration of practitioners in the Prothonotary's office. Standards for medical practice were just being established. Many physicians received much of their training at the hands of preceptors, and there were no exams for licensure by the states. "Correction of abuses and protection of themselves against quackery and from irregular practice had to come from the physicians themselves and from within their own organization." Some of the schemes that flourished in the Wyoming Valley were a sex lecture game at the Cinderella Ballroom by a "Doctor" Taylor; a food-fad racket using radio to publicize his "health" bread by a "Doc" Springer; an "Oriental Herbalist" named Iris; and a "perfect man" named "Samsted" who posed unrobed before an audience of women to push the sale of products for women only.

In addition to policing its own members and acting to prevent the practice of charlatanism in the county, the Medical Society lobbied at both the county and state levels for public health issues. A major step forward was the establishment of the State Board of Health which brought about compulsory vaccination. Lobbying efforts to effect this are first cited in the Society's minutes in 1881. They included petitions and visits by concerned physicians to Harrisburg, as well as local contacts with state representatives and senators. Bills introduced

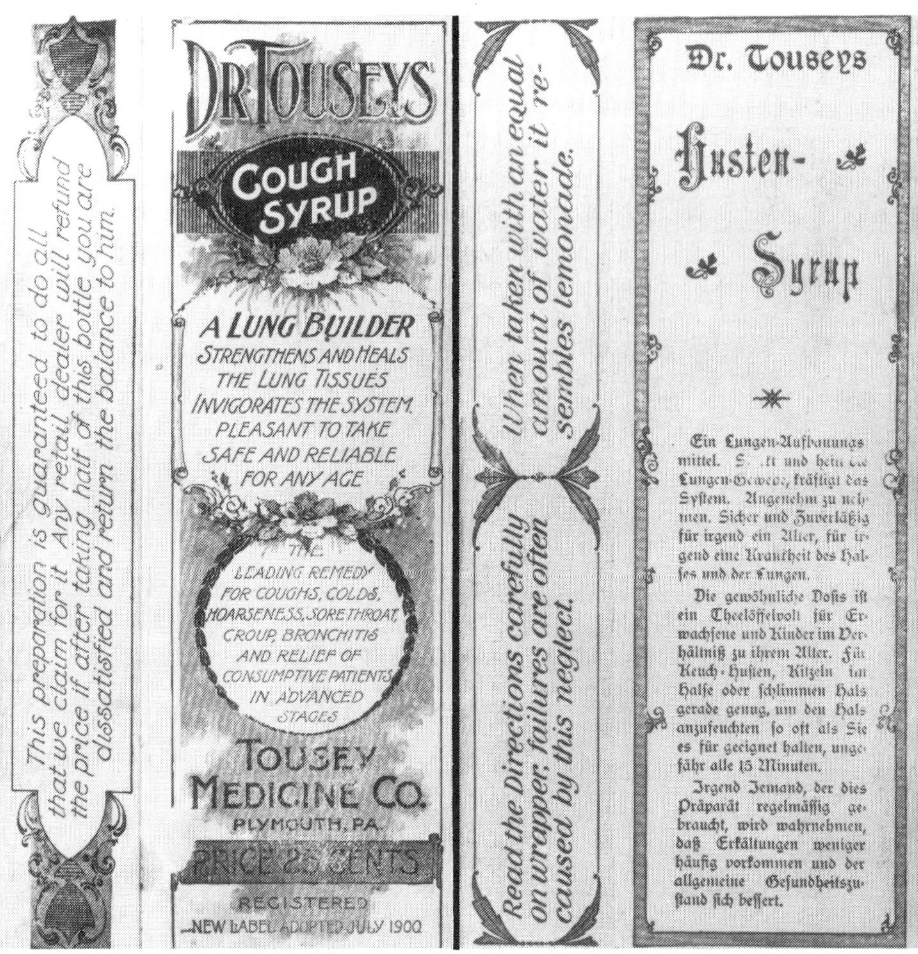

This patent medicine box dating from 1900 is part of the Wyoming Historical and Geological Society Collection. Typical of medicines of the time is both the absence of any list of ingredients and the presence of extravagant claims. The sales pitch is repeated on the back of the box in German. WHGS

at every session of the General Assembly for a decade were finally passed in 1891. Similar efforts eventually led to the creation of a State Board of Medical Examiners and Licensers.

Locally, the society was interested in improving sanitation and water quality. The 1885 typhoid fever epidemic in Plymouth led to the dissemination of information about boiling water and disinfection. An 1889 epidemic in Laurel Run led to the recommendation first that resevoirs be drained and cleaned, and finally that the upper resevoir be abandoned. An 1892 cholera outbreak led to resolutions on prompt collection and incineration of garbage. In 1895, a committee appointed by the society began to work for the organization of a board of health for Wilkes-Barre. The society also pressed for the appointment of a sanitary officer and the establishment of a city bacteriological laboratory.

The Luzerne County Medical Society Building, completed in 1915, still serves as the headquarters for the organization. It is located at the rear of 132 South Franklin Street, Wilkes-Barre. LUZERNE COUNTY MEDICAL SOCIETY

In 1899, the society again pressed the city to establish a board of health. After fourteen years of effort, the city council passed an ordinance to create one; and although the mayor was unenthusiastic and noncommital, he eventually signed it.

Resolutions of the society addressed needs of the County Poor House, recommendations for the construction of a hospital for the insane, and the need for a tuberculosis hospital. Steps were taken to deal with milk quality, communicable diseases, care of babies' eyes, public education on cancer, the examination of crippled children, and numerous other concerns.

Many new professional organizations have been formed relating to hospital interests and to the medical specialties. But the Medical Society continues to be the forum, at the local, state, and national levels, at which the broad concerns of medicine, medical care, and continuing medical education are addressed. The establishment of standards of medical practice; the optimal forms of health care for the community; and the integrity of the individual practitioner are still the society's goals, as they were in its original constitution of 1861.

A Postscript

In 1937, Lewis T. Buckman, M.D. compiled *A History of the Luzerne County Medical Society* from the records and minutes of the society. He brought the publication up to date in 1961 for the society's centennial. Since these minutes and notes were lost in the 1972 Agnes Flood, his careful and detailed history—the source for this chapter—is now invaluable.

Pauline von Mallinckrodt (1817–1881). FROM *Die Liebe zahlt nicht; nur die Liebe zahlt,* BY SISTER M. ADALBERTA METTE, TRANSLATED BY SISTER M. JULITTA GAUL

Mother Pauline von Mallinckrodt

PAULINE VON MALLINCKRODT was born at Minden in what is now Germany on June 3, 1817, two years after the defeat of Napoleon at the Battle of Waterloo. By the time of her death on April 30, 1881, the balance of power in Europe had been radically altered. The great surge of nationalism which had swept through France and brought Napoleon to power had found further expression in the unification of Italy in 1867 and the establishment of the German Empire in 1871. German nationalism, which provided the basis for Otto von Bismarck's success as architect of this unified Germany, was the dominant theme of the German Empire under its Prussian king, Kaiser Wilhelm I.

Meanwhile, as nationalism was increasing in intensity and expression, the Roman Catholic Church was becoming increasingly internationalist. Pope Pius IX convened the first Vatican Council in 1870. While it was sitting, the new Italian state annexed Rome, eliminating the last territorial holding of the Roman Catholic Church. According to R. R. Palmer, author of *A History of the Modern World,* "It is now widely agreed that with the loss of local temporal interests, the spiritual hold of the papacy on Catholics throughout the world has been enhanced." The first Vatican Council, by proclaiming the dogma of papal infallibility—that is the doctrine that the pope, when speaking *ex cathedra* on matters of faith and morals, speaks with authority that no Catholic may question or reject—resolved an internal conflict of centuries and took a major step, in a world become more national, toward internationalism.

Fearful that the internationalism of the Roman Catholic Church would undermine national loyalty, that Catholics would divide their allegiance between church and state and ultimately obey the pope rather than their own government, Germany broke off relations with the papacy. The German *Kulturkampf*—a movement to elevate German culture and enhance German nationalism—was under way. As a result, C. J. H. Hayes says in *Nationalism: A Religion,* "Jesuits were banished from Germany, candidates for the priesthood

Pauline von Mallinckrodt as a young woman.
FROM *The Woman Who Couldn't Be Stopped,*
BY SISTER DELPHINE WEDMORE, S.C.C.

were required to study at secular universities, . . . and disobedience was made punishable by fines and imprisonment. For a time every German Catholic bishop was in jail or in exile and in over 1300 parishes Catholic worship ceased." Bismarck's goal was a national German church cut off from the pope.

What does this have to do with Wilkes-Barre, Pennsylvania? And how does Pauline von Mallinckrodt enter the picture? In the clash of these great nineteenth-century movements—nationalism and internationalism—Pauline von Mallinckrodt emerged as a major force in her own right, and Wilkes-Barre became a direct beneficiary of that force.

Pauline was the oldest of the four children of Bernardine von Hartmann and Detmar von Mallinckrodt. She was educated at St. Leonard's School in Aix-la-Chapelle where she studied under Luise Hensel—a great teacher and poet who was sensitive to the dire poverty of those displaced by the industrial revolution. She involved her students in her work with the poor and sick and inspired a lifelong concern not only in Pauline but in three of her classmates as well. After a term at finishing school in Liège, Belgium, Pauline returned to live with her parents at Aix-la-Chapelle. There she led an active social life, meeting many of the men and women who would shape the conflicting futures of both Germany and the Roman Catholic Church. Her father was appointed temporary president of the Rhine Province and hoped to receive the job per-

The first Institute for the Blind at Paderborn, founded by Pauline von Mallinckrodt, opened in 1847. It grew out of the nursery she had started as a home for the street children of Paderborn. One day her family's physician and friend, Dr. Schmidt, brought her two small blind children for the nursery. In order to help these two who were doubly poor, she learned to be a teacher of the blind. By the end of that year, 1842, she had five blind children in the school. FROM *Pauline von Mallinckrodt up to Her First Profession Written by Herself*

manently. But he was passed over and the appointment given to another Protestant, one who had not married a Catholic and had not allowed his children to be raised as Catholics.

The von Mallinckrodt family retired to Boedeken and Paderborn. At Paderborn Pauline became involved in an organization for the care of the poor. There she perceived the need for a nursery for the small children who were barely surviving life in the streets. Beginning with eight children, ages two to six, under the care of Pauline, her aunt, and a friend, the nursery was supported by the women in the Association for the Care of the Sick Poor.

As the number of children in the nursery increased rapidly, Pauline responded by finding larger quarters and more funds. In 1842 she added the care of blind children to her responsibilities, learning braille and handicrafts in order to teach them. For example, she devised embroidered raised maps for teaching geography, and learned how to pour braille molds.

In 1843, the fourteen-year-old Mathilde Kothe joined Pauline's staff. She had just graduated from the teachers' school for the blind. While Pauline was tall and had learned to hold herself regally, Mathilde is described by Wedmore

Luise Hensel was an unusual teacher, raising her students' awareness of society's needs. Although St. Leonard's Academy for Girls was a secular school, its alumnae included Clara Fey, founder of the Sisters of the Poor Child Jesus, and Franziska Schervier, founder of the Sisters of the Poor of St. Francis of Aix-la-Chapelle. Anna von Lommessen, Pauline von Mallinckrodt's classmate and friend, joined the Mesdames of the Sacred Heart and became superior of their convent. Pauline said of Luise Hensel that she was "a very amiable, intelligent, wise and interesting woman, who, in an eminent degree, possessed the gift of fascinating the hearts of children and leading them to God." FROM *Pauline von Mallinckrodt up to Her First Profession Written by Herself*

in *The Woman Who Couldn't Be Stopped* as small and seemingly fragile, hiding "an unexpected strength of will and a tremendous power of accomplishment."

By the time Pauline's school friend Anna von Lommessen entered the Convent of the Sacred Heart, Pauline knew that she also wanted to commit herself to a religious life. Unable to find an order that would allow her to continue the care of her poor and blind children, Pauline visited another classmate, Clara Fey, founder of the Sisters of the Poor Child Jesus. She then turned to Bishop Claessen of Cologne. Both believed the solution was in her: She was to found a new religious congregation.

After long study, Pauline chose the Rule of St. Augustine as the basis of her new order. Her dedicated teaching staff of four, including Mathilde Kothe, chose to remain with her and to become religious also. On August 21, 1849, the first five Sisters of Christian Charity began a one-year novitiate; and in 1850, they took their first holy vows. In 1850 they also accepted their first mission. Postulants began to join the congregation, and in five years there were forty-five sisters teaching in five schools. Within twenty years, the order had grown to 250 sisters in twenty-one missions which, in addition to the Blind Institute and the nursery at Paderborn, included academies, elementary schools, orphanages, day nurseries, and a home for the aged.

The movement to establish a national German "Kultur" and to eliminate the Catholic influence on the nation was first felt by the congregation in 1871. Two sisters at Krim were not paid, and Dusseldorf replaced its religious with lay teachers. In Baden, all religious teachers were outlawed in 1872. Sisters of Christian Charity were withdrawn from Viersen and Anrath, and the school at Solingen was closed. Ironically, the celebration of the 1100th anniversary of

Hermann von Mallinckrodt (1821–1874), Pauline's brother, was the leader of Germany's Centre party and leader of the resistance to the passage and implementation of the May Laws in 1873. FROM *Pauline von Mallinckrodt up to Her First Profession Written by Herself*

the introduction of Christianity into Germany coincided exactly with the expulsion of the Jesuits by the German government.

In *A History of the Early Foundations,* Sister M. Lauretta Schreiber describes the order's response to the Kulturkampf. Mother Pauline rented a building vacated by the Jesuits for her own refugees, already forty in number. In addition, "she immediately established five new foundations in the neighboring countries of Bohemia, Leichtenstein, and Belgium with enrollments of pupils from Germany."

Even more stringent restrictions on Catholicism were embodied in the May Laws of 1873, passed despite the very vocal opposition of the Centre party, particularly that of Hermann von Mallinckrodt, Pauline's brother. Mother Pauline confronted Herr Falk, minister of education and author of the May Laws, to no avail. The support of the queen of Dresden and other staunch and formerly influential persons could not help the order as the Kulturkampf movement peaked, and seventeen more of their institutions were taken over by the German government.

In 1856—seventeen years before the May Laws—Mother Pauline had received the first request for sisters to go to America, and several women had studied English in preparation for the proposed move although it was later cancelled.

In 1872, another call came from the United States, this time from New Orleans. Also in 1872, Father Peter C. Nagel, pastor of St. Nicholas Church in Wilkes-Barre, visited the motherhouse in Paderborn "to view the grounds and buildings." Shortly afterwards he wrote, not only inviting teachers for his school (already operating and staffed by a lay teacher), but proposing the establishment of a motherhouse in the Scranton Diocese.

In May 1873, the Sisters of Christian Charity established their first American colony in New Orleans. In order to guide the congregation successfully into this new area, Mother Pauline and her secretary, Sister Gonzaga Kreymborg (later provincial superior for South America), toured the United States. They landed in New York on June 7, 1872.

Mother Pauline wrote: "We informed Father Nagel of our coming and took the train. . . . At last the conductor called, 'Wilkes-Barre.' As the train approached the station, I looked out of the window curiously and saw little girls dressed in white and boys in their Sunday suits hurrying to reach the train. We thought they were going on an excursion, but upon stepping out of the train, we saw that the children with their teachers were there to greet us. They formed a guard of honor through which the Reverend Father Nagel passed to welcome us to the Land of Liberty."

In addition to the parish school for St. Nicholas, Father Nagel requested the opening of a select school for girls. He took Mother Pauline and Sister Gonzaga to meet the Right Reverend William O'Hara, Bishop of the Scranton Diocese, and Father Schelle, pastor of St. Mary's Parish, Scranton, who also wanted them to open a parochial school. Mother Pauline consulted with Bishop O'Hara about the possibility of a provincial motherhouse from which to draw for future American missions. Bishop O'Hara gave her his blessing, and on her return to Wilkes-Barre on July 25, having traveled to Philadelphia, Baltimore, Washington, Cincinnati, New Orleans, Chicago, Detroit, Niagara Falls, and Buffalo (where they visited the Jesuits expelled from Paderborn), Mother Pauline chose a six-acre site on Park Hill "overlooking the city of Wilkes-Barre, the Susquehanna River, and a beautiful mountain range." The general plan for the prospective motherhouse was already under way before she returned to Germany. Sister Mathilde Kothe was appointed Provincial Superior for North America, and ten sisters left Bremen to arrive in Wilkes-Barre on October 15, 1873. Within two years, eighty sisters came to the New World, and nineteen missions were established.

Although Mother Pauline von Mallinckrodt returned to Paderborn to continue her efforts to keep Catholicism alive in Germany, by 1877 the Order of the Sisters of Christian Charity was officially located in Belgium. Meanwhile, although Pauline's brother Hermann von Mallinckrodt had died in 1874, the Centre party continued to gain strength in the Reichstag. In 1878 Bismarck ceased the persecution of Catholics and turned his attention to the extermination of socialism. Unfortunately, although no longer enforced, many of Bismarck's anti-Catholic measures remained part of German law until after World War I when they were reactivated by the Nazis.

What was the effect of the Kulturkampf on the Sisters of Christian Charity? Before it, there was one novitiate. By 1878 there were four—in the United States, Chile, Bohemia, and Belgium. Before it, the sisters had twenty-one houses. By 1877 there were twelve in Europe, twenty-seven in North America, and five in South America, totaling forty-two. Rather than fade docilely into oblivion under pressure, Mother Pauline von Mallinckrodt, with great courage and overriding faith, confronted the German government at every turn, fought every inch of the retreat, and turned retreat into victory. And the Sisters of Christian Charity became a truly international order.

Construction of this central portion of the Mallinckrodt Convent—the original building housing both the motherhouse for North America and St. Ann's Academy—was planned for 1873. It opened, despite seveal serious setbacks, in 1878. FROM *The Mallinckrodt,* ST. ANN'S ACADEMY, 1935

Sisters of Christian Charity

A New Home in Wilkes-Barre

On October 15, 1873, seven Sisters of Christian Charity arrived in Wilkes-Barre, Pennsylvania. They had traveled from Bremen, Germany, by way of New York, to fulfill Mother Pauline von Mallinckrodt's commitment to St. Nicholas's pastor, Father Peter C. Nagel. In addition to their parish teaching duties, they were charged with establishing a new North American motherhouse for their order in Wilkes-Barre.

Several factors had led to the sisters' arrival here. First, because of Bismarck's Kulturkampf, they had become refugees from their own German convents. Second, during the mid-nineteenth century, German immigration to America had soared. This growing population, many of them Roman Catholic, created a language barrier within many Catholic parishes and led to a demand for religious institutions that reflected the national identity of the immigrants. In response to this demand, the concept of the ethnic parish developed and spread.

In Wilkes-Barre, the Irish Catholic members of the original mission congregation of St. Nicholas of Tolentine received permission during the 1850s from the Bishop of Philadelphia, Blessed John Nepomucene Neuman, D.D., to build their own church, St. Mary of the Immaculate Conception. (The Scranton Diocese had not yet been created.) Father Nagel became the resident pastor of the mission's German Catholics, and the mission congregation was raised to the rank of an ethnic parish. A new brick church was built on the northwest corner of Canal (now Pennsylvania Avenue) and South streets, and a parochial school was established.

The German bishops and clergy were particularly ardent champions of parochial schools. Jay P. Dolan, in *The American Catholic Experience,* points out that "Within these communities the school became a key part of the local parish culture, and the . . . crusade to preserve culture through religion strengthened its importance." Centered in the national churches, these ethnic groups were cultural rather than residential. They established a web of social relationships that bound each group together and created a world of the mind where they could hear the word of God spoken in a familiar tongue and watch their children grow up speaking and praying as they did.

The German-speaking Sisters of Christian Charity, prepared to teach a new generation in their native tongue, were able to fill a great religious and cultural need for the German Catholics of Wilkes-Barre. They immediately went to work at St. Nicholas' Parochial School, already operating under the guidance of Mr. Stenger and his two daughters. Mr. Stenger continued with the upper boys' class. Sister Raphaele Sasse took the upper girls. Sister Caroline Horstmann and Sister Gertrudis Hense took the lower two classes. Sister Engelberta Ruessing took care of the household.

St. Ann's Academy also had its first beginning that fall of 1873, but lack of room and lack of funds, combined with the financial misfortunes of the order in Germany, forced its discontinuance until a new beginning could take place five years later. On April 28, 1874, sixteen more sisters arrived in America, including Mother Mathilde Kothe, the new Provincial Superior, and Sister Philomena Schmittdiel, her assistant.

Although Mother Pauline von Mallinckrodt had already purchased the land for the new provincial motherhouse during her 1873 visit to Wilkes-Barre, the order could not afford to proceed with construction. Without a motherhouse the order could not accept candidates for the novitiate or train them to teach. As a compromise measure, the first American motherhouse was opened in the small dwelling near St. Nicholas Church where the first arrivals had been living. A nearby house was also acquired, one home used for sleeping quarters and classrooms and the other for chapel, parlor, kitchen, and dining room.

Sister Domitilla Keller, a candidate for the novitiate during that first year, recalls, "The dining room was rather small, so we younger sisters had to sit two by two on the steps leading upstairs. The dishes of food were passed up and down. . . . The food was not very plentiful and often the candidates ate a hardened piece of bread and molasses with as much relish as a child enjoys a peppermint stick." Sister Prudentia Blank described the dormitories with their washstands made of egg crates with little curtains to hide their contents. Schreiber tells us that in order "to enable the sisters to earn a little money, a sewing class was opened which Mother Mathilde herself conducted. Soon after, a piano was purchased and Sister Veneranda gave lessons."

On one occasion, when they feared their piano and other furniture would be taken to pay a large bill, Mother Mathilde interrupted the class of novices to ask for their prayers. They had been praying for a long time when the doorbell rang. Upon her entrance to the parlor, a gentleman handed Mother Mathilde an envelope and left without a word of explanation. In the envelope, Mother Mathilde found a sizable donation, so she asked the novices to say another prayer—this time one of thanksgiving. This story was told by Sister Theobalda Hoffman, who also described how one day she found Sister Marcellina, who was in charge of the kitchen, in tears at the pump. When Sister Theobalda asked why she was crying, Sister Marcellina said, "I do not know what to cook, we haven't any food in the house. For fourteen days we have drunk black coffee and eaten dry bread, and we have no money." Sister Theobalda, who lived nearby, ran home and told her mother who exclaimed, "Had I known that! I shall go directly to the store and buy groceries." From then on, the neighbors kept the sisters' larder filled.

Despite the hardships, the struggle with the new language and customs, and the homesickness they must have felt when they celebrated the twenty-fifth anniversary of their community so far from home, Mother Mathilde Kothe and her colleagues persevered. Schools were established in Scranton, Honesdale (northeast of Scranton), Williamsport, and Bastress (south of Williamsport), as well as in Wilkes-Barre. Facilities in Wilkes-Barre were expanded by the acquisition of a third house near the original two, and a year and a half after the first sisters' arrival, eleven young American women were received into the community. Finally, in 1877, with the novitiate now numbering thirty-five members, construction on the motherhouse began. Because of the 1873 financial panic and subsequent depression, the cost of the building was about half what had first been estimated. But the whole cost had to be raised by the new foundations in America, for in Germany the order was reduced to poverty.

The new building, to be called the Mallinckrodt Convent, was 100 feet long and 50 wide, with a basement, three stories, and a "very large garret." The sisters moved there on October 4, 1878. "Here on the heights," say the chronicles, "We can serve God unhindered, disturbed only by the sound of the machines of distant mines and the puffing of the locomotive making its way around the mountains. We gaze on the beauty of God's nature, with the apparently quiet city at our feet. Its bustle does not reach our ears."

The Sacred Heart Chapel at St. Ann's Academy, built in 1885. FROM *The Mallinckrodt,* ST. ANN'S ACADEMY, 1935

St. Ann's Academy

On November 4, 1878, St. Ann's Academy enrolled its first six students. Its founding order, the displaced Sisters of Christian Charity, had endured five years of hard times in inadequate quarters since their arrival in Wilkes-Barre in 1873. They attempted to open an academy when they arrived, but lack of space in their rented homes and lack of funds necessary for the purchase of basic supplies forced them temporarily to put aside that goal.

The establishment of a female academy was part of Mother Pauline von Mallinckrodt's original plan for the new provincial motherhouse. It was dear to the heart of Father Peter C. Nagel, pastor of St. Nicholas Roman Catholic Church, Wilkes-Barre, who had been instrumental in introducing the Sisters of Christian Charity to the city. It also had the full support of Bishop William O'Hara of the Scranton Diocese, since it would provide a secondary level of Catholic education as well as an elementary level. Very few parochial schools at that time were able to go beyond the elementary level.

By the second half of the nineteenth century it was generally accepted, as Frederick Rudolph asserted, that the "American female was capable of being educated—up to a point," and that education would help young American women become better mothers and homemakers, as well as moral guardians of the home.

Although the primary goals of the founders of early educational institutions for girls were religious and moral, at St. Ann's Academy a supportive environment was created where a high value was also placed on excellence of achievement. Where teachers shared their students' delight in learning, it is not surprising that young women excelled. They went far beyond the limits implied by Frederick Rudolph, achieving new goals through academic and professional training. They became lawyers (the first woman in Pennsylvania to be admitted to the state bar exam was a St. Ann's alumna), physicians, scientists, musicians, artists, teachers, missionaries—and even mothers who were the moral guardians of their families.

Field day marked the end of the year's physical training course at St. Ann's. The contests included volley ball and ended with ice cream and cake. FROM *The Mallinckrodt,* ST. ANN'S ACADEMY, 1935

In 1878, in addition to the opening of St. Ann's Academy at the new Mallinckrodt Convent, a normal school for the order's teaching sisters was also established in Wilkes-Barre, allowing them to earn both New York and Pennsylvania teaching certificates. The convent was the North American Motherhouse for the Sisters of Christian Charity until 1916. By that time, despite the addition of two large wings and a chapel in 1885 and 1894, there was still not enough space for both school and motherhouse. The latter was accordingly moved to a new building in Wilmette, Illinois. The school then occupied the entire building, and in 1929 a gym and an auditorium were added.

Attendance varied. The 1920s were the peak years for boarding students, who slowly declined in number until 1948, the last year boarders were accepted. Over the years, boarders had represented twenty-two different nations and eighteen states. After 1919, two sisters accompanied those traveling by train to and from the New York metropolitan area for summer and holiday breaks. Total enrollment generally ranged between 325 and 350, peaking in 1946–47 at 423. The graduating classes, small in the early years, ranged from 25 to 33 for most of the last forty years for which figures are available. After 1932, boys were admitted at the primary level.

The school shone academically. Its students periodically won local, state, and national contests in Latin, German, Spanish, history, debating, music, art, and science. A three-year commercial course of study—preparation for a business career—was offered in addition to the original academic curriculum until 1936 when commercial subjects were made elective for eleventh and twelfth

The Guardian Angel in the park at St. Ann's Academy. F. CHARLES PETRILLO

grades. A sewing class was added in 1950. Etiquette was still taught weekly in the 1940s. And supplementing that course, as described by one alumna, were the school meals: formal three-course dinners served with a massive dose of good manners.

Art and music were outstanding. Ethel Tischler Groh, a local artist who was honored at the 1988 Cider Painters' Exhibit at College Misericordia, attended St. Ann's from 1913 to 1920, following her graduation from Wilkes-Barre High School. She studied water color, oil painting, and china painting with Sister Viventia, a dynamic teacher, in the beautiful and well-equipped art studio.

The music program under Sister Alphonsine and Sister Mary Magdalene supported both a junior and a senior orchestra. The orchestras' annual concerts grew in importance; and when the school's 700-seat auditorium could no longer hold the audience, the event moved to the Irem Temple. A guest conductor was invited each year. Leroy Anderson, a composer and conductor closely associated with the Boston Pops, was one of the most prominent. Arthur Cohn, another well-known conductor and composer, said he had never found such precision and responsiveness anywhere.

The annual concerts were important fundraisers, as were the sauerkraut suppers. Another alumna can recall the pervasive odor of sauerkraut during the weeks preceding this community event, which also grew from year to year in size and complexity, as well as fund-raising importance.

A look at tuition fees—still only $300 per year in 1969—shows why these fund-raising events were so important. The Alumnae Association and the Mothers Club were major supporters. The Fathers Club, organized in 1965,

The Mallinckrodt Convent and St. Ann's Academy overlooked the park. The chapel and the large west wing were added in 1885 to provide quarters for the sisters. In 1894 the east wing was built to provide additional classroom space. The auditorium and gym were added in 1929. A nursing home, Little Flower Manor, now occupies the academy's site.

According to Adam Drayer, although every Catholic secondary school in the Scranton Diocese was founded as an academy—a school privately operated by a religious community independent of parish jurisdiction—by 1951 St. Ann's was the only one that had not been brought under parish control. F. CHARLES PETRILLO

spearheaded the effort to keep the school open through the late 1960s. But in addition to the problem of the dwindling supply of teaching sisters and the steady inflation of costs, the order faced major problems pertaining to the building itself. The Mallinckrodt Convent had survived a cyclone almost intact in 1928, but by the 1960s, there were the usual problems of deterioration associated with an old structure. Much worse, however, were the increasingly large cracks that began to appear and to grow in size. Regardless of their origin—undermining of the area, fluent subsoil, or dynamite blasting in the nearby strip mines—they were a very serious concern. In June 1971, St. Ann's Academy closed.

An era had ended. Alumnae recall the beauty of the chapel, dedicated to the Sacred Heart of Jesus, and the straight backs and shallow seats of the very uncomfortable pews; the entrance hall with its statue of St. Ann, donated by Mother Gonzaga of the South American Province, who had been Mother Pauline's traveling companion on her first visit to Wilkes-Barre; the wonderful smell of baking bread; the quiet, single-file line in which students moved from room to room; the precision drills; the very high expectations; the beautiful commencements—the graduates in matching long white dresses and white gloves proceding beneath the arch of raised swords of the Knights of Columbus; a wonderful garden and a beautiful hilltop campus; scholastic, musical, and artistic challenges; lifetime friendships and lifelong principles.

In September 1971, the new Bishop Hoban Central Catholic High School opened. It was designed to accommodate students from thirty-two separate territorial and ethnic parishes, as well as St. Ann's Academy. A new era had begun.

The Indian maiden Kankakee dominated Public Square from her perch above the central fountain installed in 1910. This work of sculptor Orestes Formiglia of Luzerne was done in imitation marble. The base of the statue had eight muskrats, and the base of the shell four dolphins. Water poured from Kankakee's gourd and from the mouths of the muskrats and dolphins. In addition, gone from the fountain by the time this picture was taken, were four cupids holding symbols representing coal, agriculture, industry, and the city. Under the shell and inside the dark granite of the fountain's base were three tables decorated with the arms of Pennsylvania, Luzerne County, and Wilkes-Barre and a fourth containing a centennial memorial. WHGS

Public Square

WILKES-BARRE IS a uniquely beautiful city. Its setting—beside a broad river amid rolling hills and mountains—and its fine architecture are major factors. Its River Common, unmarred by canal bed, railroad tracks, or super highway, is an unusual asset. But the gem of Wilkes-Barre's center city is its Public Square.

Wilkes-Barre's and Wyoming Valley's residents owe the Public Square to Major John Durkee and the committee of the Susquehannah Company that assisted him in laying out the five settling townships. The original surveying work, dividing the valley into townships, was done in 1769, and the business of dividing each township into lots began in 1770. Major Durkee placed the two-hundred-acre town plot of Wilkes-Barre on the level stretch of land parallel to the river. Bounded by North and South streets, by Front Street (now River Street) and Back Street (now Pennsylvania Avenue), it was intersected by Union, Centre (now Market) and Northampton streets and bisected by Main Street. Main Street was also the Main Road, continuing north to Pittston and south to Hanover. Washington and Franklin streets were not included in Durkee's original plan. They came into existence more or less spontaneously as buildings accumulated. A diamond-shaped space of four acres and forty-one perches was retained as part of the "common, or public, undivided lands of the township" along with the thirty-five acres now known as the River Common. (See drawing of town plot on page 47.) This was consistent with the Susquehannah Company's directive at its meeting at Hartford, Connecticut, on June 6, 1770. The meeting mandated that rights or shares in the land be reserved for the public benefit.

This diamond-shaped open space became known as Center Square and later as Public Square. Its changing character in these two hundred and twenty-some intervening years clearly reflects the changing nature of this community.

In 1774, Fort Wyoming, located on the River Common near Northampton Street, was torn down. The need for the fort seemed to have passed. But in 1776, after settlers had reported several separate incidents with hostile Indians,

The second courthouse, completed in 1804, provided a community meeting room on the second floor for a wide variety of occasions. Fifty years later, the thriving county (which still included the boomtown of Scranton) needed much more space, and every building on the Square was pulled down to make way for the third courthouse. The first can be seen in the background of the sketch of Old Ship Zion on page 102, converted into a school. In this drawing, George W. Leach, Jr., makes the building appear more monumental than it was by making the human figures disproportionately small. FROM OSCAR J. HARVEY, *History of Wilkes-Barre*

Harvey tells us that "it was decided that a fort should be built in Wilkes-Barre large enough to include a building to be used both as a town hall and a jail." The committee chose the southern half of the unoccupied diamond as the site. Work began in September 1776, but the fort was not completed until the spring of 1778.

Fort Wilkes-Barre, according to Charles Miner, was "built by setting yellow pine logs upright in the earth, close together, fifteen feet high, surrounded by a trench." Sheldon Reynolds, author of *Frontier Forts of Pennsylvania,* adds, "The structure was in the form of a parallelogram, with flanking towers

Designed by a New York architect, the third courthouse was originally two stories with a steep roof. In 1875, it was expanded by adding a third story without adding much height to the original roof line but with the addition of considerable ornamental brickwork. Far larger than its predecessors, it stood in the center of the Square with its tower facing West Market Street. The company that provided the iron fencing threw in a cast iron deer as a bonus. In 1910, the deer was moved to the lawn of the fourth courthouse, where it stands to this day. WHGS

at the angles, and was provided with a single gateway opening towards the river, northwest. The sides were pierced with loopholes to enable the garrison to deliver its fire without exposure; and one four-pound gun was mounted on the rampart, but, inasmuch as there happened to be no suitable ammunition, it served as an alarm gun only. Barracks or huts were built along the walls within the works, which, together with the room afforded by the public buildings, was sufficient to shelter the occupants. . . . The water supply was taken from a spring either within the enclosure or near at hand."

The victors burned Fort Wilkes-Barre after the Battle of Wyoming in 1778, but two log buildings, serving as jail, court, and meeting place, were repaired sufficiently to serve the community until 1788. The act of the Pennsylvania General Assembly that created Luzerne County in 1786 also directed the erection of a court house and jail. Some effort was made to move the seat of the new county to Kingston, but the commission determined that the square in Wilkes-Barre was the preferred location. The last remains of Fort Wilkes-Barre were razed. A new structure about 24 feet by 30 feet with the lower floor to be used as a jail and the upper as a courtroom was begun. This first court house was completed in 1791. In 1806 in a "Geographical Description of Pennsylvania" by Joseph Scott, Luzerne County is credited with a population of 18,826. The Wilkes-Barre area is credited with 835 people, and the village is said to have "fifty houses, a court house and a jail."

The second structure built on the square was the meeting house or church, commonly known as Old Ship Zion. This building demonstrated that Wilkes-Barre was indeed under Pennsylvania law rather than that of Connecticut. In Connecticut, all persons were obliged to contribute to the support of the meeting house, minister, and general expense of the church. But the division of church and state in Pennsylvania meant that the church had to be funded by private contributions. A committee was chosen to determine a site, develop the fund-raising strategy, and prepare a plan for the building. The fact that they placed a religious structure on public land—the square—shows that the concept of separation of church and state was much less developed in 1791 than it is today.

Having decided on a brick church, the committee learned that sufficient brick could not be had. Stone was substituted in the plan, but by 1795 the committee was instead directed to contract for frame and siding "to build a frame meeting house early next spring." The building was still not fully subscribed, however, and work was deferred. In 1800 the shell was finally constructed, and by 1801 it was sufficiently completed to hold a few public meetings. Finally, in 1811, with funds from lotteries held in Wilkes-Barre and Philadelphia, the structure was completed and the pews (high-walled and locked) were auctioned off. In 1812 the bell was hung—the first ever provided for religious purposes for this county—and for fifty years the Old Ship Zion served as the place of worship to the Congregational (reorganized as Presbyterian in 1829), Episcopalian, Methodist, and Baptist congregations of the community and a landmark to all.

In 1801, when Old Ship Zion was still a shell, the county commissioners proposed a new court house both to house the accumulating county records and to reflect the status of the growing community. First, however, they had to resolve the issue of who actually owned the square and the River Common. Both were surveyed. Then in 1804 title was transferred from the Connecticut claimants, represented by the township committee of Lord Butler, Matthias Hollenback, and Jesse Fell, to the new town committee constituted under Pennsylvania law—composed of Matthias Hollenback, Jesse Fell, and Lord Butler (*Lord,* by the way, was the Christian name of the son of Zebulon Butler, not any kind of title).

The log structure of the first court house was moved to another part of the square. It continued to be the county jail until 1808, when a new jail was built on the south side of East Market Street near the intersection with Washington Street. It then became the home of the Wilkes-Barre Academy. In June 1801, the timbers of the second court house were raised by volunteer workers. Pearce comments, "There were thirty-two and a half gallons of whiskey used at the raising of this building; a fact which demonstrates either the great capacity of the people of that day for ardent spirits, or else the presence of a large number of consumers."

The new building was in the form of a cross, with a low tower and belfry. The main courtroom was on the lower floor and the county offices were situated in the other three wings. The second story was one large room, used as a sort of community center, as a place of worship by congregations awaiting the church's completion, as a dancing school, and upon occasion, as a ball room. The basement was leased first as a butcher shop, later as a restaurant and bar. The building was chiefly red, painted to resemble stone, with handworked cornices.

In this first half of the nineteenth century, the square was intersected by Main and Market streets to form four triangles. The new court house occupied the triangle now facing the Kirby Center for the Performing Arts, between South Main and East Market streets. The Old Ship Zion occupied the triangle between West Market and South Main streets. The Wilkes-Barre Academy occupied the triangle facing the Ramada Hotel, between West Market and North Main streets. And in the fourth triangle, between East Market and North Main streets, facing the Martz Building and the new First Eastern Plaza, was a small structure known as the "Fire Proof," built by the county "for a Public Building, Fire Proof, sufficiently large for the accommodation of the several public offices, and safe keeping of the public records and papers of the County."

The square remained essentially unchanged until the second half of the nineteenth century, when the county's population reached 44,000. By that time, the second court house was deteriorating and the second floor meeting hall was no longer adequate for public meetings and events.

Whether or not to site the next court house on Public Square was again debated at length. The most telling argument against the site was the cost of facing the building on all four sides. But the Wilkes-Barre Council proposed to the county commissioners that if office space for Wilkes-Barre were provided without rent, the borough would issue bonds to share the cost of the structure. As a result, the third court house was also located on the square.

Construction on this third court house began in 1856; and in 1858 the building was occupied. In 1857, Old Ship Zion was pulled down. (The bell from its steeple—after much wandering—is now displayed on Public Square.)

A century and a half in Public Square. TOP LEFT: About 1830, the unpaved Market and Main streets crisscrossed the Square (the viewer is looking up North Main Street). BOTTOM LEFT: About 1915, young trees begin to spread where the third courthouse once stood. North Main Street is to the left, and Coughlin High School (then Wilkes-Barre High School) is visible rising above the buildings to the right. TOP RIGHT: By 1925, cars and trucks began to dominate the landscape, but trolleys were still essential transportation. The building vacated by Pomeroy's

Department Store stands at the upper left as it looked before a modernistic facade was added in the 1950s. BOTTOM RIGHT: By 1984, the city had assumed its post–Agnes Flood configuration, viewed here looking southeast. ALL PHOTOS WHGS

The second court house was razed in 1858. Finishing the detail work on the new court house, particularly the tower, dragged on until July 4, 1860, when the flag was flown from the new flagstaff above the completed building. This court house was lighted by gas, and the windows of the courtroom were of stained glass, the woodwork painted to resemble oak, and the arched ceiling "ornamented in good taste."

Enlarged in the 1870s, the third court house served until 1909 when it was replaced by the grandeur of the fourth and present Luzerne County Court House at River and North streets on the site of the former canal basin. At that time, Public Square became entirely a park, enhanced by a pool in its center. Above the pool rose a fountain and a statue of the Indian maiden Kankakee. Kankakee's view of the industrial city rising around her was in sharp contrast to the log and frame buildings of a century earlier.

"Wilkes-Barre," wrote Theodore Dreiser in 1916, "proved a city of charm—a city so instinct with a certain constructive verve that merely to enter it was to feel revivified. . . . It was pleasant to see the welter of thriving foundries and shops, smoky and black, which seemed to sing of prosperity; the long, smooth red brick pavement of the street by which we entered, so very kempt and sanitary; the gay public square, one of the most pleasing small parks I have ever seen, crowded with long distance trolley cars and motors—the former bearing the names of towns as much as a hundred and a hundred and fifty miles away. The stores were bright, the throngs interesting and cheerful. We actually, spontaneously and unanimously, exclaimed for joy."

In 1992, Wilkes-Barre's Public Square is the crown jewel of the city. Site of the Fine Arts Fiesta, the Farmers' Market, and numerous public events, it was redesigned after the Agnes flood by architect Peter Bohlin and his colleagues to be used as an outdoor community center as well as an informal gathering place. We are deeply indebted to Major John Durkee and his far-sighted town plan.

Bishop Francis Hodur

The Polish National Catholic Church

FRANCIS HODUR, priest, bishop, and founder of the Polish National Catholic Church, arrived in Wyoming Valley in 1893 through the action of the Reverend Dean Benvenuto Gramlewicz, pastor of the Polish Roman Catholic Church of St. Stanislaus, Nanticoke. Polish immigration to Nanticoke began in 1875, making it one of the earliest of the large Polish settlements in Pennsylvania. Similar Polish communities grew rapidly during the 1880s and 1890s in industrial centers across Pennsylvania and throughout the Middle West, wherever there were jobs in coal mining, meat packing, garment making, and steel blasting. This rapid growth intensified the ethnic conflict within the Catholic churches in these communities.

The conflict between different national cultures within the Roman Catholic Church in the United States erupted in the 1880s when German Catholics in America appealed directly to the pope for equal rights for German parishes and pastors. The Vatican recognized the legitimacy and independence of separate parishes for diverse language groups—a practice already widespread in the United States—but refused to grant the Germans further privileges and left the resolution of disputes over language in a parish to the decision of the local bishop, according to J. P. Dolan in *The American Catholic Experience.*

At that time the bishop of the Scranton Diocese, which comprised all eleven counties of Northeastern Pennsylvania, was the Right Reverend William O'Hara. With great tact and diplomacy, Bishop O'Hara negotiated the establishment of numerous ethnic churches and gave them his blessing. As the century drew to its close, he was failing in health and relied upon the support of Bishop Michael Hoban, diocesan coadjutor.

When Francis Hodur arrived in America, he had already had some experience with church conflict. Born at Zarki, near Cracow, on April 1, 1866, he was one of seven children of Mary Kosowska Hodur and Jan Hodur, farmer and part-time tailor. His early education had been delayed until age ten, the

Bishop Francis Hodur of the Polish National Catholic Church at the time of his consecration, September 29, 1907. GOOD SHEPHERD POLISH NATIONAL CATHOLIC CHURCH

The Good Shepherd Parish in Plymouth was formally organized in 1898, the first Polish National Catholic congregation formed in Luzerne County. This old frame church at 269 East Main Street, whose cornerstone was laid on December 26, 1898, has been replaced by a modern church complex. Officially blessed and dedicated in July 1991, it has incorporated many features of the original church—including stained glass windows, pews, altar appointments, statuary, and bell (named Zygmunt in honor of the Polish king). Like the old church, it has a chapel dedicated to the Blessed Mother Mary of Czestochowa, its patron saint. GOOD SHEPHERD POLISH NATIONAL CATHOLIC CHURCH

village school having been closed by the local Roman Catholic pastor because of conflict with the parish teacher. Despite this late start, Francis demonstrated exceptional ability and completed four grades in three years. His teacher persuaded his parents to let him continue, so at fourteen he traveled thirty-three miles barefoot to Cracow, carrying only the address of St. Ann's High School.

In 1889 Francis Hodur began the study of theology in the Roman Catholic Seminary affiliated with Jagiellonian University in Cracow. He passed all his

Bishop William O'Hara (1816–1899), the first ordinary of the Scranton Diocese of the Roman Catholic Church, served from 1868 to 1899. In 1896, when his health was failing, Bishop Michael J. Hoban became his coadjutor and gradually assumed major responsibility for administering the diocese. Bishop O'Hara had maintained the delicate political balance of the diocese for almost thirty years of extremely rapid growth and increasing ethnic diversity. Young Bishop Hoban's hard line, however, left no room for compromise, and the schism with the Polish National Catholic Church became inevitable. FROM *The Mallinckrodt,* ST. ANN'S ACADEMY, 1935

exams "summa cum laude," but did not complete his studies. Although he received minor orders, he and ten other seminarians were dismissed in 1893.

According to Father Stephen Wlodarski, author of *The Origin and Growth of the Polish National Catholic Church,*

> *The only reasonable explanation for the expulsion of eleven seminarians was their social activities, which the Bishop of Cracow considered unorthodox. Such activities in Galicia at that time were inspired by the Rev. Stanislaus Stojalowski, who was known as "The People's Tribune." The aim of his activities was not so much to fight against the Austrian invaders, but rather to develop a social awareness among the Polish peasants . . . [and] to organize a peasant party. . . . During his entire life [Francis Hodur] was a great admirer and sympathizer of the Rev. Stojalowski.*

Since no Roman Catholic bishop in Poland would ordain a follower of Father Stojalowski, Hodur sought refuge in the only part of the world where he could pursue his goal of the priesthood—the "fourth region of Poland—America." He worked his way to New York on a freighter. Knowing no one, with no friends to meet him, he was unable to leave the immigration quarantine quarters until someone paid the United States thirty dollars or agreed to take responsibility for him. Francis wrote a letter to the Polish newspaper *Kurier Polski* describing himself and his problem. This letter caught

St. Stanislaus Bishop and Martyr Cathedral at 529 East Locust Street in Scranton is the first parish of the Polish National Catholic Church. Its rectory was Bishop Hodur's home from 1897 to 1953. ST. STANISLAUS B&M CATHEDRAL

the interest of Father Gramlewicz of Nanticoke who sent his assistant to New York to satisfy the immigration authorities and bring Francis to Nanticoke. After getting to know the young Pole, Father Gramlewicz asked Bishop O'Hara to help him complete his studies. Francis Hodur was sent to St. Vincent Roman Catholic Seminary in Beatty, Pennsylvania. After a few months of study, he passed all the examinations; and Bishop O'Hara ordained him on August 19, 1893.

Father Hodur served first as assistant pastor to Father Richard C. Aust at the Sacred Heart of Jesus and Mary Roman Catholic Church in South Scranton. He then became administrator of the Slovak Roman Catholic Parish in Scranton; and in August 1895, he became rector of the Holy Trinity Polish Roman Catholic Parish in Nanticoke.

Holy Trinity had grown out of a splinter group from St. Stanislaus, Father Gramlewicz's own church. The issues involved in that split were similar to those that led to the creation of the Polish National Catholic Church, but in the creation of Holy Trinity, Bishop O'Hara and the dissenters worked through to a resolution of the conflict. Part of that resolution was asking Father Gramlewicz to recommend a priest for the dissenters. According to Father Wlodarski, "Rev. Gramlewicz knew of only one suitable candidate, the Rev. Francis Hodur." Of Hodur's work in Nanticoke, Father John P. Gallagher, official historian of the Scranton Diocese, wrote, "Father Francis Hodur had done ex-

Bishop Franciszek Hodur (1866–1953). This portrait, based on a photograph of Bishop Hodur taken shortly before his death, was painted by Edward Jazgier, a parishioner of Good Shepherd Polish National Catholic Church. GOOD SHEPHERD POLISH NATIONAL CATHOLIC CHURCH

cellent work in the interim by taking charge of the dissidents who had established their own rival Holy Trinity Parish. Both factions had adjusted to the split and peace was restored to that distant Luzerne County community."

During the summer of 1896, the Sacred Hearts Parish of South Scranton was torn apart by violence and riots. The dissident faction was protesting what Gallagher calls the "assertedly Prussian mannerisms of Father Richard C. Aust." In October, 250 families seceded from Sacred Hearts Parish to organize St. Stanislaus Polish Roman Catholic Church. They formed a committee that bought property, immediately began construction, and sought the advice and assistance of Father Hodur. When the committee requested diocesan recognition, however, it was not Bishop O'Hara but Bishop Hoban, newly appointed coadjutor, who set the tone. To quote Father Gallagher, "The younger prelate favored the hard line. . . . With no room for compromise, the conflict broadened into definitive schism. The result was the creation of the Polish National Church."

The conflict of the Polish congregations with the bishops grew out of the issues of property ownership and the management of parish affairs. Dolan tells us that "in virtually every city where they settled, Polish Catholics went to battle over the issue of the ownership of church property. From their point of view, the tradition of the old country allowed for lay involvement in parish affairs and they sought to continue this in the United States. . . . The bishops and the clergy, many Polish priests included, would not go along. For them, the clergy, not the people, should run parish affairs and hold title to all church property. . . . The Polish did not give in on this issue. They resisted strongly and even accepted excommunication, rather than go along with the Irish-Roman tradition of clerical control in parish affairs."

Father Francis Hodur, already known as a "social-minded priest," and an admiring follower of Father Stojalowski, the People's Tribune, identified with the Polish people rather than the church hierarchy. He left Nanticoke to accept the congregation's call to St. Stanislaus on March 14, 1897. On March 21, Bishop Hoban suspended him. On July 4, St. Stanislaus Church was consecrated by a priest rather than a bishop and with the support of sympathizers from other Polish Roman Catholic parishes. In September 1898, Father Hodur agreed to Bishop Hoban's request for submission to his authority, but he imposed three conditions: retention of the deed by St. Stanislaus, lay control of finances, and committee approval of pastoral appointments. These conditions were rejected.

Father Hodur journeyed to Rome, hoping to get papal approval for his church despite the bishop's opposition. He was unsuccessful; and on October 15, 1898, he was excommunicated by Bishop Hoban. Continued appeals to the Pope did not bear fruit. In 1900, Father Hodur approached Bishop Hoban through an intermediary, Father Stanislaus Siedlicki of St. Adalbert's, Glen Lyon. Precedents had been established elsewhere in America for independent parishes returning to the Roman Catholic Church after proper expiation. But the meeting, although courteous, was not successful. Father Hodur's congregation was unwilling to accept the conditions set forth by Bishop Hoban. Instead, the schism widened when the Polish Congregation replaced Latin with Polish in the liturgy of the mass. This revolutionary change took place for the first time in St. Stanislaus Church at midnight mass on Christmas Eve 1900.

Father Hodur became Bishop-Elect of the National Church at its First Synod in 1904. At Utrecht, Holland, in 1907 he was consecrated a bishop in the Old Catholic Cathedral of St. Gertrude by the Old Catholic Archbishop Gerard Gul. The Polish National Catholic Church now possessed apostolic succession, recognized by both Orthodox and Roman Catholic theologians. Bishop Hodur became the approved head of the entire independent movement, and the National Catholic Church became part of the worldwide family of Old Catholic Churches.

The great majority of Polish Catholics stayed within the Roman Catholic Church. When necessary, they turned ownership of church property over to the local bishop and clergy. Poles across the United States, however, continued their tradition of lay involvement in parish affairs through popular election of parish committees. Democracy in church affairs has remained a strong trait of Polish Roman Catholic parishes in Northeastern Pennsylvania, in addition to its key role as the foundation principle of the Polish National Catholic Church and its founder, Bishop Francis Hodur.

Ellen Webster Palmer. A statue commemorating her work stands on the River Common in Wilkes-Barre. FROM HENRY W. PALMER'S *Fifty Years at the Bar and in Politics*

Ellen Webster Palmer and the Breaker Boys

WE LIVE IN a world where child labor laws and compulsory education have wiped out the grim use of children in the coal industry of a hundred years ago. They lived in a world without worker's compensation for injuries, Social Security for widows and children, or disability insurance in any form. The work of boys in the mines and collieries was essential for the food and shelter of their families, and the need was greatest in those families where the father was dead or disabled—not uncommon in the high-risk occupation of coal mining.

Although Pennsylvania made it illegal in 1885 to employ children under fourteen inside the mines or children under twelve in surface jobs, much younger boys continued to be exploited. The mine operators wanted a continuous supply of cheap labor, and parents desperately needed the additional income, small as it was (forty-five cents a day for a ten-hour day, six days a week). So the usual age for entering the mines continued to be about eight or nine, and the entry job was sorting coal in the breakers.

The breaker boys, wrote Stephen Crane, "live in a place of infernal dins. The crash and thunder of the machinery is like the roar of an immense cataract. The room shrieks and blares and bellows. All the structure is atremble from the heavy sweep and circle of the ponderous mechanism." Miller and Sharpless describe the bleeding fingers—"redtop"—that were the common condition of the boys and say that the "oldtimers claim that the paths the boys took home after work could be followed by the drops of blood in the snow." Despite, or because of, the whips and clubs of the foremen and the harsh and dangerous nature of the job, these boys were tough and independent.

How do we fit Ellen Webster Palmer into this context? How did this woman, mother of eight, of whom five were living in 1885, come to focus on the needs of the breaker boys of Wyoming Valley? We know that two very important changes were taking place in late nineteenth-century thought. First,

The B. I. A. Drum Corps. Mrs. Palmer included this photograph in a pamphlet she wrote and distributed to attract support for the Boys' Industrial Association. WHGS

the Christian social movement had recognized both the distress of the working class created by the Industrial Revolution and the inadequacy of the traditional charitable means of the churches in dealing with it. The American offspring of the Christian social movement, the social gospel, with its emphasis on the social-ethical tasks of the church, was gaining widespread influence. Second, and closely related, the attitude toward poverty itself was changing. Despite social Darwinism and its harsh belief in "survival of the fittest," the concept of poverty as a vicious and self-perpetuating cycle had been born. The need for developing new means for relieving and preventing poverty had become apparent.

In 1888 Jane Addams visited Toynbee Hall in London. Founded in 1884, Toynbee Hall was located in the heart of London's Whitechapel industrial district. Its purpose was to help individuals move out of the cycle of poverty by acquiring the necessary knowledge and skills, and it became the prototype for the settlement house.

Addams was determined to use Toynbee Hall as her model in the United States. She acquired a large vacant mansion, former residence of Charles Hull in Chicago; and in 1889, she and Ellen Gates Starr moved in and began their work. As the services they offered were expanded, so was the institution. Eventually Hull House included thirteen buildings and a playground, as well

Boys as young as eight were employed in the collieries picking unburnable slate out of the coal. They perched above the vibrating sieves as the coal worked its way down to the loading areas. FROM A PHOTOGRAPHIC POSTCARD CIRCA 1907 BY W. J. HARRIS, WEST PITTSTON. F. CHARLES PETRILLO

as a camp outside the city. There were a day nursery, a gymnasium, a community kitchen, and a boarding club for working girls. Programs included training in art, music, and crafts such as bookbinding, as well as amateur dramatics and college-level courses.

Mrs. Palmer's work with the breaker boys was not, as was Hull House, a social settlement. It did not try to develop and improve a neighborhood. It did, however, use very much the same approach, by providing attractions to draw participants and supporting activities and educational opportunities for self-development. One cannot help speculating that Mrs. Palmer, whose daughter Louise M. Palmer married George E. Vincent, professor of sociology at the University of Chicago, was aware of Jane Addams' work in Chicago.

Ellen Webster Palmer was born in Plattsburg, New York, on October 20, 1839. In September 1861 she married Henry W. Palmer, who had been admitted to the Luzerne County Bar in August 1861. In 1879, at age 40, he was appointed Attorney General for Pennsylvania by Governor Henry M. Hoyt. When Palmer's term expired, he resumed his law practice in Wilkes-Barre.

Eight years after the Palmers' return to Wilkes-Barre, Mrs. Palmer initiated her work with the breaker boys. On March 9, 1891, she met with nearly a

Pictured here with Ellen Webster Palmer are some of the members of the Boys' Industrial Association. Sitting on the floor in front are a boy identified only as Pascal and Daniel Litz. In back are three Ashman brothers, John Peters, and a boy named Nottrass. WHGS

hundred boys employed chiefly as slate-pickers by the mines. A second meeting drew an even larger crowd and led to a series of Saturday evening entertainments that became so popular that it was "necessary to close the doors promptly at 7:30 to prevent overcrowding." Classes in reading, writing, and arithmetic were instituted at meetings held in vacant stores.

Impressed by these developments, the Wilkes-Barre City Council allowed the new organization to use a large room on the fourth floor of City Hall. Activities expanded to include a singing class, a debating club, and a junior literary branch. The organization became known as the Boys' Industrial Association.

In 1899 the B.I.A. constructed its own building on land to the rear of City Hall. This four-story structure provided space for training in manual skills such as carpentry, shoemaking, and seatcaning, as well as standard classrooms, auditorium, gallery, gymnasium, parlors—one for boys and one for young men—and two rooms for the debating clubs. The association also had its own band.

Like the settlement houses, the B.I.A. provided opportunities to prepare for a livelihood outside the coal mines. Perhaps more important, it provided those who participated with a chance to improve their quality of life and it gave them (an estimated 75 percent were foreign born) a chance to be a part of the mixture of cultures that is still evolving and is called "American."

In 1903, the Pennsylvania legislature raised the age for employment in the mines to fourteen for surface and sixteen for underground jobs. Although this law, like that of 1885, was not well enforced, mechanical slate pickers eventually eliminated the need for breaker boys. The YMCA, formed in 1871, added a Boys' Department in 1907. After Mrs. Palmer's death in 1918, the Boys' Industrial Association building was used less and less. In 1920 the City Council assumed control and turned the building over to Wilkes-Barre Post 132 of the American Legion.

Ellen Webster enlisted the help of many capable people, especially Mary L. Trescott, Luzerne County's first woman lawyer, who managed the finances of the B.I.A. and acted as secretary of the organization. Mrs. Palmer found the funding and made the contacts that created an institution to ameliorate an evil we find hard to visualize—the grueling, almost unending labor of children whose future was very bleak. Perhaps one of Ellen Webster Palmer's most important contributions was helping to create a bridge from that world to ours.

Mr. Peanut symbolizes both Amadeo Obici's marketing genius and Planters Peanuts. This elegant gentleman is far removed from the lowly goober or groundnut. ELENA ENGLISH HORRIGAN PARKHURST

Achievers and Achievements

Some came to the valley to achieve their destinies. Others began here and made their marks here. Still others went elsewhere for their rendezvous with fame. The valley itself survived depression, the slow death of its major industry, and a devastating flood—always planning for tomorrow.

"Rose O'Neill and Her Kewpies," a self-portrait. FROM *Cordially Yours,* GIFT OF MARY BARRETT TO WHGS

Rose O'Neill

The Kewpie Creator

A HISTORICAL MARKER in Branson, Missouri, cites Wilkes-Barre, Pennsylvania, as the birthplace of Rose O'Neill, "artist, sculptress, writer, poet, illustrator, and creator of the Kewpie, Scootles and Ho-Ho dolls." Born in Wilkes-Barre on June 24, 1874, Rose Cecil O'Neill was the daughter of William Patrick O'Neill and C. Alice Asenath Smith O'Neill. The family lived in Emerald Cottage on Meade Street in the Heights section of the city. Mr. O'Neill was first a realtor, maintaining offices with Attorney Daniel L. O'Neill at 108 North Main Street. He then went into the auction and commission business as the firm of O'Neill and Whyte, finally specializing as a bookdealer. Mrs. O'Neill taught school, was musical, and had a theatrical flair. When hard times hit, Mr. O'Neill outfitted a Conestoga wagon and moved his family west, where they came to rest "in a tumbled-down shanty on the top of a clay bank" in Battle Creek, Nebraska. Later they moved to Omaha, where Rose attended the Sacred Heart Convent School.

Rose O'Neill's career as an illustrator began when she won the Omaha *World-Herald's* art contest at the age of thirteen. The paper promptly hired her to do a weekly cartoon series; she published some poems and illustrations in a Denver magazine; and in 1893 she headed for New York City. Legend has it that this trip was financed by her mother's sale of the family cow. In New York she lived at the Convent of the Sisters of St. Regis and sold illustrations. In 1896 she married Gray Latham, a Virginia aristocrat whom she had first met in Omaha. They were divorced in 1901. Throughout this marriage and her subsequent one to Harry Leon Wilson, editor of *Puck,* O'Neill continued to sell drawings to a list of magazines that included *Life, Harper's, Collier's, Good Housekeeping,* and *Cosmopolitan,* as well as *Puck,* where she worked on the staff. She illustrated Wilson's first novel, *The Spenders,* completed her own novel, *The Loves of Edwy,* then illustrated three more of Wilson's books before their divorce in 1907.

Kewpies were everywhere—even on postcards.
GIFT OF MARY BARRETT TO WHGS

Despite these early successes, O'Neill might have been lost in obscurity had it not been for Edward Bok, editor of *The Ladies' Home Journal.* At Bok's urging, O'Neill created the first Kewpie drawing for the December 1909 issue of the *Journal,* which was printed with an explanatory footnote: "The reason why these funny, roly-poly creatures are called kewpies is because they look like Cupids. You can tell by their tiny wings. Kewpie means a small Cupid, just as a puppy means a small dog." Kewpies were "extremely wigglesome and disposed to hop out on the balcony to play with the birds."

O'Neill recalled:

> *The idea of the Kewpies first came to me about twenty years ago in a dream. But their origin dates further back to my childhood when I used to be enraptured with my baby brother and was always making little drawings of his funny lovely little looks and gestures. It was all those stored-up memories of babyism that came out in the Kewpie—the things that made me call the baby "The Tender Clown." The Kewpie top-knot was the little lock that used to stand up from the baby's head on the pillow. The tiny wings came naturally from the baby character, half elf, half angel.*
>
> *The quality of Kewpishness is not only to be smiling and round and ridicu-*

"Terror Without" was among the drawings Rose O'Neill exhibited in Paris in 1922. These bizarre and powerful images—which show the strong influence of German artist Käthe Kollwitz—are the antithesis of the lighthearted Kewpies. FROM *Cordially Yours,* GIFT OF MARY BARRETT TO WHGS

lous but also loving and wise. The Kewpie Philosophy is doing kind deeds in a funny way. I have put it in a nutshell in these verses:

Philanthropists need
A spice of wit,
Or else they make
Dull work of it.
But the Kewp's idea,
If understood,
Is to make you laugh
While they do you good.
—*Quoted in* Celebrity Doll Journal, *No. 4, 1972*

That quality of Kewpishness continued to appear regularly in *The Ladies' Home Journal, Women's Home Companion,* and *Delineator.* In *Good Housekeeping,* the Kewpies danced through a monthly page for children until 1923. O'Neill wrote and illustrated over five thousand Kewpie stories for magazines and wrote several Kewpie books. In addition, Kewpies appeared in comic strips, cutouts, calendars, and on everything imaginable—soap, fabric, napkins, letter paper and greeting cards, mugs, plates, salt and pepper shakers, creamers, sugar bowls, pitchers, planters, vases, pillows, lamps, inkwells, jewelry, buttons, and even radiator caps. O'Neill wrote,

I had been publishing the Kewpie drawings and verses in magazines about a year when I modeled the first Kewpie figure. Children had begun writing to me from various places in the world, asking if I would not make a Kewpie they could hold in their hands. . . . So I modeled nine sizes of Kewpie dolls and they went all around the earth, made in . . . bisque, celluloid, rubber, composition.

The dolls were first manufactured in Germany in 1913. Joseph L. Kallus, a young student at Pratt Institute, had worked with Rose O'Neill in sculpting the earliest Kewpies. He remained her principal associate; and upon her death the trademarks and copyrights were passed to him, enabling him to continue production of the Kewpies into their fourth generation. "As I worked on Kewpie models, I tried to reproduce the boundless joy of Rose's spirit," said Mr. Kallus. "Whenever the lid of a Kewpie box was raised, the recipient responded with happiness."

While the Kewpies swept the nation and the world, O'Neill continued to write and draw. In 1921, at the Galerie Devambey in Paris, she exhibited a group of drawings "remarkable for their kinship to the sensuously semi-religious visionary art of William Blake and Kahlil Gibran." Carlin T. Kindilien noted that her writings dealt with "the duality of sex, unconsummated love and treacherous lovers; . . . fairies and stags and lost souls, and occasionally, as in the poem 'Love-ending,' achieved a sensuous grasp of human experience." A 1922 exhibit in New York of her "Monster" drawings was described as "intensely sincere and searchingly emotional," showing a deep interest in legend, folklore, and myth. In 1929 her novel *Garda* was published, followed by *The Goblin Woman* in 1930.

Described by *Time* as "exquisitely beautiful" and in one biography as "a large extravagant blonde, sometimes given to babytalk," Rose O'Neill preferred to dress in flowing red velvet robes and go barefoot. A song hit of the early 1920s, "Rose of Washington Square," was written about her. Always generous, and known for her perpetual open house, at one time she had twenty young artists staying with her at once. About 1936, with her mother ill and her money running out, she retired to Bonnie Brook, her home in the Ozark Mountains near Branson, Missouri, where she lived until her death in 1944. There the historical marker, the School of the Ozarks' permanent exhibit, the Rose O'Neill Museum at Shepherd of the Hills Farm, and her most outstanding sculpture, *Embrace of a Tree,* memorialize this complex and creative individual.

Amadeo Obici

The Peanut King

AMADEO OBICI developed an industry by changing the eating habits of a nation. His innovation, together with an idea of Dr. John Kellogg, superintendent of the Battle Creek Sanitarium, also changed the country's agricultural patterns. As the *Encyclopaedia Britannica* says, "The peanut is grown mainly for its edible oil, except in the United States, where it is produced for grinding into peanut butter . . . for roasted salted nuts; and for use in candy and bakery products."

Kellogg, a vegetarian, tried grinding peanuts into a nutritional paste to provide concentrated protein for his patients. (He also served his patients flaked wheat and flaked corn for breakfast—an idea his brother W. K. Kellogg used to revolutionize American breakfast habits.)

Peanuts (also called groundnuts, earthnuts, or goobers) are like soybeans. They enrich the soil with nitrogen and restore the nutrients that other crops, particularly cotton, deplete. George Washington Carver, a scientist at the Tuskegee Institute and one of the first black Americans to win fame for his achievements, saw commercially farming peanuts as a way to restore agricultural viability to the South, where dependence on cotton had exhausted the land and created a cycle of poverty. He directed most of his research to the development of approximately three hundred products derived from peanuts to try to ensure the marketing of a crop so ideally suited to the needs of southern agriculture. (He even succeeded in making peanuts taste like dill pickles.)

In 1890, peanuts were not even a recognized cash crop. Within half a century, they had become one of the six leading crops in the United States and the second cash crop, after cotton, in the South.

What was Amadeo Obici's contribution to this nutritional and agricultural revolution? Amadeo Obici was born on July 15, 1877, in Oderzo, in the province of Treviso, Italy. In 1889 his mother, a widow faced with raising

LEFT: Amadeo Obici was president and general manager of Planters until his death. He created and expanded the market for peanuts while providing the product to meet the increasing demand. RIGHT: Like her husband, Louise Mussante Obici operated a peanut stand in Wilkes-Barre, where she met and married Obici. The Louise Obici Hospital in Suffolk, Virginia, is her husband's memorial to her.

four children, sent Amadeo by steamer and train to an uncle in Scranton, with his destination on a label tied through his buttonhole. At the age of twelve, he spoke no English. In Scranton he attended school and worked with his uncle, a tailor, then went to work in a cigar factory. At fifteen he moved on his own to Wilkes-Barre where he worked for friends selling fresh fruit at a street stand for six dollars per month plus board.

Obici next took a job tending bar for Andrew Lynch. Lynch, who was very involved in politics, asked Obici to locate any Italians in Luzerne County and persuade them to support his candidates. Obici went looking for Mario Peruzzi, who had also come from Treviso, and found him in a basement in Hazleton oiling a large cheese for the wholesale grocery firm where he worked. They became friends at once.

Obici's used his savings from barkeeping to open his own small fruit stand and peanut roaster. Fruit and peanut stands had operated continuously in the downtown area of Wilkes-Barre for a number of years—but Obici's is said to have been the first to have a whistle attached to the pipe where the steam escaped. In three years, he had saved enough money to bring his family from Italy.

LEFT: Mario Peruzzi, vice president and treasurer of planters, became president after Obici's death. He was Obici's partner in the original incorporation of Planters Nut and Chocolate Company and manager of the Wilkes-Barre operation. RIGHT: Frank A. English was secretary of Planters when this picture was taken. He later became vice president, succeeding Mario Peruzzi as president. In addition to his responsibilities to Planters, he was executor of Obici's estate. FROM THE SUFFOLK, VIRGINIA, *Suffolk News-Herald,* 200TH ANNIVERSARY EDITION, COURTESY ELENA ENGLISH HORRIGAN PARKHURST

At this point, with $600 cash to pay his agent's fee, Obici purchased a building for $39,000—covered by a mortgage for $39,000. The rest of his cash went to install an oyster bar and soda fountain. As a sideline to what he regarded as his future in the restaurant business, he also purchased a bigger peanut roaster and installed it above the store in order to sell roasted peanuts to other storekeepers and bars. This venture went so well that he soon hired someone to roast and package the peanuts and spent his time delivering the salted nuts in Wilkes-Barre and the surrounding towns. On his wagon, drawn by an ancient gray called Old Dick, he painted a sign: "The Peanut Specialist."

By 1906, at the age of twenty-nine, Amadeo Obici had decided that there was a future in the peanut business. He persuaded Mario Peruzzi, by that time head of the confectionery department of C. P. Wentz Co. in Scranton, to borrow $2000 on a personal note. Together they formed Planters Peanuts. "Planters," said Obici, "sounded important and dignified." They never did actually own any peanut acreage. They rented a small factory for $25 a month, installed two large roasters and some machinery, and employed six people.

Store owners were supplied with glass display jars and cups to measure the peanuts. Ten-pound cans were supplied as refills.

In 1908, with Obici still serving as president and general manager and Peruzzi as secretary-treasurer and director, the firm was incorporated as Planters Nut and Chocolate Company and capitalized at $50,000. Of this, only $10,000, representing a hundred shares of common stock, was actually paid in. Some stock was sold to friends in and around Wilkes-Barre, but most was absorbed by Obici (50 percent) and Peruzzi (20 percent).

> *One major asset of the company was a process Obici had discovered for roasting peanuts so that they could be readily blanched of their red skins before salting, without breaking in half. Its major premise was that people preferred whole blanched salted Virginia peanuts to the small, round red-skinned Spanish nuts that at that time dominated the market. (*Fortune, *April 1938)*

Another asset was the creative combination of peanuts with chocolate and syrups. And perhaps most important was his family's strong support.

Elizabeth Obici Peruzzi, Amadeo's sister and later the wife of Mario Peruzzi, recalled during a 1974 interview with the *Sunday Independent* on her ninetieth birthday, "I had charge of our first plant in Wilkes-Barre when my brother first started selling peanuts in large quantities. There were more than 100 employees working under me, and we put in twelve hours a day, six days a week."

Obici also introduced his own business formula, according to *The Obici Story,* persuading dealers that "prices and first profits were not nearly so important as repeat business. Quality, brand name, and creation of consumer demand were far more important to the retailer and his continued success."

Obici's marketing genius was first demonstrated in the days when "The Peanut Specialist" distributed bags of roasted peanuts to children on the way to pick up raw peanuts at the railroad station. The parade he staged through Wilkes-Barre with his first full carload of raw peanuts was repeated several decades later when Planters introduced roasted peanuts to England and Obici staged a parade all around London.

Mr. Peanut—that elegant trademark with his top hat, cane, and spats, was far removed from the lowly goober—became the universal symbol of Planters. Many of us can remember him, nine feet tall, walking through Wilkes-Barre's Public Square, distributing bags of peanuts to a new generation of peanut-lovers. Mr. Peanut literally walked the streets of cities all over the United States, and the electric sign above Times Square in New York City, where Mr. Peanut was embodied in 6,700 lamps, was a familiar landmark. Single-page cartoon stories about "Mr. Peanut's Nutty History" were printed in millions of comic books. Ham Fisher, Wilkes-Barre's creator of Joe Palooka,

Planters Nut and Chocolate Factory at 45 South Main Street, Wilkes-Barre, as it looked about 1915. PHOTO BY JOHN JENNINGS, COURTESY F. CHARLES PETRILLO

drew some of these ads out of gratitude to Mario Peruzzi, who had helped him when he was a struggling advertising solicitor.

A large percentage of the advertising budget was directed toward premiums that would appeal to the peanut eaters of the future—coloring books, stamp albums, and the all-time favorite, the Mr. Peanut mechanical lead pencil. Adults could exchange their hoarded candy bar wrappers and peanut bags for the Ingersoll watch. National advertising of the popular "Nickel Lunch" enabled Planters' sales to hold up well during the Depression.

Innovative packaging was another strength of Planters. In 1904 glassine was introduced into the United States from Germany. By 1912, with the development of a machine that could make the material into see-through bags, Planters was merchandizing prepackaged peanuts. In 1932 cellophane replaced glassine.

In 1912, Obici and Peruzzi found themselves at the mercy of commodity speculators in Virginia peanuts. Accordingly, they decided to take steps to secure their supply. Taking letters from his Wilkes-Barre bankers, Obici approached a Suffolk, Virginia, bank with a proposal to buy a peanut-cleaning plant there. By 1913 the plant had been renovated, and peanut production near the source of supply took over from the Wilkes-Barre operation, although the executive offices and the premium redemption center continued to operate in Wilkes-Barre.

By 1927, with the purchase and modernization of two more plants in Virginia and the construction of cold storage for 600 carloads of peanuts, Planters was an industrial giant. It also manufactured and printed its own bags, boxes, and tins. In addition, plants had been set up in San Francisco in 1921 and in Toronto in 1924. Other plants followed in Philadelphia, Chicago, Boston, Atlanta, and Memphis. Two subsidiaries were also created. The National Peanut Corporation, founded in 1929, consisted of thirty-five retail stores selling all varieties of nuts and operating chiefly to promote Planters Peanuts. The Planters Edible Oil Co. pressed undersized and broken nuts for their oil, marketed as Hi Hat, Kosher Hi Hat, and Ali D'Italia. The dried remnant was sold as fodder for hogs and cattle. The ground peanut hulls were also sold for a variety of uses, from insulation to an abrasive for silverware. Other peanut by-products ended up in cosmetics and soap. Nothing was wasted.

The one major peanut product that Obici and Peruzzi did not manufacture was peanut butter. When asked about this in an interview, Obici said it was unseemly to compete too vigorously with one's best customers. The peanut butter manufacturers were the largest buyers of the processed peanuts that were not used in making Planters' own products. In fact, the raw nut market did not always make money for Planters, but it secured the supply for Planters' products.

Amadeo Obici became known as the Peanut King. Just over five feet tall, he was described in *Fortune* as impressively proportioned, with a big nose, double chin, and pudgy and expressive hands. "The most notable things about him are two: one is his personal likableness; . . . the other is the nature and design of the inside of his head. Mr. Obici is smart, with an extra smartness that is known in the business as 'peanut sense.' "

Obici was considered a demanding employer, expecting a day's work for a day's pay, and the company was run on paternalistic lines. Planters never faced a strike, however. According to an article in the Suffolk, Virginia, *News-Herald,* "Obici pioneered the five day work week in the peanut industry. He was among the first to pay blacks and whites equal wages for equal work, and shocked many in the community by bidding up the area's hourly wages."

In 1916 Obici married Louise Musante, who had also operated a peanut and confectionery stand in Wilkes-Barre, and from the 1920s on, they had a home at Bay Point Dairy Farm on the Nansemond River near Suffolk, in addition to their residence at 38 Dagobert Street, Wilkes-Barre. Mario and Elizabeth Obici Peruzzi continued to have their chief residence at Pine View, Nuangola.

Louise Musante Obici died in Mercy Hospital, Wilkes-Barre, in 1938, and in 1942 Amadeo Obici formed a corporation to hold funds from a variety of sources with which to build a hospital in her memory. After his death, also at Mercy, on May 21, 1947, additional funds became available through his will and through a favorable ruling on the Obici Trust, enabling construction to begin. The Louise Obici Memorial Hospital opened to the public in September, 1951, in Suffolk, Virginia. In addition to numerous other bequests, funds were made available through Obici's will for a small hospital at his birthplace in Oderzo, Italy.

Mario Peruzzi, who succeeded Obici as president of Planters, died in December 1955. In 1960 Planters was purchased by Standard Brands, Inc., for a total cost of almost $20 million. Standard merged with Nabisco in 1981 to form Nabisco Brands, Inc., which in turn merged with R. J. Reynolds to become RJR Nabisco.

Did Horatio Alger ever make up a story more dramatic than this one? This real life rags-to-riches adventure changed the eating habits of America and helped turn around Southern agriculture, but it started with a fruit and peanut stand in downtown Wilkes-Barre operated by a very bright, very creative, and very hard-working man.

Arline Phillips posed with her dog Cindy for this portrait in 1951. PHOTO BY BERT HUSBAND, COURTESY WILKES-BARRE BRANCH, PENNSYLVANIA ASSOCIATION FOR THE BLIND

Arline Phillips

Opportunity, Not Sympathy

IN WYOMING VALLEY, persons faced with the loss of their sight are fortunate to have the Wilkes-Barre Branch of the Pennsylvania Association for the Blind. Here those who need them can acquire useful aids and appliances, from Talking Books to white canes; learn necessary skills for independence; obtain counseling through tough times; and enjoy social events bringing people with the same problems together. The services provided by the Blind Association range from help with copying class assignments for blind students to supplying a crochet hook and yarn for a blind prison inmate. The association has also mounted a comprehensive effort toward the prevention of blindness through early childhood screening.

The education of blind persons took a giant leap forward in the nineteenth century with the establishment of special schools and the development of braille as the system of writing universally used by blind persons. By the beginning of the twentieth century, however, it became apparent that although blind persons were being educated and trained to work in public industries, they had difficulty getting hired. Problems of mobility, acquisition of daily living skills, and simply coping with the world at large could be nearly insurmountable challenges to the blind and visually handicapped.

In 1903, the Massachusetts Association for Promoting the Interests of the Adult Blind was organized in Boston. By 1908, a group of concerned persons and organizations began to address the needs of the adult blind in Pennsylvania. First organized as the Pittsburgh Association for the Adult Blind in 1910, within six months they became the Pennsylvania Association for the Blind (P.A.B.). The first branch organized outside Pittsburgh was formed in Scranton in 1913. In 1917, thanks to the efforts of Arline Phillips, Wilkes-Barre became the site of the second branch of the P.A.B. The Dauphin County Branch began its work in 1923, and 1927 and 1928 saw the establishment of branches in Lancaster, Venango, Blair, Cambria, Beaver, Lehigh, Philadelphia, and

This Yuletide celebration by the Blind Association was probably held in the basement of their building at 35 East Union Street in Wilkes-Barre. Note Santa Claus among the Girl Scouts

Northampton. In 1929, the Pittsburgh Branch set up a board of directors separate from that of the statewide organization, the Association's bylaws were revised, and the branches were formally represented on the board of trustees of the Pennsylvania Association of the Blind.

Arline Phillips, founder of the Wilkes-Barre Branch, was a remarkable person. Totally blinded at age two from scarlet fever and meningitis, she refused to let the handicap impede her in achieving her goal of enabling other blind persons to live full lives. Her father, a funeral director in north Wilkes-Barre, wanted to learn everything he could about dealing with blindness and traveled to New York, Philadelphia, and Boston to get the latest information. From a young age, Arline attended the Overbrook School for the Blind in Philadelphia. She learned braille, conquered the basics of independent living, and even mastered roller skating. As a graduate of the Pennsylvania Institute for the Instruction of the Blind (the former name of Overbrook), she returned to Wyoming Valley and began work as a home teacher of the blind. In a 1965 interview with Lou Rauscher of the *Sunday Independent,* she said, "I grew rather tired of hearing about blind people begging on the streets. Every time I threw some

along the back wall. PHOTO BY ACE HOFFMAN, COURTESY WILKES-BARRE BRANCH, PENNSYLVANIA ASSOCIATION FOR THE BLIND

money into their tin cups I felt that I just had to do something to get them off the streets."

In 1917, Arline Phillips opened an office in a small room donated for that purpose at 15 South Franklin Street, Wilkes-Barre. She found her first clients by talking to blind people she met on the streets. She also made regular visits to the state office on Pennsylvania Avenue where the blind dole was distributed to recruit clients for the association. In addition, she met with Attorney Paul Bedford—a meeting she later recalled as the most fruitful of any contact she ever made on behalf of Wyoming Valley's blind—and on Friday, November 8, 1918, the first meeting of the "Wilkes-Barre Committee of the Pennsylvania Association for the Blind" was held. Paul Bedford was elected president and Arline Phillips, secretary.

The organization had already moved to larger quarters at 44 North Main Street when Abram G. Nesbitt made a generous contribution. With this as "seed money," an additional $50,000 would enable the association to build a permanent center. In twenty-one days the building fund raised $53,000, with Miss Phillips speaking before as many local groups as she could find.

The display window of the Miners National Bank Building (now Mellon Bank Building) that faced South Franklin Street in Wilkes-Barre was used to show the development of technical aids for the blind in honor of the fiftieth anniversary of the Wilkes-Barre Branch, Pennsylvania Association for the Blind. PHOTO BY ACE HOFFMAN, COURTESY WILKES-BARRE BRANCH, PENNSYLVANIA ASSOCIATION FOR THE BLIND

The new building, at 35 East Union Street, Wilkes-Barre, opened in October 1921, making possible a workshop where blind persons could earn a living through articles crafted for sale to the public. Following the 1972 Agnes Flood, this building was sold, and the site is now a parking lot and track adjacent to Coughlin High School. The association moved to the YMCA in 1972 and into its present quarters at 63 North Franklin Street, Wilkes-Barre, in the fall of 1980. The workshop program is now operated by United Rehabilitation Services.

Arline continued to raise funds for the association. She later worked with Rose Brader of the United Way, raising money for that organization. Rose, Arline, and Arline's guide dog, who accompanied her everywhere, would meet with the workers at a construction site between 6:00 and 6:15 A.M. to do a brief presentation. They also visited the garment shops together. Rose was impressed that Arline could be ready to go with her in a minute when an opportunity presented itself. When the United Way redirected its allocations

Arline Phillips and her 13-year-old seeing-eye dog Ginger, as they prepare to make an official visit to a visually handicapped client. This would be one of Arline's last visits. PHOTO BY PAUL BIELEY, COURTESY WILKES-BARRE BRANCH, PENNSYLVANIA ASSOCIATION FOR THE BLIND

policy from deficit funding to program funding in 1973–74, the Blind Association decided to operate independently of the United Way and rely solely on its own resources.

In addition to her unique fund-raising ability, Arline's greatest gift was her strong spirit, combined with her empathy and concern. An editorial tribute to Arline states, "She truly loved all creatures great and small. She enjoyed being with people—all kinds of people, whether prominent or obscure, blind or sighted. . . . It brought her a special kind of pride and satisfaction when any one of her blind proteges, whom she had held in her arms as an infant, was graduated from college and embarked upon a career."

For many years, Miss Phillips relied upon the bus system to get to her home visits. She knew all the bus drivers and once said, "If I live to be a thousand I'll never forget the feeling I had when I went on a bus alone for the first time." From the late 1950s on, however, the Council of Jewish Women made the commitment to supply her with a driver, which greatly eased her daily routine.

Mildred Shapiro, a certified braille transcriber, was with her braille instructor one day when a call came from Miss Phillips requesting a driver for that Friday morning. She recalls saying that she could drive her on Friday if it was just that Friday. But that Friday turned out to be the beginning of a long relationship. For the next fourteen years, Mrs. Shapiro not only drove

Miss Phillips every Monday afternoon but began her own career of home visiting to the blind.

Home visiting served a variety of purposes. In addition to teaching braille, Miss Phillips taught handicrafts to her students, and showed them how to deal with the daily chores of living. She also taught them to cope emotionally with their blindness, both by direction and by example. And although she had great empathy, she had no sympathy for self-pity. On one visit she and Mrs. Shapiro found the client crying, saying, "Oh Miss Phillips, I can't see." Arline snapped, "I can't see either, but I don't cry about it."

Marion Comer, her former student and close friend, describes Arline as very witty and jolly. Marion was sixteen when she lost her sight. When she made her first visit to the Blind Association with her mother, her mother was very depressed. When they walked in the door, Arline quipped, "I forgot to turn on the lights." Here was this cheerful, positive person, living a full and dedicated life, and reaching out to help. Marion says her mother smiled for the first time in weeks.

Later, after Marion and Arline had become friends, they would argue about whether it was better to go blind at two and have no visual memory and no limits to the imagination or to lose one's sight at sixteen, with a storehouse of images but a sharp awareness of what was lost. In addition to braille, Arline taught her to type. Marion then went on to the Hadley correspondence courses, which were in braille, and studied almost everything from Latin to business. In 1992 Marion graduated from College Misericordia.

Miss Phillips lived most of her life in north Wilkes-Barre at 42 West Hollenback Avenue. After a brief, unhappy marriage, she took a job outside the area in November 1932 as editor of the Matilda Ziegler Magazine for the Blind. The Pennsylvania Association of the Blind publication noted, "In her promotion, the Association is losing a charming, wide-awake, and personally acceptable Supervisor, and the Ziegler Magazine for the Blind is adding to its staff a personality." But homesickness caused Miss Phillips' stay with the magazine to be relatively short, and she returned to Wilkes-Barre where she could continue her work with those who were learning how to live in darkness. She was honored in 1967 for her fifty years as founder, director, and worker with the Wilkes-Barre Branch of the Pennsylvania Blind Association. She retired in 1973 and died on December 27, 1974, at the age of 81.

The Hoyts and the Hoyt Library

THE NAME *Hoyt* is now almost synonymous with *library* to most Kingston and West-Side-community residents. This public library is now sixty-four years old and better than ever, despite its terrible losses in the 1972 flood. But why is it the *Hoyt Library?* Near *Hoyt Street?* And what is that historical marker about *Henry M. Hoyt* further north on Wyoming Avenue? As one might guess, they are all connected. The Hoyt family history interweaves the history of the community, the state, and the nation.

Daniel Hoyt, a Connecticut farmer, came to Wyoming Valley from Danbury in 1795. He built his frame house on the corner of what is now Wyoming Avenue and Hoyt Street, almost surely accounting for the name of the street. He was known as Deacon, and his younger brother, Ard Hoyt, was pastor of the Kingston and Wilkes-Barre congregations at the time the Forty Fort Meeting House was constructed in 1808. In 1817, Ard Hoyt left these Presbyterians and Congregationalists to become a missionary to the Cherokees. Meanwhile, Daniel Hoyt's younger son, Ziba Hoyt, who had distinguished himself on the western frontier during the War of 1812, accompanied General William Henry Harrison (later president of the United States) to the Battle of the Thames in which the great Shawnee Chief Tecumseh was killed.

Elias Hoyt, Ziba Hoyt's older brother, did not venture off to war but stayed in Wyoming Valley and ran a store in Kingston until his death in 1853. He was active in one of the valley's first railroad projects. When the Susquehanna Railroad Company was incorporated on April 9, 1833, Elias Hoyt was elected president. The railroad languished and died unbuilt in the financial Panic of 1837, but the idea of a west side railroad was well established. In the late 1840s, when the Lackawanna Iron and Coal Company was turning the area known as Slocum Hollow into a boom town—the genesis of Scranton—the plan was revived.

Pennsylvania Governor Henry M. Hoyt was born in this house in 1830. It stood on Wyoming Avenue near the site of the present historical marker in an area then called Goose Island because—it is said—the Hoyt family always kept a flock of geese. WHGS

This Lackawanna and Bloomsburg passenger train appears on a poster promoting a special excursion to the Northern Luzerne County Fair in Waverly on September 25, 1861. The train was to leave Kingston at 8:00 and arrive in Waverly at 10:00, returning from Waverly at 5:10 and arriving back in Kingston at 7:15. Excursion tickets to Waverly and return cost one dollar from Kingston and ninety cents from Pittston. Formally merged into the Delaware, Lackawanna and Western Railroad in 1873, the Lackawanna and Bloomsburg's eighty miles of track were the DL&W's greatest producer of revenue—the direct result of the great volume of coal shipped over this line. WHGS

Built by railroad entrepreneur Samuel Hoyt, this house on Wyoming Avenue in Kingston became the Hoyt Library. Note the front and side porches and Italianate tower, as well as Wyoming Avenue's graceful elm trees. Daniel Hoyt sold the lot in 1812. It had changed hands many times before Samuel Hoyt acquired it in 1846. He replaced the old frame house with a new brick one—the middle portion of the house pictured above. It was attached to an even older frame building to the rear, which Hoyt later replaced with a brick wing. Sometime later, perhaps after the Civil War, he built the elaborate structure in front, making his home one of Kingston's showplaces. WHGS

To the north of Wyoming Valley, the Scrantons constructed a railroad between Scranton and Great Bend in Susquehanna County where a connection was made with the Erie Railroad to New York. To the south of the valley, a railroad from Catawissa in Columbia County to Tamaqua in Carbon County made a connection at Tamaqua with the Reading Railroad to Philadelphia. That made it possible to link the Wyoming Valley with both New York and Philadelphia by adding just one more section, a line from Scranton to Rupert, below Bloomsburg.

Henry M. Hoyt (1830–1892) was a man of conscience with a wide range of interests and concerns. For the Historical Society of Pennsylvania he wrote the definitive legal summary of the old conflict over land claims, "Brief of a Title in the Seventeen Townships in the County of Luzerne: A Syllabus of the Controversy between Connecticut and Pennsylvania." In his campaign for governor, Hoyt declared a hard money position: "Professing to be an honest man, and the candidate of an honest party, I believe in honest money." Despite both the unpopularity of his position and his refusal to equivocate about it, his appeal was so great that he won anyway. As governor, Hoyt worked to prevent the imprisonment of juveniles with adults in the hope of restoring them to society as useful and honest citizens. In order to accomplish this goal, he initiated the construction of the first state reformatory for young offenders. While in public office, he spoke out sharply—and at the expense of some personal friendships—against the use of public trusts for private and personal schemes, asserting that "peace will never come until the moral forces in politics . . . prevail." His house on South Franklin Street in Wilkes-Barre was demolished in 1985. FROM OSCAR J. HARVEY *History of Wilkes-Barre*

The incorporators of this proposed line included Samuel Hoyt, son of Elias Hoyt and husband of Ann Nesbitt. On April 5, 1852, the Lackawanna and Bloomsburg Railroad was formed; and on June 24, 1856, the first locomotive drawing passenger cars entered Wyoming Valley with more than 300 passengers aboard. In his *History of Certified Kingston Township,* William Brewster writes:

> *Shortly after daybreak on a fine June morning, the crowds began to gather in the fields about Kingston depot. They came up the river from as far away as Berwick and Bloomsburg; from over the mountain; from Wilkes-Barre and all parts of Luzerne County. Most of them had never seen a locomotive before, and the day was a great event in their lives. . . . Shortly after eight o'clock the many anxious eyes turned northward saw a little curl of steam rising in the air from the long stretch of straight and level track below Wyoming; and many who would not believe before the road would be a success, beheld the little locomotive puffing along at a great speed, for those times, and drawing a number of gaily painted coaches filled with people. As the engine approached the depot, the driver blew his whistle. It was the signal. The cannon roared, church bells were rung, a*

Elinor Wylie, née Elinor Morton Hoyt, was a highly esteemed poet and novelist of the post–World War I era. FROM NANCY HOYT, *Portrait of an Unknown Lady,* COURTESY WHGS

great cheer went up, and the people knew that . . . Wyoming Valley had at last modern connection with the outside world.

By these mid-1850s, Samuel Hoyt's first cousin, Henry M. Hoyt, one of Ziba and Nancy Hurlburt Hoyt's six children, had been admitted to the Luzerne County Bar. Born in 1830 in a small frame house near the intersection of John Street and Wyoming Avenue (where the historical marker stands), he had worked on his family's farm until, at fourteen, he left to attend the Wilkes-Barre Academy, Wyoming Seminary, Lafayette College, and Williams College. He taught for several years and became professor of mathematics at Wyoming Seminary before deciding to read law under George W. Woodward, later chief justice of the Supreme Court of Pennsylvania. Prior to the Civil War he was defeated in a race for district attorney.

With the onset of the war, Henry M. Hoyt helped to raise and lead the 52nd Regiment of Pennsylvania Volunteers. He was captured, escaped, and was recaptured by the Confederates. When released at last through an exchange of prisoners, he returned to Wyoming Valley and was breveted Brigadier General for meritorious conduct. In 1867 he was defeated in election for judge of Luzerne County. He nevertheless became chairman of the Republican State Committee in 1875 and was elected governor of Pennsylvania in 1878.

While Governor Hoyt pursued his political career, Samuel Hoyt, active in the successful effort to bring a railroad to the valley, built a large brick

This rendering from architects Pyros and Sanderson shows the new wing of the Hoyt Library, including the new children's library. The project entailed major renovations of the original building as well. HOYT LIBRARY

mansion on Wyoming Avenue near his grandfather's original home. This was not a single structure but a large new addition to the front of an older house that had already acquired a newly built wing to the rear. Samuel Hoyt's son, Frank Weston Hoyt, great grandson of Deacon Daniel Hoyt, the farmer from Danbury, was born in Kingston in 1866.

Frank Weston Hoyt resided near Philadelphia at the time of his death in 1909. He left this fine old family home to Kingston Borough for a public library. Perhaps he was influenced by Andrew Carnegie, who in an article called "Wealth," published in 1889, outlined his ideas on how large fortunes should be used for the betterment of society, his own going to education, public libraries, and the world peace movement.

Perhaps Frank Weston Hoyt's cousin, poet and novelist Elinor Wylie (1885–1928), inspired his bequest. Born Elinor Morton Hoyt, Wylie was the granddaughter of Governor Henry M. Hoyt and the daughter of Anne MacMichael and Henry Martyn Hoyt, who served as assistant attorney general and then as solicitor general of the United States under presidents William McKinley and Theodore Roosevelt. Elinor Wylie is buried in the Forty Fort Cemetery. She was noted both for her beauty and for the fine craftsmanship of her work, which reflected the changes in American attitudes in the wake of World War I. Her poetry collections include *Nets to Catch the Wind, Black Armour, Angels and Earthly Creatures,* and *Trivial Breath.* Her novels are *Jennifer Lorn, The Venetian Glass Nephew, The Orphan Angel,* and *Mr. Hodge and Mr. Hazard.* Her third husband, poet William Rose Benet, published her *Collected Poems* and *Collected Prose* after her death. *Last Poems* appeared in 1943.

Frank Weston Hoyt's bequest came as a surprise to the Kingston Borough Council. A public meeting of the town's residents held several days later passed a resolution that the council accept the gift. The house continued to be rented, and the rents accrued in a special fund, along with an additional $500 to be set aside by the council each year. After extensive remodeling, the Hoyt Library opened on January 2, 1928. As on that day in 1856 when the first locomotive came to Kingston, there was a great celebration, "and the children came in such numbers that a double line was formed, reaching far beyond the library doors."

Meanwhile, the older Hoyt house on the corner was torn down to make way for the American Auto Store. Now it, in turn, has given way for the expansion of the library. With great interest and enthusiasm, residents of Kingston and the West Side communities celebrated the construction of the new wing, which has extended the building and grounds of the Hoyt Library right to the corner site of the original Hoyt farmhouse.

According to his biographer Richard Meryman, lunch was the high point of Mankiewicz's day—"an impromptu party [lasting] long after other diners had left and waiters were resetting tables." As a young man in New York, Mankiewicz lunched regularly with the other wits of the famous Algonquin Round Table. FROM RICHARD MERYMAN, *Mank,* COURTESY FRANK MANKIEWICZ

Herman J. Mankiewicz
From Wilkes-Barre to Hollywood

IT IS SAID that Sir Arthur Sullivan, in spite of the phenomenally successful operettas he composed with W. S. Gilbert, wanted to be remembered as a serious musician and held the form in which he achieved fame in low regard. In much the same way, Herman J. Mankiewicz achieved his masterpiece in a medium he openly derided and always felt that his best and greatest achievement would be a serious literary endeavor.

Working with Orson Welles and John Houseman, Mankiewicz wrote the screenplay for *Citizen Kane,* one of the greatest films ever produced. In it, his comprehension of American politics and the culture of which he was a part coalesce with his wit. He drew on at least two experiences from his own life to create unmatched poignant moments in film history. The loss of his beloved bike, stolen from in front of the Osterhout Free Library in Wilkes-Barre, was the model of the famous lost sled "Rosebud." And his drunken collapse over his typewriter and consequent failure to complete a review of *The School for Scandal* for *The New York Times* brought his boss, drama editor George S. Kaufman, to an unmatched rage and almost cost him his job. In *Citizen Kane,* Joseph Cotten, as the reporter Jedidiah Leland, does lose his job in a similar scene.

Mankiewicz's sense of competition, first with his brilliant father Franz Mankiewicz and later with his much younger (and perhaps even more brilliant) brother Joseph L. Mankiewicz, compounded his sense of failure; and he died believing that his talent had been wasted. Nevertheless, once movies had begun to be recognized as a legitimate art form, *Citizen Kane* came to be almost an icon. Richard Meryman calls it

> *the most important and seminal American movie ever made. Filmed in 1940, it was a synthesis and extension of everything innovative in film to that date. As a totality, Kane was so revolutionary in its techniques, so devoid of sentimentality,*

so advanced in its use of psychology, that the movie became a springboard for future motion pictures—and eventually a landmark in cinema history. Perhaps no other script has provided a movie with a structure at once so complex and so perfectly machined."

An impoverished Franz Mankiewicz had left Berlin for New York City in 1892, and in 1904 he took a job in Wilkes-Barre as editor of the German-language newspaper *Demokratischer Waechter.* In 1896 he had married Johanna Blumenau, and they brought to Wilkes-Barre with them Herman, born in 1897, and Erna, born in 1901. Joseph was born in Wilkes-Barre in 1909. Their first home was at 32 Sullivan Street, five blocks south of Public Square.

Franz Mankiewicz believed there was no future in foreign language newspapers in America and felt fortunate to obtain a position as tutor, and later as teacher, of German and French at the Harry Hillman Academy. After he became a professor of foreign languages, the family moved to 238 Academy Street. Herman became a scholarship student at the academy and completed the requirements for graduation by the time he was fourteen. He had already passed the entrance exams for Columbia University a year earlier, but was considered too young to matriculate. He got a job in the mines for a year as assistant to a surveyor.

In 1912, Professor Mankiewicz found a job with the prestigious Stuyvesant High School in New York City, and the whole family moved when Herman started at Columbia. After his graduation, Herman went to work for the *Tribune.* Sam Hoffenstein, who had grown up next door in Wilkes-Barre, had become a theater press agent and supplied Herman with free theater tickets and introductions to George S. Kaufman and Alexander Woollcott, theater editor and drama critic respectively of *The New York Times.*

During World War I Mankiewicz did a stint in the Marines and spent two years living adventurously in postwar Berlin with his young wife Shulamith Sara Aaronson before he returned to New York. There he wrote theater reviews for the *Times,* became one of the founding staff members of *The New Yorker,* and worked on writing plays, both on his own and with several colleagues. He became an important part of the Algonquin Round Table, despite his youth, under the sponsorship of Kaufman. This lunch club of playwrights, critics, essayists, and reporters idolized cleverness and appreciated Mankiewicz's quick wit and humor, although they found his strong political opinions and his already well-developed social consciousness rather tedious.

In 1925, Mankiewicz was offered $500 a week to go to Hollywood to write a scenario for a silent movie about the Marines. The money was a powerful magnet, and he went. Instead of the Marine scenario, however, he wrote his first movie, *The Road to Mandalay,* for that master of disguises Lon Chaney.

The Harry B. Hillman Academy was Herman Mankiewicz's alma mater. Founded as the Wilkes-Barre Academy in 1878, successor to the old Wilkes-Barre (Wyoming) Academy, which once stood on Public Square, it actually was located for a few years on Academy Street in Wilkes-Barre. The school was renamed in 1884 in memory of young Harry Hillman and moved into its new quarters in 1886. Located near the corner of West River and Terrace streets in Wilkes-Barre, this red brick building designed by W. W. Newer was a spacious and airy school. Harry Hillman's grandfather, Col. H. B. Hillman, had been a business partner of Asa Packer's at Mauch Chunk. In 1842 he moved to Wyoming Valley, and went into business as a coal operator. H. Baker Hillman, young Harry's father, was a director of the People's Bank, Vulcan Iron Works, Glen Summit Hotel, and the Electric Light Company. In 1939 the Harry B. Hillman Academy (for boys) consolidated with the Wilkes-Barre Institute (for girls) to form the Wilkes-Barre Day School (now the Wyoming Seminary Lower School) and moved to Wyoming Avenue in Forty Fort. The old school building, which was converted into apartments about 1947, is now covered with tan stucco. FROM A 1915 POSTCARD, COURTESY F. CHARLES PETRILLO

As he became more and more involved in the world of Hollywood, he moved steadily away from the serious writing of his early ambition. He enticed Ben Hecht to Hollywood with this telegram: "MILLIONS ARE TO BE GRABBED OUT HERE AND YOUR ONLY COMPETITION IS IDIOTS. DON'T LET THIS GET AROUND." Hecht went, and commented, "Movies were rarely written. They were yelled into existence at conferences that kept going in saloons, brothels, and all-night poker games."

Herman Mankiewicz posed with his new bicycle, obviously his pride and joy. The emotions he endured after it was stolen from the front of the Osterhout Free Library are echoed in *Citizen Kane's* central theme, the loss of the sled Rosebud. FROM RICHARD MERYMAN, *Mank,* COURTESY FRANK MANKIEWICZ

When silent films gave way to talkies, Mankiewicz was in his element as one of the few writers with a background in the Broadway theater. And when the two plays he had co-authored failed on Broadway, he became even more deeply entrenched in film. He was officially involved as writer in at least seventy-five movies and did behind-the-scenes rewrites on about a hundred more. His best known credits include *Pride of the Yankees,* and the first two Marx Brothers flicks, *Monkey Business* and *Horse Feathers.*

Critic Pauline Kael observed in a 1971 *New Yorker* article that, "if [Mankiewicz] was at that time [1926–40] one of the highest-paid writers in the world, it was because he wrote the kind of movies that were disapproved of as 'fast' and immoral. His heroes weren't soft-eyed and bucolic; he brought good-humored toughness to the movies, and energy and astringency. And the public responded because it was eager for modern American subjects."

Kael believes that Mankiewicz's downfall from that Academy Award winning peak of *Citizen Kane* was forcefully abetted by William Randolph Hearst, who viewed the film as a personal betrayal and mounted a vendetta against everyone who had anything to do with it. Kael traces Hearst's harassment of Mankiewicz and relates it to his dwindling output during the 1940s. By the end of the decade, he could barely find work at all. He completed an epic screenplay about the evangelist Aimee Semple McPherson but ran into numerous production blocks. Nevertheless, and in spite of deteriorating health, he continued to support his family with whatever despised hackwork he could land until the time of his death in 1953.

Herman Mankiewicz lived a high-speed life. He gulped liquor, smoked constantly, and gambled on everything. He literally lived by his wits. His joy was conversation. Ben Hecht wrote, "Most of Manky's utterances, even his deepest philosophical ones, stirred laughter. Even his enemies laughed. He could puncture egos, draw blood from pretension—and his victims, with souls abashed, sat still and laughed. The swiftness of his thoughts was by itself a sort of comedy. Never have I known a man with so quick an eye and ear—and tongue—for the strut of fools."

Mankiewicz once said, "The best thing that can happen to a man working in this petal factory is that he makes ten thousand dollars a week and only spends twelve thousand—before taxes—and that he's buried in a gold-plated, rhinestone encrusted coffin. . . . And while he sleeps beneath the sod, his life's work is occasionally projected on the walls of converted grocery stores—and then the film is cut up into mandolin picks." Never would he have foreseen that *Citizen Kane* would still be showing today on VCRs in millions of homes across the United States, universally acknowledged as one of the very best movies ever written.

C. Edgar Patience (1906–1972). COURTESY ALICE PATIENCE

C. Edgar Patience

Black Coal Sculptor

IN 1981, at the Afro-American Cultural Museum in Philadelphia, two pieces made up northeastern Pennsylvania's contribution to an exhibit called *Three Hundred Years of Black History.* One was a venerable piece of artisanry: the "Crown Point powder horn decorated with pictures of houses and ships by Gershom Prince, a black soldier who was the slave of Captain Robert Durkee of the Connecticut militia." Prince fought with Durkee in the battle of Quebec during the French and Indian War and died on July 3, 1778, during the Battle of Wyoming.

"Amalarice," the other contribution, was executed almost two hundred years later by one of Pennsylvania's outstanding artists, C. Edgar Patience. It was the only sculpture in the exhibit. The sculptor noted at an earlier exhibition of "Amalarice" that the name, in one of the many African dialects, meant "The Meek One" and quoted, "The meek shall inherit the earth." It is probably not simple coincidence that Amalarice is also a play on the name of Alice Marie Patience, the artist's wife.

C. Edgar Patience was unique. Born in West Pittston on August 27, 1906, he—like his five brothers—was recruited into his father's business while still a boy. His father, Harry B. Patience, was the son of a slave who came north with a hospital unit during the Civil War. Born in Northmoreland in Wyoming County, he began work as a breaker boy in the collieries near West Pittston. He taught himself to carve the coal he sorted and eventually opened a coal souvenir business. Later, with the help of his sons, he supplied these trinkets to stores throughout the state. Edgar Patience learned to carve as a boy and continued in the souvenir business for many years.

Edgar Patience, however, made the leap from craftsman to artist. As we contemplate a work of art, we may forget that the artist must first be a skilled craftsperson, deeply familiar with the materials and the means of modifying them, in order to make possible the creation of art—the unique expression of the ideas of the artist in such a way as to capture the imagination and emotions of the viewer.

By the time he had reached his early forties, Patience knew that he wanted to take the leap from the hard working but more secure souvenir business into the equally hard working but very insecure life of an artist. This meant abandoning the production of numerous small objects carved from coal whose marketability was predictable throughout the coal regions of the state. It also meant trading a regular income for a period of no income that might or might not eventually become productive. Alice Marie Patterson Patience made this gamble possible by providing for the family's support for a five-year experimental period. By the end of those five years, they knew that Edgar had a future as an artist. Although Alice continued to work at her job as manager of the Customer Info-Center of Blue Cross of Northeastern Pennsylvania, Edgar Patience was established in his new role as an artist and freed from the repetitiveness of the souvenir trade.

As a sculptor of coal, Patience had to deal with the mechanics of the coal industry. He found the Mammoth Vein near Tamaqua and Hazleton to be the best source of the high-density coal that could be handled without cracking. He searched to find the flawless pieces necessary for a flawless product, but the larger the piece, the less predictable the material, despite careful probes to test quality. As a result, two of his largest pieces had to be executed twice. When flaws emerged after months of work, he discarded them and began again. A finished piece was developed from a raw chunk of coal more than three times its final size.

The machinery in Patience's shop, behind his home at 82 Loomis Street in Wilkes-Barre, ranged in size from the heavy equipment necessary for moving the large pieces of coal, through lathes and power saws, to the finest jeweler's tools. Polished surfaces were truly a labor of love, for they were meticulously achieved with jeweler's rouge.

Self-taught artist that he was, Patience studied the work of many sculptors, traveling to museums and special exhibits whenever possible and making use of illustrated books on art. He particularly admired Henry Moore and made many trips to the Museum of Modern Art in New York to study his work, as well as the other modern and impressionist pieces on display there. Patience continued to experiment with the interaction of coal—with its unique properties of blackness, density, matte finish, satiny gleam, and vivid iridescence—and the wide varieties of form it could assume as he transformed it from pressed carbon to work of art.

During the early years, Patience exhibited his work and demonstrated his skill at numerous arts and crafts shows and meetings, including Wilkes-Barre's Fine Arts Fiesta, in which he participated from the beginning. As his fame as a sculptor spread, he began to receive special commissions and honors. Con-

"Amalarice"—one of Patience's most beautiful and unusual pieces of sculpture. PHOTOS BY RICHARD M. ROSS, COURTESY ALICE PATIENCE

gressman Dan Flood purchased and presented coal pieces to every president of the United States from Franklin Delano Roosevelt to Richard M. Nixon. A Hoover vacuum cleaner in coal is housed with the Hoover Company archives, and a Mack Bulldog of coal decorates the Mack Truck Company offices.

Some of Patience's works found their way into the collections of Lady Bird Johnson and Wendell Wilkie. When the late Representative Joseph Semanoff of Lehighton was named honorary ambassador of good will to Holland in 1973, he presented Queen Juliana of the Netherlands with one of Patience's coal sculptures. Soldiers of the 101st Airborne Division returning to Holland to take part in the 25th anniversary celebration of the liberation of that country from Germany also presented Queen Juliana with one of Patience's works.

More significant was the commissioning of the official seal of Barbados at the time of that nation's independence from Great Britain. Alice Patience recalls that on the cruise ship that took them to the ceremonies, her husband was the honored guest of the new nation and the center of attention. He loved it.

In 1969, Patience responded to a special invitation and introduced his head of John F. Kennedy at the Cooperative Crafts Exhibit sponsored by the U.S. Department of Agriculture. Patience also received attention from the Canadian prime minister and press at the 1971 Canada Expo in Montreal where his work was on exhibition by special invitation. His abstract pieces led to a display at Grippi's Gallery in New York. His last display and exhibit was part of "Pennsylvania Excitement" at Gimble's–Center City, Philadelphia, in May 1972.

In March 1970, *Ebony* magazine featured Patience in an article that described him as "one of the nation's most unusual sculptors—creating masterpieces of art from chunks of penny-a-pound hard coal." He was named in *Who's Who in the East, Who's Who in America,* and *Who's Who in the World.* He had also been proposed for inclusion in the National Social Directory at the National Register of Prominent Americans and International Notables.

C. Edgar Patience died June 7, 1972, only three days after being hospitalized with pneumonia. He was sixty-five. In his twenty years as an artist, he created many works ranging from miniatures to monoliths. On one twelve-by-twelve-by-eighteen-inch diorama he represented the complete operation of a coal mine, from the men at work underground to the automobiles parked in front of the company office.

Another minature, "Coaltown, USA," can be seen at the William Penn Museum in Harrisburg. It is the result of fifteen to eighteen years of continuing work—Patience's recreation from his other sculpting. It portrays a mining town of a generation ago with homes, streets, breakers, coal cars, miners, and company store. Like the diorama, it is minutely detailed. In contrast to these are the monolith on permanent exhibit at the Smithsonian Institution in Washington, D.C., a highly polished three and a half ton chunk of coal, and the coal altar to be found in the chapel of King's College, Wilkes-Barre, weighing nearly four tons, with thousands of highly polished jewel-like surfaces.

The Pennsylvania Historic and Museum Commission has acquired, in addition to "Coaltown, USA," Patience's "Bust of George Washington." This piece portrays the first president with the extremely broad shoulders that Patience saw as the foundation of the nation. It is a dramatic contrast in style to his portrait of "Mama," a fertility figure that is full-busted and stooping, with extended pelvis and massive buttocks, and his very abstract "Stone upon Stone"—carved and highly polished coal pieces assembled to create a beautiful form.

Patience's works are perfect symbols of one of the most important themes of the civil rights movement, "Black is Beautiful." But they are far more than that. As the 1981 Afro-American Museum catalogue states, "Edgar Patience's anthracite coal sculptures are among the [world's] most unusual and moving works of art."

Significant Women in Wyoming Valley History

DURING THE 1960S, women's history emerged as a legitimate field of research and historical analysis. As a result, we have had a wonderful explosion of information: First, about women, who as individuals, have had an important impact on their communities—whether local, state, or national in scope; and second, about the lives of women in general. As a result, we now know much more about the role of women in the westward movement, about the influence of women on immigration decisions, how women have affected the development of cities, on women as the developers of social institutions, women's influence on and in the paid work force, and much more.

Janice H. McElroy says in *Our Hidden Heritage,* "Significant figures in history traditionally have meant those associated with power, influence, violence, and visible activity in political and economic affairs." The significant women in Wyoming Valley's history do not fit that traditional profile. Instead, their impact has been felt across the entire fabric of our community, as shown by Mary Beard in the first important work to analyze women's place in history. In *Women as Force in History,* published in 1946, Beard demonstrated that women have been "active, competent, and recognized in their own times and in a wide range of endeavors and circumstances."

Here are a few brief descriptions of some women who have had an impact on Luzerne County and Wyoming Valley. Harry Truman once said that there were twenty-five men in his home town capable of being international statesmen—and ten of them would have made excellent presidents of the United States. And he didn't think his town was unique. He believed every community in the United States could produce a similar list. Nor did he believe that the quality of the leadership they exercised was less important than that of national leaders, since the quality of our lives depends on the integrity and ability of our leaders at every level of our society.

Frances Dorrance was a scholar, graduating from Wyoming Seminary in 1896 and from Vassar in 1900 (Phi Beta Kappa). She studied at Berlin University and at Columbia; and using her skills in German and botany, she translated German botanical works into English. In 1916 she attended the New York State Library School, receiving her Bachelor of Library Science degree in 1918. After heading the circulation department at the Trenton Public Library in Trenton, New Jersey, she returned to Wyoming Valley where she worked at the Osterhout and Hoyt libraries and served as executive director of the Wyoming Historical and Geological Society. WHGS

The Wilkes-Barre Institute stood at 78 South Franklin Street. It had earlier occupied two rooms in the old Wilkes-Barre Academy building on Public Square, then had a home of its own on South River Street before moving into this former residence in 1881. Education beyond the elementary level first became available to Wyoming Valley's women with the opening of its predecessor—the Wilkes-Barre Female Seminary—in 1839. F. CHARLES PETRILLO

In the interest of balancing the books, our local history books in this case, the following is a list of women whose concern about this community and involvement in it have had an important impact on our lives. The challenge is not one of locating significant women in Wyoming Valley's history. The challenge is keeping the list manageable, while attempting to portray something of the variety of endeavors we regard as significant.

We get dramatic glimpses in the early historical record of the lives of two women in Wyoming Valley at the time of the Battle of Wyoming. The first is Esther Montour, known as Queen Esther (see "The Bloody Rock"). The second is Martha Espy Stewart, wife of Captain Lazarus Stewart.

Martha Espy Stewart's story represents the degree of heroism to which women have risen when safeguarding their families from disaster: On the day of the Battle of Wyoming, widowed when her husband died on the battlefield and only two days after giving birth to her seventh child, Martha Stewart gathered her children and the most valuable of their family possessions into two canoes, lashed them together side by side, and guided them down the Susquehanna River to her sister's home in Bloomsburg. After several days rest, she and her sister decided that Bloomsburg was not really a safe place either and continued downstream to the Harrisburg area, where they had been born. About three years later, Mrs. Stewart and her children returned to their

Mary L. Trescott (left) and S. M. R. O'Hara (right) were Luzerne County's first two women lawyers. FROM OSCAR J. HARVEY, *History of Wilkes-Barre*

home in Hanover Township and rebuilt the cabin and farm—not only a courageous act but a backbreaking undertaking.

Shortly after the Battle of Wyoming, a little girl named Frances Slocum was kidnapped from her home and became Maconaqua (see "The Wonderful Story of Frances Slocum"). Wyoming Valley's first female physician was Eunice Chapman Poyner Sprague (see "Medicine on the Frontier").

In the nineteenth century, education was changing from the privilege of the few to an opportunity for many. Women played an important role in accomplishing this change, both by making education available for women and by making education available for the entire community.

Three separate educational movements occurred: the development of the common schools, now known as the public schools, supported by taxation; the development of the "public" schools, now called "independent," open to all but paid for by student fees; and the development of the parochial schools, sponsored by and usually subsidized by religious institutions, and usually requiring some payment of fees.

Despite both a tax of three pence on each pound levied in 1773 for the support of a free school in each township of the original settlement and recorded meetings of school committees dating from 1774, no common school is known to have been formally established. The earliest formal school in Wyoming Valley was begun in 1807. At that time, the lower floor of the former jail was reorganized as a schoolroom for elementary students. Called the Wilkes-Barre

Wyoming Seminary, established in Kingston in 1844, was Wyoming Valley's first coeducational secondary school—providing young women with the opportunity for truly equal education. The original building was Swetland Hall, the first on the left, now on the National Register of Historic Places. The school was already eighty years old when this picture was taken in the 1920s. WHGS

Academy, this school was public in the sense that it was open to all who could pay tuition—meaning both boys and girls. The upper floor of the former jail, housing the upper grades of the school, was limited to boys. The first free school in Wilkes-Barre operated at public expense was opened in 1836.

In 1839, the Wilkes-Barre Female Seminary on River Street opened. A forerunner of the Wilkes-Barre Institute, which was chartered in 1844, it made more advanced education available to girls. In 1844 Wyoming Seminary also opened its doors to both men and women on the west side of the river, making secondary education more widely available. Almost all these educational developments relied on the efforts of women as well as men, particularly as teachers.

The earliest establishment of a Roman Catholic secondary school in Wyoming Valley was the work of Sister M. Cephas and her six colleagues from the Reading motherhouse of the Immaculate Heart of Mary who established St. John's Academy in Pittston (see "Luzerne County's First Catholic Secondary School"). The most dramatic story of the founding of an educational institution, one that spans the distance from Germany to Wilkes-Barre, is that of Mother Pauline von Mallinckrodt (see "Mother Pauline von Mallinckrodt," "Sisters of Christian Charity: A New Home in Wilkes-Barre," and "St. Ann's Academy"). Ellen Webster Palmer promoted education outside the school

This scene from the 1959 strike against Jenkins Sportswear on North Main Street in Pittston shows Min Matheson—top center, wearing black—in the center of the action. Beside her is David Gingold, director of the Northeast Department of the International Ladies Garment Workers Union. Ann Little is on the left end, carrying the sign about piece rates. Seated in front are Stella Krivak, Ann Kizis, Marian Narcum, Marian Lockus, and Mary Ann Tilley. ILGWU

structure through the Boys' Industrial Association (see "Ellen Webster Palmer and the Breaker Boys").

Edith Brower (1848–1931) was primarily a writer. Her work appeared both in *Atlantic Monthly, Lippincott's,* and *Catholic World* and in local publications. It is her work for the beautification of Wilkes-Barre, particularly the River Common, that makes us most grateful to her today. That work led her to become the founder of the organization known today as the Wyoming Valley Women's Club. She was also instrumental in founding the Visiting Nurses Association of Wilkes-Barre. Another writer of the same era, poet Elinor Wylie, had Wyoming Valley roots and is buried in the Forty Fort Cemetary (see "The Hoyts and the Hoyt Library"). Artist Rose O'Neill's work is described in "Rose O'Neill: Kewpie Creator."

Two Wyoming Valley women were pathfinders into the legal world. The first woman admitted to the Luzerne County Bar was Mary L. Trescott (1861–1935). She was also the first woman in Pennsylvania to run for judge and the first to be appointed a referee in bankruptcy. Mary Trescott was the second woman in the entire United States to be admitted to practice before the United States Supreme Court. She was also the first woman elected to the Wilkes-Barre School Board and the first to become its president. She worked hard to establish regular raises for teachers. In addition, Trescott worked closely with Ellen Webster Palmer in establishing and maintaining the Boys' Industrial Association.

S. M. R. O'Hara (1882–1954) was the first woman in Pennsylvania to hold a cabinet office—Secretary of the Commonwealth (1939–1943). She then became the first Secretary of Welfare for the Commonwealth of Pennsylvania (1943–1947). Incidentally, she was the second woman to be admitted to the Luzerne County Bar.

Among the many women who have had a significant impact on the quality of life in Wyoming Valley, several stand out because of their work in filling needs they identified in the community.

Anna Bertels (1850–1931) was born at Lambaheim, Bavaria. She came to America with her husband, Jacob Bertels, in 1870. Mrs. Bertels was appointed the first matron of the newly organized United Charities (forerunner of the Family Service Agency) in 1895. She opened its first headquarters in a room in the old Raeder hotel on West Northampton Street, using a soap box as her chair. From this makeshift office, she took on the care and supervision of young people at risk and started the work of alleviating suffering and straightening out domestic difficulties. A forceful and dominant personality, Anna Bertels made the organization a success.

Fannie Sax Long (1876–1959) came to Wilkes-Barre as the wife of Dr. Charles Long. It was she who took the initiative in founding the Visiting Nurses' Association. She was also the organizer and first president of the Wilkes-Barre Parent-Teachers Association; and she organized Wilkes-Barre's first Girl Scout Troop. She had a lifetime interest in prison reform, served on Pennsylvania's Penal Commission, was named by President Hoover to a federal commission to study European prisons, and attended meetings of the International Congress of Prisons and Penitentiaries in The Hague, Prague, and Berlin.

The lives and work of Anna Bertels, S. M. R. O'Hara, and Edith Brower have been researched in detail by Rita Wolberg, who presented her material at workshops at the Luzerne County Women's Conferences at Penn State Wilkes-Barre. Dr. Sheldon Spear, in *Chapters in Wyoming Valley History,* has published the stories of Edith Brower, Mary L. Trescott, Fannie Sax Long, and Anna Bertels in a section entitled "Notable Valley Women."

Arline Phillips, founder of the Wilkes-Barre Branch of the Pennsylvania Association of the Blind, was herself handicapped by blindness (see "Arline Phillips: Opportunity, Not Sympathy").

Min Matheson, born in 1910, was Wyoming Valley's postwar organizer of the International Ladies Garment Workers Union. She achieved the seven-hour day for garment workers and established the ILGWU Health Center on South Washington Street. She also actively involved unions in the Community Chest, now the Wyoming Valley United Way, laying the groundwork for today's organization, and building one of the community's most important bridges between labor and business.

Frances Dorrance (1877–1973) played a key role in initiating the 1924 statewide archeological survey, with the goal of preserving the remaining Indian village sites for future excavation and study and preventing the loss of the information they contained. As executive director of the Wyoming Historical and Geological Society, she was a founder of the Pennsylvania Historical Association, parent of the Pennsylvania Federation of Museums and Historical Organizations, which works in partnership with the Pennsylvania Historical and Museum Commission. Also the Hoyt Library's first head librarian, she was active as well in establishing kindergartens for underprivileged children. For her many contributions, she became the first woman in the United States to receive the American Legion's Distinguished Service Award. She provided for the delight of several generations of Wyoming Valley residents by acquiring Chief Sitting Bull's clothing and artifacts and having a model made in his image. He greets visitors to this day as they approach the Indian exhibit at the Wyoming Historical and Geological Society's Museum.

Annette Evans (1893–1969) also belongs on this list. She was the founder of Wilkes-Barre's Fine Arts Fiesta. Her interest in art is shown in her excellent study of Catlin's work, cited earlier in "George Catlin." She also established the Little Theater of Wilkes-Barre and served as its executive director for many years. She chaired the Experiment in International Living, which brought ten Fulbright scholars to the valley, and she was the first general chair of the Wyoming Valley United Nations Committee.

This list is a sampling, and by no means complete. We do not lack significant women in Wyoming Valley history. The challenge is deciding which stories to tell.

The Transportation Hub

THE CONNECTICUT AND PENNSYLVANIA settlers who struggled to establish their civilization in Wyoming Valley saw this area through the eyes of their seaboard communities. Transportation in the seventeenth and eighteenth-century American settlements was chiefly by ship along the Atlantic coast and up the navigable rivers. Driving their wagons over the barrier mountains of the great Appalachian chain, the settlers could not appreciate that—from another point of view—they were traveling an already well developed route to a major transportation center.

The Indians of the northeastern United States had an altogether different view from that of the settlers. As a civilization, the Six Nations of the Iroquois viewed the Appalachians not as a mountain barrier but as a part of a domain that stretched from the St. Lawrence River to Tennessee and from Maine to Michigan.

Wyoming Valley was a natural crossroads, and paths for all purposes—diplomacy, war, trade, seasonal travel, and hunting—traversed the valley from every direction of the compass. In his speech at the 1951 Wyoming Monument ceremonies, Paul Wallace observed that the Indian paths, designed for the moccasin-clad feet that used them, were functional and efficient highways, planned and maintained to get their users from place to place with as little trouble as possible. In fact, "between given points, the routes . . . were often much shorter than those we travel today. Whereas many of our present roads loop about, picking up towns along the way and circumnavigating important properties, the old trails went as nearly straight as the conformation of the land would allow." Also, the foot traveler would climb a steep pitch to save miles while the easier grades (demanded first by wagons and later by cars) required much more mileage.

This system of good trails enabled the Six Nations of the Iroquois Confederacy to establish and maintain their Great Peace over an area as large as Western Europe. The trails formed a continental network with numerous local feeders and interconnections. The valley was an important hub in this network.

This tollgate stood at Georgetown, just outside Wilkes-Barre, on the Easton and Wilkes-Barre Turnpike (Northampton Street). Imagine paying a toll to drive up Giant's Despair. WHGS

Trails connected here from the north (Great Bend), northeast (Cushetank), east (Minisink, connecting with the shell fisheries on the New Jersey coast), southeast (Stroudsburg), south southeast (Easton), south (Reading), south southwest (Wapwallopen), southwest (the Wyoming Path to Sunbury, forming a section of the Great Warriors' Path through Pennsylvania to Maryland, Virginia, and the Carolinas), west (Muncy), west northwest (Harvey's Lake), and north northwest (the northern section of the Great Warriors' Path to Athens, formerly Tioga).

The events that form the early history of the valley took place along these routes. The early Connecticut settlers first entered Wyoming by the path from Cushetank, where the Connecticut settlement on the Delaware was located. Because they were bringing heavily loaded wagons and livestock over a trail designed to be a footpath, they found it necessary to fell trees, creating a road as they went. They also had to struggle with steep grades, not at all suited to wheeled vehicles. The path from Minisink to Wyoming Valley traveled through Bear Swamp and the Great Swamp, including the area called "The Shades of Death" by the refugees escaping from the aftermath of the Battle of Wyoming. It was scary, since the lofty white pines (described as reaching over two hundred feet) and the close-needled hemlocks combined to "blot out the sun and depress the traveler's spirits." Also, this area was still the home of bears, wildcats, and rattlesnakes. The trail was not dangerous, however, unless one had an enemy following close behind. Today Bear Swamp is long since drained, but Bear Creek, which ran through the middle of it, is still there. The Great Swamp began about two miles beyond Bear Swamp, in the vicinity of Thornhurst. The road through the Great Swamp was fifteen miles long, with the area called "The Shades of Death" the darkest and most dismal part. Route 115 is a more direct route through much of the same territory.

The British, Tory, and Indian forces attacking Wyoming in 1778 moved south along the Great Warriors' Path from Tioga. In 1779, the Sullivan Expedition sent by General George Washington to eliminate the Indian threat to this frontier came to Wyoming Valley from Easton. After assembling sufficient supplies, the army moved north along the Great Warriors' Path to lay waste the Indian villages. General John Sullivan, leader of this punitive expedition, was responsible for constructing the first proper road leading into Wyoming Valley. In order to move his force of 3,500 men and their supplies, Sullivan had the "Lower Road to the Delaware," as the widened trail was then known, systematically surveyed, redesigned, and built to the army engineers' specifications. Thus this road became not merely a converted trail but a planned thoroughfare for heavy-wheeled vehicles and artillery. Northampton Street, from River Street in Wilkes-Barre, through Georgetown, past Prospect Rock, and over Wilkes-Barre Mountain to Laurel Run, is still almost identical to the original Sullivan Trail. It connected Wilkes-Barre to Easton and the Delaware

Turnpike tickets were issued by the Easton and Wilkes-Barre Turnpike. Note that in those uninflated days it was necessary to divide 25¢ into increments of 12½¢ and 6¼¢. F. CHARLES PETRILLO

General John (Black Jack) Sullivan (1740–1795) was an attorney from New Hampshire. He served in the First Continental Congress and in 1775 was appointed brigadier general in the newly formed Continental Army. After commanding the retreat of the American Army from Quebec, he was taken prisoner at Long Island but exchanged in time to participate in the attack on the British in Trenton, before Washington commissioned him to lead the retaliatory expedition against the Iroquois allies of the British. The numerous British-inspired Indian raids against the frontier settlements along the North and West Branches of the Susquehanna, as well as those along the Mohawk River in upstate New York, were demoralizing the American cause. Sullivan and his troops routed the Iroquois, burned their villages, and destroyed their crops—the major food source both for the British troops in the north and for the Iroquois themselves. Sullivan retired from the military shortly after his expedition ended but continued to serve—as delegate to the Continental Congress, as New Hampshire's attorney general and president (governor), and then as presiding officer of the New Hampshire convention that ratified the U.S. Constitution in 1788. WHGS

River via the Wind Gap. For years residents called it "the longest street in the world," since it ended in Easton as it began in Wilkes-Barre, still Northampton Street. For many generations, the Easton and Wilkes-Barre Turnpike was the chief road in and out of Wyoming Valley for stage coaches and wheeled freight.

American roads built during this period were literally "high ways" in the sense that once the area of the road bed was cleared, ditching was dug on both sides and the dirt thrown toward the middle to raise the road surface above the surrounding ground. The traffic moving on it was the chief method of compaction. In low-lying areas, where ditching was not sufficient to keep the road surface drained, two or three logs were laid lengthwise in the dirt and topped with logs laid side by side to form a corduroy road. Dirt was thrown over the logs to help even the surface, but these roads did not lend themselves to a smooth ride. In marshy spots, tightly tied bundles of brush were laid first, then the lengthwise logs were placed, and finally the surface was finished with the crosswise logs for the roadbed.

These corduroy and dirt roads were a far cry from those of the Romans who first designed "high ways" with their layers and layers of loose stone, cut blocks, and surface paving to a thickness of three to five feet. But a new road engineering concept, developed in the 1700s in Britain, led to the con-

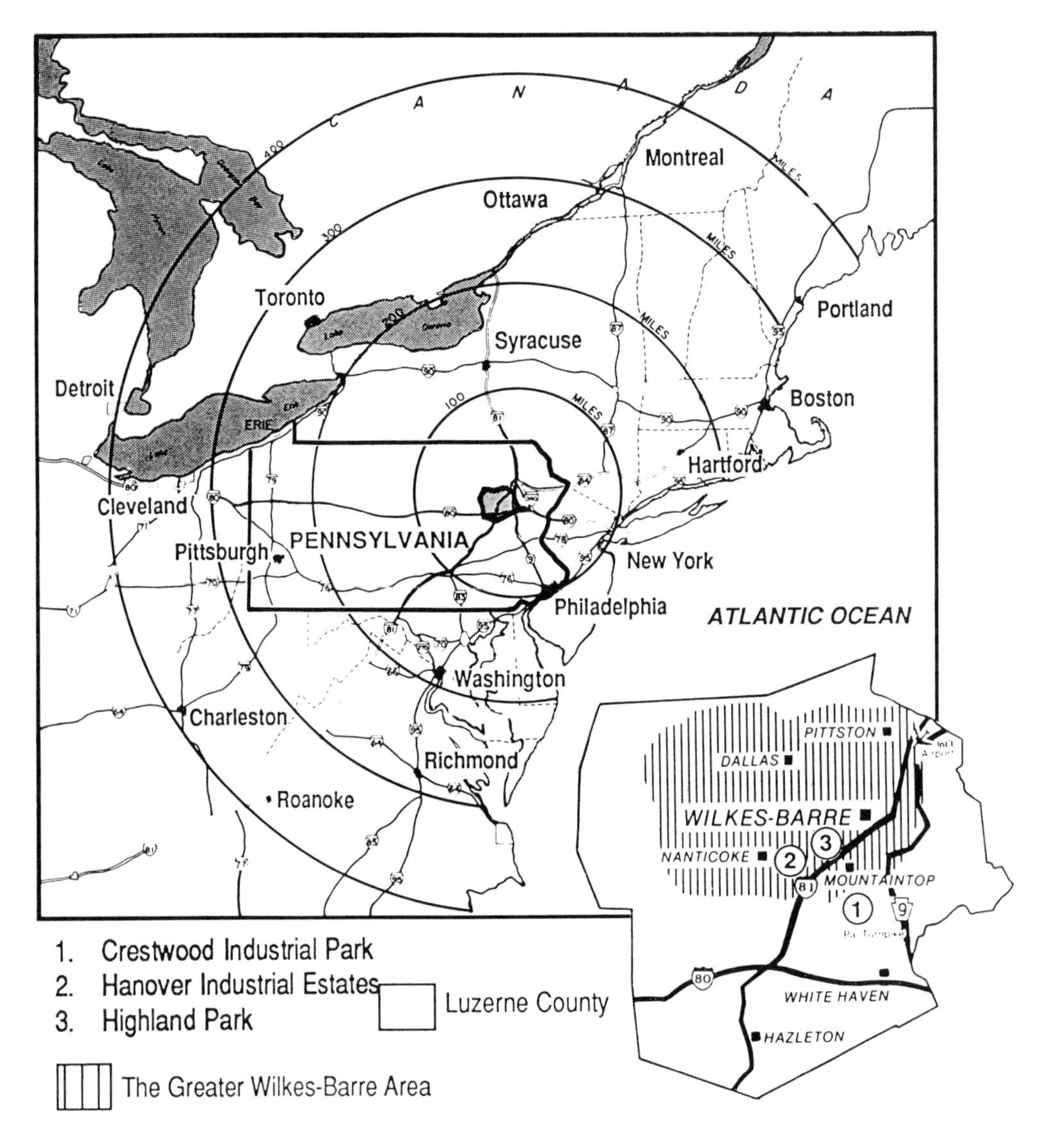

This map was developed for the Committee on Economic Growth—now part of the Greater Wilkes-Barre Partnership along with the Greater Wilkes-Barre Chamber of Commerce. It shows Luzerne County's strategic position today in the network of superhighways. SHARON WARD, COMMITTEE ON ECONOMIC GROWTH

struction of efficient and effective but much lighter-weight roads. The first such road constructed in America was the Lancaster Pike, built in 1793–94 from Philadelphia to Lancaster and surfaced with broken stone and gravel. The Cumberland Road or National Pike opened for traffic from Cumberland, Maryland, to Wheeling in what is now West Virginia in 1818. By 1838, it extended into Illinois. American road-building nevertheless ground to a near halt as the nation focused its transportation improvements first on canals and then on railroads. New interest in improving roads developed in the late nineteenth century with the spread of bicycles, but it wasn't until the twentieth century and the beginning of America's love affair with the automobile that highways began to supersede railways.

Pennsylvania's State Highway System was created in 1911. By 1931, it had grown from its original 9,000 miles to 13,500 miles. Gifford Pinchot, governor from 1923 to 1927 and from 1931 to 1935, added 20,000 additional miles through the development of the state's rural road system. By 1960, there were 41,000 miles of road in Pennsylvania—1,682 of them in the Wilkes-Barre–Hazleton Metropolitan Area. U.S. 11, running along the Susquehanna River, and Pa. 309, crossing the mountains from its junction with U.S. 6 in Tunkhannock through Wilkes-Barre to Hazleton and on to Allentown, formed the key through routes. Route Pa. 115 continues to connect the valley to areas to the southeast. These are crisscrossed by numerous roads connecting the valley to all the surrounding communities.

The first fully modern highway system was conceived in Germany in 1926. The autobahn network consisted of dual roadways separated by a substantial median, with all access severely limited. Construction began in 1934; and largely because of its military purpose, it was completed in a few years.

The Pennsylvania Turnpike Commission, established in 1937, raised funds to build the first such divided, dual-lane, limited-access highway in the United States. Designed for large volumes of traffic moving at high speed, the Pennsylvania Turnpike from Harrisburg to Pittsburgh, later extended eastward to Philadelphia and westward to Ohio, was an immense popular success. It contributed significantly not only to the post–World War II toll-road boom but also to the later interstate highway program. The interstate system, which includes many of the earlier toll roads, carries at least 20 percent of the nation's traffic on about 1 percent of the total road and street system. These interstate highways, thanks to modern engineering, are able to carry our wheeled vehicles along routes that much more closely approximate the Indian trails than could the old roads. Both road surfaces and means of transportation have undergone radical changes, but the Indian skill in road viewing—the art of finding the shortest and most direct route—is unsurpassed.

Wyoming Valley is again the center of a transportation network connecting the heart of America with its coastal margins. The east–west (I-80) and the north–south (I-81) interstates with their rayed linkages (I-84 and I-380), as well as the Northeast Extension of the Pennsylvania Turnpike, have put us in a prime commercial position, with overnight truck delivery to 62,500,000 people—27.6 percent of the United States' population—and two- to four-hour driving time to New York City, Philadelphia, Baltimore, and Washington,

D.C. In addition, the great beauty of the valley and its environs is still easily accessible to us on the fine network of local and state roads built and rebuilt many times since the first logs were felled to make room for a wagon on an Indian trail.

A Concluding Thought

THINK OF THIS BOOK as a sampler. There are thousands of fascinating stories rooted in Wyoming Valley—stories of people and stories of places. How did Sir William Osler, the greatest medical teacher of his day, come to donate $100 to the Luzerne County Medical Society Library? Where did Wilkes-Barre get the generous grant of land for the Hollenback Golf Course? Why does the Medical Society have a tradition of passing a gold-headed cane from the outgoing president to the incoming? These three questions are tied together in the person of Dr. Lewis H. Taylor (1850–1928).

Some of the valley's most notable figures include Father John J. Curran, who worked with the United Mine Worker's organizer John Mitchell to get President Theodore Roosevelt to force the mine owners to deal fairly with the unions, and Father Joseph Murgas, pastor of the Sacred Heart (Slovak) Church of Wilkes-Barre, who was the true inventor of a really practical form of wireless communication.

There is at least one good story for each ethnic group that has made Wyoming Valley its home, at least one good story for each of its religious and educational institutions, and at least one for each of the industries and service organizations that have developed here. The union movement has passed through many exciting moments, and its roots are a critical part of northeastern Pennsylvania's history.

Each flood has had its own unique character, from the Pumpkin Flood of October 1786, named for the pumpkins that came downstream in such enormous quantities that in Harrisburg (according to legend) one could walk across the river on them, to the Agnes Flood of 1972, whose twentieth anniversary was noted in 1992.

There are exciting stories about each of the wars of the past two hundred years—who went off to fight, who stayed behind, and how life was sustained during these crises. And there are the stories of how the valley's people have overcome the economic disasters of the downturns in the business cycles—unemployment, depression, bank failures—and survived them. There are the stories of political and civic leadership, especially in times of crisis, that have brought the community to a new level of understanding and appreciation of what it means to be a community.

The interweaving of all these threads is the history of Wyoming Valley. We are fortunate to have such a fascinating tapestry creating the backdrop that shows us who we are and where we are today.

Carl Sandburg described us:

Twilight and little mountain
towns along the Lehigh, sundown
and grey lavender flush.

Miners with dinner buckets and
headlamps, state constabulary on
horses, guns in holsters, Scranton,
Wilkesbarre, the Lackawanna Trail.

Twilight and the blessed armistice
of late afternoon and early evening.

Twilight and the sport sheets, movies,
chain programs, magazines, comics,
revival meetings.
Twilight and headlights on the new
hard roads, boy friend and girl friend,
dreams, romance, bread, wages, babies,
homes.

A Brief Chronology

Prehistoric Era

8000 B.C. to 1000 B.C.	Archaic cultures in Wyoming Valley
1000 B.C. to 300 B.C.	Early Woodland period
300 B.C. to A.D. 1000	Middle Woodland period
A.D. 1000 to 1550	Late Woodland period

Historic Era

1550–1625	Indirect contact with European culture begins
1625–1675	Europeans invade North America
1675	Iroquois control Wyoming Valley
1683	William Penn's Great Treaty
1701	First Shawnee settlement in Wyoming Valley
1727	Munsee settlement in Wyoming Valley
1728	Second Shawnee settlement
1736	Mohegan village observed in Wyoming Valley
1737	Infamous Walking Treaty
1741	Moravian settlement at Bethlehem
1743	Lenapes move to Wyoming Valley from the Forks
1748–1753	Nanticokes live in Valley; Tuscarora noted
1753	Mahicans settle in Wyoming Valley
1753	Susquehannah Company organized
1754	Lenapes under Teedyuscung settle in valley
1754	Susquehannah Company "purchases" valley
1755–1763	French and Indian War
1762	Susquehannah Company makes first foray
1763	Teedyuscung dies and most Indians leave
1763	Connecticut settlement begun and destroyed
1765	Captain Amos Ogden opens trading post in valley
1768	Treaty of Fort Stanwix
1769–1775	First Yankee–Pennamite War

1775–1783	American Revolution
July 3, 1778	Battle of Wyoming
1778	Frances Slocum kidnapped from family farm
1779	Sullivan's March
1782	Decree of Trenton
1783–1786	Second Yankee–Pennamite War
1786	Pennsylvania creates Luzerne County
1788	First Luzerne County Courthouse and jail built
1795	Post Office established in Wilkes-Barre
1805	Easton and Wilkes-Barre Turnpike begun
1806	Borough of Wilkes-Barre incorporated
1807	Wilkes-Barre Academy opens
1807	Abijah Smith markets coal in Maryland
1808	Jesse Fell burns anthracite in an open grate
1819	First Market Street Bridge opens
1821	William Gildersleeve moves to Wilkes-Barre
1829	George Catlin begins painting among the Indians
1830	North Branch Canal completed to West Nanticoke
1834	Wyoming Division of the canal completed
1837	Frances Slocum located by her family
1839	Wilkes-Barre Female Seminary opens
1843	First passenger train reaches Wilkes-Barre
1849	Wilkes-Barre Law and Library Association organizes
1850	First telegraph line operates in Wilkes-Barre
1852	Lackawanna and Bloomsburg Railroad forms
1856	Wilkes-Barre Gas Company begins operation
1856	First train comes to Kingston
1858	Wyoming Historical and Geological Society organizes
1860	Third Luzerne County Courthouse completed
1861	Luzerne County Medical Society organizes
1864	St. John's Academy opens in Pittston
1866	First street car and first cobblestone street
1871	Wilkes-Barre incorporated as a city
1872	Mother Pauline von Mallinckrodt visits city
1872	Canal north of Pittston closed
1874	Rose O'Neill born in Wilkes-Barre
1878	St. Ann's Academy opens in Wilkes-Barre
1878	Henry M. Hoyt elected governor of Pennsylvania
1878	First telephone line constructed
1879	First electric lights installed in Wilkes-Barre
1882	Canal through Wilkes-Barre closed
1889	Osterhout Free Library opens
1891	Boys' Industrial Association organized
1895	First woman admitted to the Luzerne County Bar
1895	Board of Trade (Chamber of Commerce) organized

1897	Polish National Catholic Church founded
1901	North Branch Canal closed below West Nanticoke
1902	Anthracite miners strike
1905	Rev. Joseph Murgas transmits on his wireless
1906	C. Edgar Patience born in West Pittston
1908	Planters Nut and Chocolate Co. founded
1911	Lyman Howe's studio produces first films
1917	Association for the Blind established in city
1928	Hoyt Library opens in Kingston
1929	Present Market Street Bridge opens
1935	International Ladies Garment Workers Union, Northeast Department, organizes
1939	O'Hara becomes first woman in governor's cabinet
1940	*Citizen Kane* filmed
1953	First television station in Wilkes-Barre
1971	Shad lifted above dam to breed in the Susquehanna
1972	Agnes Flood inundates Wyoming Valley

Selected Bibliography

Andrews, Ronald Linn. "Historic Sites Survey of Wilkes-Barre: Final Report." Wilkes-Barre: Wyoming Historical and Geological Society, 1979. Unpublished.

Atlas of Pennsylvania. Temple University, University of Pittsburgh, and Pennsylvania State University Cooperative Project. Philadelphia: Temple University Press, 1989.

Beck, John. *Never Before in History: The Story of Scranton.* Northridge, California: Windsor Publications, 1986.

Bodnar, John. *Anthracite People: Families, Unions and Work, 1900–1940.* Harrisburg: Pennsylvania Historical and Museum Commission, 1983.

Brewster, William. *History of the Certified Township of Kingston, Pennsylvania, 1769–1929.* Kingston: School District of the Borough of Kingston, 1930.

Buckman, Lewis T. *One Hundred Years with the Luzerne County Medical Society, 1861–1961.* Wilkes-Barre: Luzerne County Medical Society, 1961.

Cox, Harold E. *Wyoming Valley Trolleys: Street Railways of Wilkes-Barre, Nanticoke and Pittston, Pennsylvania.* Forty Fort: Harold E. Cox, 1988.

Dolan, Jay P. *The American Catholic Experience: A History from Colonial Times to the Present.* Garden City, New York: Image Books, 1985.

Drayer, Adam M. *A History of Catholic Secondary Education in the Diocese of Scranton, Pennsylvania.* New York: Fordham University School of Education, 1953.

Farr, Judith. *The Life and Art of Elinor Wylie.* Baton Rouge: Louisiana State University Press, 1983.

Gallagher, Reverend John P. *A Century of History: The Diocese of Scranton 1868–1968.* Scranton: The Diocese of Scranton, 1968.

Garrahan, Francis D. "Airport II Site: A Clemson Island/Owasco Settlement on the North Branch of the Susquehanna River." *Pennsylvania Archaeologist,* Vol. 60, No. 1 (February 1990).

Hanlon, Edward F., with John Beck. *The Wyoming Valley: An American Portrait.* Woodland Hills, California: Windsor Publications, 1983.

Harvey, Oscar Jewell (completed by Ernest Gray Smith). *A History of Wilkes-Barre and Wyoming Valley,* 6 volumes. Wilkes-Barre: Harvey and Smith, 1909, 1927, 1929.

Henwood, James N. J., and John G. Muncie. *Laurel Line: An Anthracite Region Railway.* Glendale, California: Interurban Press, 1986.

Historic Resources Study: Delaware and Lehigh Canal National Heritage Corridor. Easton: Hugh Moore Historical Park and Museums, 1991.

Hoyt, Nancy. *Elinor Wylie: The Portrait of an Unknown Lady.* Indianapolis: The Bobbs-Merrill Company, 1935.

Immaculata, Sr. M., C.I.M. *Mother M. Theresa Maxis Duchemin.* Scranton: Marywood College, 1945.

John Wilkes and Isaac Barre: Politics and Controversy in Eighteenth Century Graphics. Wilkes-Barre: Wilkes College, Sordoni Art Gallery, 1988.

Kent, Barry C. *Susquehanna's Indians.* Harrisburg: Pennsylvania Historical and Museum Commission, 1984.

Klein, Philip S., and Ari Hoogenboom. *A History of Pennsylvania.* University Park: Pennsylvania State University Press, 1973.

Kohler, Dave, and John Orlandini. "The Golomb Farm Site," *Pennsylvania Archaeologist,* Vol. 55, No. 3 (September 1985).

Kulp, George B. *Families of the Wyoming Valley,* 3 volumes. Wilkes-Barre: Yordy, 1885.

Mancall, Peter C. *Valley of Opportunity, Economic Culture along the Upper Susquehanna, 1700–1800.* Ithaca, New York: Cornell University Press, 1991.

Meryman, Richard. *Mank: The Wit, World and Life of Herman Mankiewicz.* New York: Morrow, 1978.

Miller, Donald L., and Richard E. Sharpless. *The Kingdom of Coal: Work, Enterprise, and Ethnic Communities in the Mine Fields.* Philadelphia: University of Pennsylvania Press, 1985.

Miner, Charles. *History of Wyoming, In a Series of Letters from Charles Miner to his son William Penn Miner, Esq.* Philadelphia: J. Crissy, 1845.

Moss, Emerson I. *African-Americans in the Wyoming Valley, 1778–1990.* Wilkes-Barre: Wyoming Historical and Geological Society, 1992.

Musser, Charles, and Carol Nelson. *High Class Moving Pictures: Lyman H. Howe and the Forgotten Era of Traveling Exhibition, 1880–1920.* Princeton: Princeton University Press, 1991.

Myers, Wilbur A. *Historical Album of Wilkes-Barre and Wyoming Valley in Luzerne County, Pennsylvania.* Wilkes-Barre: Luzerne County Bicentennial Commission, 1976.

Myers, Charles E. *The History of Shad Fishing on the Susquehanna River and Current Efforts to Restore the Species.* Wilkes-Barre: Wilkes University Press, 1991.

"Nomination of the River Street Historic District to the National Register of Historic Places." Wilkes-Barre: Wyoming Historical and Geological Society, 1984. Unpublished.

Packard, Jeremy. "The Face of the Enemy: Aspects of the Loyalists and Native Americans in the Battle of Wyoming." *Proceedings of the Wyoming Commemorative Association* (1991).

Palmer, Henry W. *Fifty Years at the Bar and in Politics.* Williamsport: Sayden & Bischof, 1913.

Petrillo, F. Charles. *Anthracite and Slackwater: The North Branch Canal 1828–1901.* Easton: Center for Canal History and Technology, 1986.

Petrillo, F. Charles. *Ghost Towns of North Mountain.* Wilkes-Barre: Wyoming Historical and Geological Society, 1991.

Petrillo, F. Charles. *Harvey's Lake.* Revised edition. Wilkes-Barre: Wyoming Historical and Geological Society, 1991.

Phillips, Edward. *History of Wilkes-Barre and Luzerne County.* 8 volumes. Wilkes-Barre: Wyoming Historical and Geological Society. Undated and unpublished.

Plumb, Henry Blackman. *History of Hanover Township Including Sugar Notch, Ashley, and Nanticoke Boroughs and Also a History of Wyoming Valley in Luzerne County.* Wilkes-Barre: Robert Baur, 1885.

Price, William E. *A Study of Frontier Community in Transition: The History of Wilkes-Barre, Pennsylvania, 1750–1800.* Kent, Ohio: Kent State University, 1979.

Proceedings and Collections of the Wyoming Historical and Geological Society, Vols. 11 (1910), 19 (1926), and 21 (1930). Wilkes-Barre: Wyoming Historical and Geological Society.

Richter, Daniel K. "A Framework for Pennsylvania Indian History." *Pennsylvania History,* Vol. 57, No. 3 (July 1990).

Roberts, Ellis W. *The Breaker Whistle Blows: Mining Disasters and Labor Leaders in the Anthracite Region.* Scranton: Anthracite Press, 1984.

Russ, William A., Jr. *Pennsylvania's Boundaries.* Pennsylvania State University, University Park: The Pennsylvania Historical Association, 1966.

Schooley, Ruth B. *The Market Street Bridges of Wilkes-Barre.* Wilkes-Barre: 1987.

Sgromo, Vito J., and Michael Lewis. *Wilkes-Barre Architecture 1860 to 1960.* Wilkes-Barre: Wyoming Historical and Geological Society and Northeastern Pennsylvania Chapter, American Institute of Architects, 1983.

Shank, William H. *The Amazing Pennsylvania Canals.* York: American Canal and Transportation Center, 1960; Anniversary Edition, 1981.

Smith, Ira F., III. "The Parker Site: A Manifestation of the Wyoming Valley Culture." *Pennsylvania Archaeologist* (1973).

Spear, Sheldon. *Chapters in Wyoming Valley History.* Shavertown: Jemags & Co., 1989.

Taber, Thomas Townsend. *The Delaware, Lackawanna & Western Railroad: The Road of Anthracite in the Nineteenth Century, 1828–1899.* Muncy: Thomas T. Taber, III, 1977.

The Sisters of the I.H.M.: The Story of the Founding of the Congregation of the Sisters, Servants of the Immaculate Heart of Mary, and Their Work in the Scranton Diocese. New York: P. J. Kennedy & Sons, 1921.

The Life of Mother Pauline von Mallinckrodt. New York: Benziger Brothers, 1917.

This is Luzerne County. Wilkes-Barre: League of Women Voters of the Wilkes-Barre Area and the Hazleton Area, 1976.

This is Luzerne County. Revised edition. Jane Elmes-Crahall, ed. Wilkes-Barre: Wilkes University Press and the League of Women Voters of the Wilkes-Barre Area, 1992.

Vale of Wyoming: Nineteenth Century Images from Campbell's Ledge to Nanticoke. Wilkes-Barre: Wilkes College, Sordoni Art Gallery, 1986.

Valletta, Clement. "Ritual and Folklore in Pennsylvania's Wyoming Region: Old to New World Wonder." *Pennsylvania Folklife,* Vol. 33, No. 1 (Autumn 1983).

Wallace, Paul A. W. "Sakayenkwarahton and General Sullivan Travel The Great Warriors Path." *Proceedings of the Wyoming Commemorative Association* (1966).
Wallace, Paul A. W. *Indians in Pennsylvania.* Harrisburg: Pennsylvania Historical and Museum Commission, 1970.
Wallace, Anthony F. C. *King of the Delawares: Teedyuscung 1700–1763.* Syracuse: Syracuse University Press, 1949, 1990.
Wedmore, Delphine, S.C.C. *The Woman Who Couldn't Be Stopped.* Sisters of Christian Charity, 1986.
Weslager, C. A. *The Delaware Indians: A History.* New Brunswick: Rutgers University Press, 1972.
Weslager, C. A. *The Nanticoke Indians—Past and Present.* Newark, New Jersey: University of Delaware Press, 1983.
Wilkes College History of the Wyoming Valley Lecture Series, 1986–1987. Wilkes-Barre: Wilkes College Press, 1989.

Index